MAYDAY

Matt O'Sullivan, the deputy business editor for the *Sydney Morning Herald* and *The Age*, has been writing on the aviation industry for more than seven years. He has also worked for the *Australian Financial Review* and for national newspapers in the UK such as *The Times* and *The Independent*, and in New Zealand for the *Dominion Post*.

Follow the author on Twitter @Mattonews

MAYDAY

HOW WARRING EGOS FORCED QANTAS OFF COURSE

Matt O'Sullivan

VIKING
an imprint of
PENGUIN BOOKS

VIKING

UK | USA | Canada | Ireland | Australia
India | New Zealand | South Africa | China

Penguin Books is part of the Penguin Random House group of companies whose addresses can be found at global.penguinrandomhouse.com.

Penguin
Random House
Australia

First published by Penguin Group (Australia), 2015

10 9 8 7 6 5 4 3 2 1

Cover design by Laura Thomas © Penguin Group (Australia)
Text design by Samantha Jayaweera © Penguin Group (Australia)
Cover photography by razihusin/Shutterstock (plane); Dean Lewins/AAP Image (Alan Joyce); Tracey Nearmy/AAP Image (Geoff Dixon); Tracey Nearmy/AAP Image (John Borghetti)
Typeset in 12/16pt Adobe Garamond by Samantha Jayaweera, Penguin Group (Australia)
Colour separation by Splitting Image Colour Studio, Clayton, Victoria
Printed and bound in Australia by Griffin Press, an accredited ISO AS/NZS 14001 Environmental Management Systems printer.

National Library of Australia
Cataloguing-in-Publication data:

O'Sullivan, Matt John, 1974- author.
Mayday : how warring egos forced Qantas off course / Matt O'Sullivan.
9780670078370
Includes index.
Subjects: Qantas Airways – Management.
Airlines – Management.
Business losses – Australia.
Aeronautics, Commercial – Australia.

387.706594

penguin.com.au

MIX
Paper from responsible sources
FSC www.fsc.org FSC® C009448

To Maki, KJ and EJ

CONTENTS

PROLOGUE

Qantas could easily have become a small footnote in history early last century when two returned war pilots travelled to Sydney to pick up its first aeroplanes. Hudson Fysh and Paul 'Ginty' McGinness served in the trenches at Gallipoli during World War I, before becoming mates in No.1 Squadron in the Australian Flying Corps. On January 21, 1921, the co-founders of the airline were living an adventure in Australia as they set off from Mascot aerodrome in Sydney. McGinness was flying an Avro, and Fysh a BE2c biplane in which he had clocked up just thirty minutes. Flying in tandem, the pair lost visual contact as clouds rolled in north of Sydney on the way to their first stop in Newcastle.[1] With an uneasy feeling in his stomach Fysh decided to fly through the darkening clouds, hoping he would quickly emerge into clear sky on the other side. But he soon realised it was the wrong decision. Before long he was on the verge of losing control of the plane as he tried to fly under the clouds, which he hoped were not shrouding hilltops. In an instant he hit a clear patch of sky to discover he was in a valley with clouds hugging the ground. After finally regaining control, he touched down on a hillside, careering through bushes and eventually coming to rest near a miner's cottage. Fysh and his passenger, Arthur Baird, had narrowly escaped disaster.

The rich history of the Queensland and Northern Territory Aerial Services stretches back to a lounge in the stylish Gresham Hotel in Brisbane in August 1920. Around a glass-topped table, Fysh, McGinness and Queensland grazier Fergus McMaster cemented plans to form a company to offer air services to the region. They were adventurers in every sense of the word, literally flying by the seat of their pants. Three months later – on November 16, 1920 – the founders signed papers in the Gresham Hotel formally registering as a company that was to become known by the acronym QANTAS, and based in the small central Queensland town of Winton. Little did they know that what they founded within just two decades of the Wright brothers' first flight would become the world's second-oldest airline after Dutch flag carrier KLM. Australia's geographic isolation and the difficulty of traversing its big, wide-open expanse explained why people quickly cast aside their concerns about unreliable flying machines in the early twentieth century to travel by air. Parts of western Queensland where Qantas was born often became difficult to pass overland during wet periods. Many parts of the state lacked roads and bridges. An air service offered a way over the onland barriers.

Qantas soon shifted its base from Winton to Longreach, and later to Brisbane, before settling on Sydney where it remains today. In the process, Qantas became indelibly linked to the Australian psyche. It connected the country to political and business capitals on the other side of the world in Europe and the United States. Australians' passion for aviation has grown in tandem with the airline since the early days of the World War I veterans who founded Qantas. It helped the country to tackle the tyranny of distance. Later nicknamed the 'Flying Kangaroo', the airline has become etched in popular culture. Playing the autistic Raymond Babbitt, who feared flying, in the 1988 film *Rain Man*, Dustin Hoffman remarked to his brother, who was trying to coax him onto a plane, 'Qantas. Qantas never crashed'. While glossing over plane crashes in its early years, the reference helped cement Qantas' place in history. As the national flag carrier, Qantas' reputation was strengthened as it mounted missions to rescue Australians from far-flung parts of the globe. At home in 1974, it achieved a world record at the time for cramming the most number of people onto a Boeing 747 jumbo during a rescue flight from Darwin following Cyclone Tracy. The airline became one of the few Australian companies to become known globally.

As it nears its centenary, Qantas has reached another fork in the road. The country's once-dominant national carrier has become an airline in decline. After the collapse of Ansett in 2001, Qantas was handed a near monopoly in the country's domestic air-travel market. Today it lurches from crisis to crisis as it is buffeted from all sides – and from within. The story of the decline of Qantas has all the hallmarks of a modern corporate tragedy. A multitude of factors have brought Qantas to where it is today – management missteps, the rise of a challenger, big egos fighting for the right to chart its path, a company of tribes resistant to change, and the opening of Australian routes to the world. After taking the reins in 2008, the Qantas chief executive, Alan Joyce, became a polarising figure. To his supporters, he tackled problems his predecessors were unwilling to confront. To his critics, he presided over an irreversible shrinking of the airline. His unprecedented decision to ground the entire Qantas fleet in late 2011 to break an industrial dispute divided the nation and made him a household name. He earned plaudits from the big end of town, but many travellers and a large slice of the airline's workforce deemed Qantas' action union busting from another era. Behind Joyce sat Leigh Clifford, the Qantas chairman who never shied away from a fight. As the aviation reporter for the *Sydney Morning Herald* since early 2008, I have covered Qantas' every step and met and interviewed its chief executive on numerous occasions. But neither Joyce nor Clifford would be interviewed for this book.

The airline's predicament echoes that of Australia, a country at the crossroads. As much as Qantas has grappled with a rewriting of the rules governing aviation, the lucky country is dealing with the challenges of globalisation in the twenty-first century. Qantas is an airline that evokes passion like almost no other. Everyone has an opinion on how it should be run – politicians, shareholders, unions, travellers, the media, the airline's board, executives and workforce, and part of the wider Australian public that still believes Qantas remains in the nation's hands two decades after government ownership ended. History helps to tell us why Qantas is where it is today, and gives us an insight into its path ahead. Rod Eddington, a former chief executive at Ansett and British Airways, remarked: 'There are no new ways of going broke; only old ways that keep getting revisited.'[2]

1

HIT IN THE ARSE WITH A RAINBOW

In early September 2001, Peter Gregg's mobile phone rang as he headed with Geoff Dixon, the Qantas chief executive, to Singapore's Changi Airport to catch a flight to Sydney. Gary Toomey, the chief executive of the Air New Zealand–Ansett group, was on the other end of the line. Gregg knew Toomey better than most from the years they had spent working together at Qantas and Australian Airlines. A year earlier, he had reported directly to Toomey, a big-framed man who had been Qantas' chief financial officer before Gregg was appointed to the role, and who was known for peculiarities such as an obsession with security. 'The price is now a dollar,' Toomey said. Weeks earlier Toomey had phoned Gregg, who had been on a biannual overseas roadshow with Dixon to meet Qantas' largest institutional investors, to ask if Qantas would consider purchasing Ansett for about $400 million.[1] Qantas had run the numbers and concluded that Ansett's debt obligations would be substantially higher than the asking price. Qantas' board rejected the offer. The airline stood to gain far more from its arch rival collapsing than it would from trying to fix it.

Now, Toomey wanted to sell Ansett for a dollar coin. After ending the call, Dixon and Gregg convened an urgent board meeting. From the airport manager's office at Changi Airport, the pair dialled into a teleconference with their fellow Qantas directors, including the chairman, Margaret Jackson. The Howard Government had given strong assurances it would support Qantas buying Ansett. The loss of an airline with an extensive domestic network would have far-reaching ramifications for Australia. Gregg told Jackson that the prime minister, John Howard, was likely to exert pressure on Qantas to at least consider the offer. The purchase of Ansett would give Qantas more than 90 per cent of Australia's domestic market. The board quickly told Dixon and Gregg to stop thinking with their hearts and start thinking with their brains. An Ansett takeover was not about to happen. The two Qantas executives were to fly home, and Qantas would deal with whatever eventuated.

After a nine-hour flight from Singapore, Dixon and Gregg walked off a Qantas plane at Sydney Airport. As they did, a Qantas staffer handed Gregg a message to inform him that he would not be heading to its head office on the outskirts of the airport. Instead, he would be sent to New Zealand. The Howard Government wanted Qantas to run a scoping study of Ansett. Thousands of jobs would be lost if the airline collapsed. Qantas' chief financial officer boarded the next flight to Auckland. A group from Qantas' finance department was already winging its way across the Tasman Sea. Over the next forty-eight hours, the team would crunch the numbers on what the real cost of buying Ansett would be. In Sydney, Dixon was in talks with Greg Combet, the secretary of the Australian Council of Trade Unions, about whether a deal could be struck to reshape Ansett's industrial agreements to make them more favourable to an enlarged Qantas. Ansett's costs were about 13 per cent higher than its red-tailed rival. In Canberra, Arthur Sinodinos, the chief of staff to the prime minister, was the point man for the government as the crisis enveloping Australia's second-largest airline unfolded. Ansett was losing

$1.3 million a day. Unless the Australian or New Zealand government intervened, or a white knight emerged, the airline that had serviced Australia for sixty-five years would cease to exist.

By the early morning of September 11, Gregg, his offsider Grant Fenn and the rest of their finance team had finished running the numbers on Ansett in their hotel in central Auckland. By their calculations, Qantas would be buying Ansett and $800 million in obligations for a buck. Their figures did not include the cost of fixing the airline. In Sydney, Dixon had told Combet that he would consider putting to Qantas' board a deal to buy Ansett if the unions allowed management to peel away some of the more generous parts of the industrial agreements for both airlines. The carrot for the unions was that Ansett would not lose its entire 16 000-strong workforce. Instead, jobs would be slashed from both Ansett and Qantas. Dixon, who knew Ansett well from his years in the early 1990s as its marketing director, was proposing a shake-up of the industry in Australia.

Late that day, the Qantas directors dialled into a meeting to consider their options. In the end, the message was emphatic: Qantas would not step in. It could not gain agreement from the trade unions to reshape the work practices at both airlines. Gregg was told to deliver the news to Air New Zealand, whose 22-storey office tower overlooking Auckland's waterfront was just a few blocks from the Regent Hotel where the bulk of Qantas' finance team was staying. Qantas' burly chief financial officer walked into Air New Zealand's headquarters where its executives had been working around the clock for days in a bid to dig themselves out of the giant hole they – and their predecessors – had created for New Zealand's flag carrier. Apart from the straight-talking Toomey, Gregg knew a large number of Air New Zealand's other managers well, including its chief financial officer, Adam Moroney. They had been among a large group of executives known within Ansett as the 'red team' that Toomey had taken with him from Qantas when he left a year earlier. Air New Zealand's acting chairman, Jim Farmer, and other directors such as banker Ralph

Norris were waiting for Gregg. Turning to its enemy to take Ansett off its hands was a final act of desperation for Air New Zealand. 'We won't go forward with the acquisition as we can't get the conditions required to make this work,' Gregg told the grim-faced Air New Zealand directors. Gregg walked out a short time later, and headed back to his hotel. Ansett's fate was almost sealed.

On the way back, Gregg phoned Arthur Sinodinos to let him know Qantas' decision. 'What's it going to be like?' Howard's chief of staff asked. 'All shit is about to break loose,' Gregg replied. A short time later, he walked into his hotel room, exhausted, and switched on the TV. A live news feed showed dark black smoke billowing from the World Trade Center in New York. Stunned by what he saw, Gregg phoned Grant Fenn, the Qantas deputy chief financial officer, in his nearby room in the Regent Hotel to tell him to quickly turn on his television. 'As soon as 9/11 occurred it was basically, well if there was any chance, there is certainly not any now – we are just not going near it,' Fenn recalled. 'Ansett was in too bad a shape and would have dragged Qantas down significantly.'[2] Gregg also phoned home in a depressed state. Both men knew what was about to unfold.

A day after two passenger jets crashed into the north and south towers of the World Trade Center. Air New Zealand cut Ansett adrift, placing the airline it had taken full control of more than a year earlier in the hands of corporate paramedics. At about 6.00 p.m. on September 12, Peter Hedge and two other accountants from PricewaterhouseCoopers walked into the foyer of Ansett's headquarters on Swanston Street in Melbourne. There to meet them was Trevor Jensen, the chief pilot at Ansett and one of the only Australian executives to survive a major cull by the Kiwis a year earlier. He escorted them up to the executive floor on Level 17 where they quickly settled into the chairman and CEO's offices. Shortly afterwards, they called a meeting of Ansett's executive staff to inform them the airline was now in administration. The executives could no longer carry out any actions without their approval. More staff from PricewaterhouseCoopers began filing into the office, some clutching boxes of pizza, in what was to become an all-nighter as they laboured to determine the true state of Ansett's finances. 'Whatever they wanted, we started to produce,' Jensen recalled. 'They worked through and then the next night at about ten o'clock we began closing the airline down. Peter Hedge instructed me to stop flying.'[3] Following the order, Jensen and about ten other managers set up an emergency control centre to prepare for a shutdown of the airline the next morning.

On September 14, Hedge fronted a media conference to declare that the 'cupboard was bare', admitting he felt like Old Mother Hubbard.[4] Ansett's fleet would officially be grounded and more than 16 000 staff put out of work in the largest single loss of jobs in Australia's history. With hundreds of flights cancelled, the travel plans of 47 000 Ansett passengers were thrown into chaos, leaving them desperate to get seats on Qantas and Virgin Blue flights. It was a stark reminder of the role airlines play in so many people's lives, and the wide-ranging impact the grounding of one could have on the nation.

For Qantas, it had been a frantic few days that left its staff dealing with their own personal tragedies. The terrorist attacks in New York and Washington, DC on September 11 claimed the lives of two Qantas employees. Alberto Dominguez, a 66-year-old baggage handler at Sydney Airport who was just three weeks from retirement, and Laura Lee Morabito, thirty-four, a sales manager for Qantas in the US, were aboard American Airlines Flight 11 from Boston to Los Angeles.[5] Sitting a few seats in front of Dominguez, a father of four and grandfather of six, in 8D in business class was Mohamed Atta, the 33-year-old Egyptian later named as the ringleader of the attacks. At 8.46 a.m. local time, the Boeing 767 carrying ninety-two people that Atta and four other al-Qaeda members had hijacked careered into the North Tower of the World Trade Center.

In Sydney, senior managers in Qantas' operational nerve centre were to make decisions well beyond their pay scale over the next three days. On September 11, Richard Cantor was duty manager in the flight despatch unit. On that night, he was also training a colleague as he kept watch over flight planning and air-space restrictions. Cantor, a twenty-five-year Qantas veteran at the time, was walking past a television when he spotted images of the first plane disappearing into the upper floors of the North Tower. Rushing back to his desk, he phoned a counterpart at American Airlines, Qantas' partner carrier in the US and the operator of the 767 plane that had just ploughed into the New York landmark. 'The guy was in tears,' Cantor recalled. 'Then we realised we had a situation that wasn't an accident.'[6] Less than half an hour later, Cantor and his colleagues learnt that American authorities had made an unprecedented order to shut down their entire country's air-space. All air traffic was to be grounded immediately, and planes flying from destinations outside the country were to be diverted. Cantor rang an official at the Federal Aviation Administration in Washington, DC who told him that planes had to land at the nearest airports unless they were 'fuel critical'. At the time, four Qantas 747-400 planes were in the final stages of their journeys from Australia to Los Angeles. The planes could only keep flying to the city if they were already committed to land there. 'It wasn't a case of having a roundtable conference – we had to act,' Cantor said. '9/11 enveloped everybody. You had to just deal with it.'

A short time later, the first three Qantas 747s landed in the US. 'The last one [of the three] had a fighter escort off the back of its tail, making sure they didn't deviate,' Cantor said. The fourth jumbo on its way to Los Angeles was in airspace near Hawaii and forced to land at Honolulu. That 747-400 aircraft was to later play a critical role in returning John Howard, who was in Washington, DC when the hijacked planes crashed into the Twin Towers and the Pentagon, back to Australia during a time of crisis. 'No one was sure when Howard was ever going to get home,' Warren Truss, a minister in the Howard Government, recalled.[7]

The next morning at 7.00 a.m., Cantor walked out of the headquarters in Sydney. 'I was just in a daze. It was like situation overload.

It was surreal – I couldn't believe it was happening,' he said. Less than two days later, Howard and his entourage, which included the outspoken head of the Department of Prime Minister and Cabinet, Max Moore-Wilton, boarded the Qantas 747 that had been diverted to Honolulu. Earlier, the prime minister had arrived in Hawaii from Washington aboard Air Force Two, the US vice-president's jet, and one of the few planes to be granted special clearance to breach the shutdown order. Apart from the crew, the Qantas jumbo carried just Howard and his staff from Hawaii to Sydney, where a RAAF jet later whisked the VIP passengers to Canberra. 'It allowed us to get the aeroplane home and Howard home, too,' Cantor recalled. 'It was the most tumultuous week of my thirty-eight years at Qantas. All US airspace was closed and then on the Friday morning Ansett went bust. I remember thinking that whatever innocence the world had, was now gone. It was also the loss of a lot of liberties.'

The calamity on September 11 threw international air travel into crisis, including Qantas' key routes. Days later, the collapse of Ansett had delivered Australia's domestic market to Qantas on a platter. At the head office on the outskirts of Sydney Airport, Qantas executives rushed between meetings as they worked to get their hands on any aircraft they could to fill the gap left by its rival. The immediate task was to shift hundreds of thousands of people booked to fly on Ansett in the days after its grounding. In the US, the shutdown of the country's entire air space presented a major dilemma for Qantas. Qantas managers, such as Richard Cantor, in the network operations control centre in Sydney at the time of the attacks in New York and Washington, DC had acted quickly to try to limit the impact of the shutdown on the airline. But by the time Ansett was grounded on September 14, Qantas still had about a quarter of its fleet of Boeing 747 jumbo jets parked at airports in the US. The Americans had reopened the country's airspace by the time Ansett was grounded but a huge backlog of flights in the US meant it would take time for Qantas to gain full use of a sizeable part of its international fleet.

After countless phone calls to other airlines, Air Canada emerged as the best bet for securing additional aircraft. Canada's flag carrier had Boeing 767 passenger jets available that were ideal for flying routes in Australia. Importantly, Air Canada also had English-speaking crews. However, in order for Qantas to lease the planes and their accompanying crews, it would need to organise work visas for the Canadians. The request went all the way to John Howard. Despite Qantas' pleas, the prime minister refused to allow visas to be issued. He demanded Ansett planes and crews be put into service or Qantas find another solution. The government did not want to be seen to be bringing in foreign airlines to ferry passengers around Australia because of the failure of Ansett. In the end, Qantas shifted as many planes as it could onto domestic routes while, much to the chagrin of Virgin Blue, Air Canada planes filled a reduction in services on trans-Tasman runs between Australia and New Zealand.

Less than a month after Ansett was grounded, Qantas negotiated a multi-billion-dollar deal to buy fifteen of the latest Boeing 737-800 planes and options to purchase another sixty. It arranged to buy planes that American Airlines had ordered at a much lower price. The US airline was in a world of pain following a slump in travel in the aftermath of the terrorist attacks on September 11 and had too many planes. It did not need more, and Qantas was able to take advantage of American Airline's purchasing power as a large buyer of aircraft. The first batch of 737s delivered to Qantas was fitted out to American Airlines' specifications with small galleys and without coat racks. For Qantas, it was a small price to pay. The airline had planes that could help it take advantage of the huge gap in the domestic market left by Ansett.

Well-heeled business travellers whom Qantas had been fighting Ansett over for years had no choice but to fly on the airline with red tails on its planes. 'We've been hit in the arse with a rainbow,' a Qantas director quipped to fellow board member Rod Eddington in late 2001. Eddington had sat on Qantas' board for less than a year as one of British Airways' three representatives. The astute businessman knew well Ansett's plight, having relinquished the reins as its chief executive in April 2000 to become boss of British Airways, replacing Bob Ayling at the world's largest international airline. He had described Ansett as a great airline but a lousy business. 'Ansett's demise was of its own making, some of which I had been trying to fix. It had far too many aeroplane types, and older planes. Qantas had a far simpler fleet. Fleet complexities killed many airlines,' Eddington recalled. Ansett had also spent too much money and time on peripheral businesses. It owned Hayman Island and half of Hamilton Island in the Whitsundays, invested in trucking and insurance companies, and controlled a majority stake in the Diners Club franchise in Australia. When Eddington was Ansett's chief executive, he recalled once trying to get hold of the airline's head of marketing and sales. He discovered that his senior executive was out of reach because he was committed to a Diners Club conference for three days. 'They had spread their capital far and wide, and management resources were devoted to these joint ventures, which distracted people from Ansett,' Eddington said. 'Running an airline is a bloody tough job and you want to be focused on your main game, not peripheral stuff.'[8]

With its rival at death's door, Australia's domestic market was there for the taking for Qantas. In the space of three months it had been handed the equivalent of seven years of growth in the domestic market. Virgin Blue had begun flights a year earlier with just two planes and was a no-frills airline bereft of business class. By the time Ansett was grounded in September 2001, Virgin was flying just nine aircraft and did not have Qantas' advantage through its relationship with American Airlines to fast-track the delivery of extra planes. Virgin was frustrated in its negotiations to buy Boeing 737 aircraft from Ansett to allow it to expand to meet the demand.

The grounding of Australia's second-largest airline was a godsend for Virgin Blue and its flashy owner, English businessman Richard Branson. Before Ansett's demise, Qantas had calculated Virgin was three weeks away from running out of cash. 'We tracked their yields, their loads. We knew what fares they were charging – it's not hard. Subsequently, it turned out to be right – they were that close,' Peter Gregg recalled later. 'But Branson is a ballsy bloke. He made a billion dollars out of that deal.'[9] Like Qantas, Branson was well aware of Ansett's precarious financial position and knew that if Virgin could last the distance it stood to benefit from the exit of a once-great airline. Months earlier, Air New Zealand had been in talks to buy Virgin as a last-gasp effort to rescue Ansett, whose underbelly was under attack from the new no-frills airlines in Australia. The talks ended in typical Branson mischief at a media conference at Melbourne Airport in early September 2001. 'After much deliberation, we've decided to sell out to Ansett. I'm off to England with my quarter-of-a-billion-dollar cheque, so thank you very much,' a straight-faced Branson told journalists.[10] Moments later, Branson ripped up a mock cheque for $250 million. 'I'm just joking,' he laughed. 'This Virgin bride is not for sale.' With Virgin facing an uphill battle to establish itself in the domestic market against two incumbents, Branson had unexpectedly found himself with a winning hand. The hole in the market left by Ansett was to put Virgin on a fast track to become Australia's second-largest airline.

Qantas executives knew Ansett was in deep trouble but they had thought there was a fair chance Air New Zealand shareholders or the country's government would inject more funds to help rescue its Australian subsidiary. Air New Zealand had fought hard to buy Ansett outright in late 1999, outbidding Singapore Airlines' $500 million offer, but less than two years later was walking away from the airline and half of Australia's domestic travel market. In turning its back on Ansett, New Zealand's reputation was also damaged. It was a point not lost on the country's prime minister, Helen Clark, who experienced first-hand the anger of Ansett staff at Melbourne Airport when they blockaded the Air New Zealand jet she had arrived on from Europe the day administrators officially grounded their airline. After they also blocked a Qantas plane she had been transferred to, Clark had to be whisked by police helicopter to an air-force base at Sale in Victoria before making her way back to New Zealand aboard an ageing Orion turboprop aircraft flown across the Tasman to collect her.[11]

Dixon, who was then sixty-one, had officially been Qantas chief executive only seven months when Ansett was grounded. In late 2000, he had beaten Toomey, a man sixteen years his junior, to the prestigious position. He was anointed as James Strong's replacement two days before the opening of the Sydney Olympics. While Toomey was an astute numbers man, the Qantas board believed Dixon was the better pick because of his strong marketing skills. Before joining Qantas in 1994, he had been Ansett's marketing boss. Dixon was also close to Strong, whose eight years as Qantas chief executive had included integrating Australian Airlines and overseeing the public float of the enlarged airline in 1995. Strong had been a mentor to his older friend. The three representatives from Qantas' largest shareholder, British Airways, were among those on the board who backed Dixon for the top job.

Branding was crucial to an airline's ability to win over customers. In early 1994, Dixon and his marketing team at Qantas were struggling to devise a new advertising campaign for the merged airline. After a lacklustre presentation from advertising agency Mojo, Dixon and his marketing executive, Peter McLaughlin, walked into The Oaks Hotel in Sydney's harbourside suburb of Neutral Bay for a few beers. 'Geoff asked me what I thought of "I Still Call Australia Home". He recapped that when he was at Ansett, he was going to pinch it for Ansett,' McLaughlin recalled.[12] Qantas had used the song by Peter Allen in an ad campaign in the 1980s, and Dixon wanted to modernise it for the merged airline. 'He told me we ought to go and get "I Still Call Australia Home", and get an agency to wrap an ad around it.' After much haggling with record label Rondor Music, Qantas bought the rights to use the song. The airline took a gamble launching its new campaign at the Australian Football League grand final between

Geelong and the West Coast Eagles on October 1, 1994. The ad, featuring Australian entertainers such as Kate Ceberano, Yothu Yindi, Tommy Emmanuel, Jack Jones, James Blundell and James Morrison, was to become as Australian as meat pies and Vegemite, linking Qantas to perceptions of what it meant to be Australian in the final years of the twentieth century. Branding was to turn out to be one of the signatures of Dixon's long tenure at Qantas.

Dixon was a shrewd, street-smart businessman. He was born four days before Christmas 1939 in the New South Wales town of Wagga Wagga, the son of a wool and skin buyer, Arthur 'Butcher' Dixon. Geoffrey James Dixon came from a generation who finished school at a young age. He left Wagga High when he was seventeen for a job as a delivery boy before joining the town's *Daily Advertiser* newspaper for a stint in journalism. By twenty-one, he was chief of staff.[13] Dixon could win people over by playing on a larrikin streak. He talked about identifying with the left side of politics, pointing to his working-class background and his father's trade-union affiliation.

In reality, the world he grew up in was light years away from the brutal, high-stakes sphere of business that he navigated with a certain ease decades later. To the unions, Dixon remained a hard-nosed senior executive who they had to battle against in labour negotiations. During heated discussions, he would swivel in his chair to gaze out the window and gather his thoughts before returning to face his adversaries. 'But if you hit the notes, you could gain his attention,' Ian Woods, a former president of the Australian and International Pilots Association, recalled.[14] His innate ability was to win people over, drawing them into his tent and making them less of a threat. He willingly shared private details, something that helped to put those he met at ease. 'Dicko' was a small bloke in stature at about 170 centimetres tall but he did not have in his early sixties the protruding waistline that besets many people in their later years.

Early on in his tenure as Qantas chief executive, Dixon showed his penchant for dealmaking and political lobbying. In mid-2001 he had tried to orchestrate the so-called Qantas Plan in an approach to the New Zealand government and several Air New Zealand directors. Under his plan, Qantas proposed to buy Singapore Airlines' 25 per cent stake in Air New Zealand, as well as a further 30 per cent shareholding owned by the corporate raider Brierley Investments, which would be placed in trust in order to circumvent foreign investment restrictions. In return, Air New Zealand would sell Ansett to Singapore Airlines, allowing it to achieve its long-stated aim to have a substantial presence in one of its largest markets.[15] The deal needed the consent of Air New Zealand's shareholders, chiefly Singapore Airlines. However, Singapore's flag carrier wanted to pursue its own plan to boost its stake in Air New Zealand to 49 per cent, creating an airline group that would challenge Qantas. After Air New Zealand rejected Qantas' proposal, Dixon turned to the New Zealand government. 'We are proposing a genuine partnership between Qantas and Air New Zealand to create an airline alliance with the economic and financial scale to compete in world markets while maintaining two separate, independently owned and controlled and locally based carriers with distinctive and popular brands,' Dixon wrote in a letter to the New Zealand finance minister, Michael Cullen, on June 25. 'I stand ready to visit Wellington.'[16] Dixon and Gregg were all too aware that Qantas would face a major challenger if Singapore Airlines gained management control of Air New Zealand and, in turn, Ansett. They feared a three-way tie-up. After intense lobbying from Qantas, the Australian government gave its full backing to Dixon's proposal. In so doing, it scuttled the only viable plan to rescue Ansett in the months before it was placed in the hands of administrators.[17] Qantas' successful campaign created serious levels of ill will at Singapore Airlines, casting a pall over their relationship for years to come.

Qantas had the domestic market stitched up, albeit with Virgin Blue slowly eating away at its leisure passengers. Attempts to resurrect Ansett proved fruitless. The airline was finally pronounced dead in late February 2002 when a consortium spearheaded by Victorian businessmen Solomon Lew and Lindsay Fox ditched a $3.6 billion bid for a slimmed-down Ansett. Mark Mentha, one of two insolvency specialists who had replaced PricewaterhouseCoopers as the administrator of Ansett within days of its grounding, summed up the feeling of the airline's staff.[18] 'They have been taken to the top of the mountain, only to have fallen back down again. It is a tragic day,' he told journalists.[19] Early on the morning of March 5, 2002, Ansett Flight 152 touched down in Sydney from Perth, saluted by water cannons from two fire engines as it taxied to the terminal. The airline founded by Reginald Ansett with a single-engined, six-seater Fokker Universal in the Victorian town of Hamilton on February 17, 1936, had flown its last commercial flight. It would be another decade before Ansett was finally put to rest when the administrator, KordaMentha, made a final payout to the airline's staff, giving them an average of 96 cents of every dollar in entitlements owed. But in 2001, Ansett's loss was Qantas' gain.

2

SHOOTING STAR

With Ansett consigned to the pages of history, Qantas was ever mindful of new threats in a rapidly changing industry. Airlines survived on the slimmest profit margins, and Ansett was another reminder that once dominant brands could quickly be left behind. Qantas went from controlling half of the market to almost a hundred per cent of the major routes in Australia following the failure of Ansett. 'It was never going to be sustainable and we knew that,' Grant Fenn, the Qantas deputy chief financial officer at the time, recalled. 'Whilst it might be okay in the short term for business, there were a lot of negative positions coming from a lot of customers who were welded-on Ansett customers and frequent-flyer holders.'[1] Under the stewardship of Brett Godfrey, Virgin Blue was a true low-cost airline, and steadily eating away at Qantas' grip on leisure travellers. The collapse of Ansett gave Virgin a new lease of life, inhibited only by its ability to get its hands on new aircraft to fill a vacuum in the low-cost segment of the air-travel market.

Even before Virgin Blue launched its first flight in August 2000, Qantas grappled with how to slow low-cost airlines' attack on its underbelly. Within six months of Virgin Blue starting services, Qantas announced it planned to launch a low-cost airline to fly routes to Asia that it had abandoned because it could no longer make money from them. In August 2001 Geoff Dixon confirmed that Qantas would resurrect the Australian Airlines brand for the new low-cost carrier, which would fly to destinations in Asia, including Japan. The brand had ceased in 1993 when Australian Airlines was folded into Qantas following the Keating Government's decision to open up the country's aviation sector. After a slight delay due to a major downturn in international travel caused by the September 11 terrorist attacks, Qantas' all-economy subsidiary Australian Airlines began its first flights in October 2002 from Cairns to the Japanese cities of Osaka and Nagoya.

Its focus firmly fixed on leisure travellers, Australian Airlines expanded to other destinations including Bali, Hong Kong, Taiwan and Singapore. But it did not provide Qantas with an answer to Virgin Blue in the domestic market. With Ansett gone, the new budget airline was expanding aggressively. 'Virgin was absolutely massacring us and we were under a lot of pressure to find a solution,' Peter Gregg, Qantas' then chief financial officer, recalled.[2] By 2002 the pressure was building within Qantas' corporate offices in the AAP Centre tower on George Street in central Sydney for its executives to find a solution. Dixon and his executive team, including Gregg, John Borghetti and the Australian Airlines' chief executive, Denis Adams, ran between meetings as they searched for answers. Qantas had toyed with all-economy seating on routes to destinations such as Adelaide but its business travellers quickly made it clear that this was not a concept they would accept. They wanted the full-service perks that they had long been accustomed to.

Qantas was prepared to give Australian Airlines time to find its feet, but it quickly dawned on its executives that the resurrected subsidiary airline was not the answer. Australian Airlines struggled to make money. Its small fleet of Boeing 767 aircraft was not suited for the routes to Asia it was flying, while its employment agreements made it an expensive operation compared with its new low-cost competitors. The Qantas executives quickly found themselves looking for a way to quietly kill the subsidiary. 'We were wondering how the hell we were going to get ourselves out of that with a bit of face,' Gregg recalled.[3] However, it could not scrap Australian Airlines without having something to replace it.

In meetings in the city office, Qantas' head of sales and marketing, John Borghetti, had favoured starting a new low-cost airline with a maximum of ten aircraft to try to halt Virgin's advance. Borghetti, the son of Italian immigrants who arrived in Australia four decades earlier, emphasised the need for a clear delineation between Qantas and a new airline to ensure that they were not competing against each other on routes. Top of his mind was the risk of a low-cost offshoot cannibalising the airline he had worked for since he dropped out of high school in Melbourne at the age of seventeen for a job in the Qantas mailroom.

In 2002 Boston Consulting Group was hired to carry out a study of the low-cost model for Qantas. The consultants from BCG and other firms had long been a regular sight in Qantas' offices as they worked away on many secret projects. Qantas needed a solution, and fast. After significant modelling, Qantas concluded that a low-cost airline could succeed so long as it limited the extent to which it took passengers from its parent. Qantas wanted a low-cost offshoot to attack Virgin, instead of it having to mount a costly rearguard action of its own. Virgin would be forced to keep fares low as it fought a new low-cost rival, preventing it from attracting some of Qantas' price-sensitive passengers. The consultants from BCG eventually proposed a low-cost airline with between twenty and thirty aircraft, which immediately raised concerns from Borghetti. He believed the aim of a new low-cost carrier was to block Virgin from dragging Qantas down to compete against it on its terms, not to expand into a large airline that threatened to pull passengers away from its parent.

Three decades earlier, Southwest Airlines in the United States had pioneered the budget airline model. Herb Kelleher, an American businessman who often had a cigarette in one hand and a glass of wine in the other, was the architect of Southwest's business model. It was based on an airline flying just one type of aircraft and simplicity to the nth degree. The book about Kelleher, *Nuts!*, became a must-read for anyone who wanted to run a successful no-frills airline. Michael O'Leary at Europe's largest budget airline, Ryanair, and Stelios Haji-Ioannou at easyJet copied unashamedly from Southwest's model as they reshaped the aviation industry across the Atlantic in Europe.

The rise of Virgin was forever on the minds of the Qantas executives. 'Virgin had been in dire straits. But then Virgin all of a sudden started to take up part of that market and was obviously going to get bigger,' Fenn recalled. 'Despite Qantas providing all this service – the frequent flyer, the lounges, the meals – when we would do our customer surveys we found Virgin and Qantas were surprisingly seen as the same. We just found this incredible – we couldn't differentiate ourselves even though we had differentiated product.'[4] In March 2002, their fears were heightened when Chris Corrigan's transport giant, Patrick Corporation, forked out $260 million for a 50 per cent stake in the airline that had started just eighteen months earlier with two planes and $11 million in start-up capital. 'All I can say is, Qantas, watch your tail because we are on it,' Godfrey boasted to journalists as he detailed plans to launch flights to New Zealand and Asia and triple Virgin's fleet to fifty planes within five years.[5] The airline had enlivened the imagination of one of Australia's most high-profile business figures at the time. Corrigan, the driving force behind Patrick, had shown he was up for a fight. Four years earlier, he had dealt a blow to the Maritime Union of Australia's grip on the waterfront in one of the most bitter industrial disputes in the country's history. It was arguably surpassed only by the great shearers' strike of 1891, which later helped lead to the creation of the Australian Labor Party. With Corrigan on board, Virgin appeared well on its way to achieving its target of 30 per cent of the domestic aviation market by the end of 2003.

Virgin Blue had started as a clean slate. Scribbling on the back of beer coasters in a London pub in 1993, Brett Godfrey, then a mid-ranking executive at Richard Branson's flagship, Virgin Atlantic, and his mate Rob Sherrard had plotted ways to challenge the two incumbent airlines back in Australia. Their first proposal was rubbished by Virgin Atlantic executives, and Godfrey's dream looked as though it would remain just that. He went on to help launch Virgin Express, a no-frills Belgian airline created out of the shell of EuroBelgian Airlines. While Godfrey rose to become its chief financial officer, Virgin Express was riddled with problems, churning through three chief executives in eight months. Born in the south Sydney suburb of Sans Souci, the second of four children yearned for Australia. After the earlier setback, the former accountant's big break came in early 1999 when he took his plan to launch an airline in Australia to Branson. By late that year, Branson had given the go-ahead for Virgin Blue, which employed staff on wages and conditions akin to a low-cost airline model. In contrast, Qantas' labour agreements had been built up over decades, and reflected its position as both a premium airline and a former government enterprise. It could not simply shift staff to a new airline and pay them less than what they had earned at Qantas to fit the low-cost model it hoped to create.

The problem had long vexed Qantas management. Unbeknown at the time, the solution had walked into an Italian restaurant in East Sydney in March 2001. Gerry McGowan, the founder of Impulse Airlines, wanted an exit strategy after a major shareholder baulked at a capital raising. Over a few beers at Beppi's, McGowan hammered out a deal with Geoff Dixon for the 'Little Aussie Battler', as Impulse promoted itself, to be swallowed by Qantas. For McGowan, the offer to buy Impulse gave him a way out of a bind. For Dixon, the $20 million outlay for Impulse was a steal, and removed a small competitor. Dixon's industrial-relations head-kicker, Ian Oldmeadow, quickly realised the importance of Impulse to Qantas. While its fleet of eight Boeing 717 planes and thirteen smaller aircraft was folded into QantasLink after the deal was consummated in late 2001, the shell of Impulse was to later create the building blocks for a low-cost airline. 'For $20 million we thought it was a great opportunity. We did that transaction against the better wishes of the rest of the management team because they'd have liked us to let it fail and just fill that space ourselves,' Gregg recalled. 'But we could see that we weren't changing structurally the business enough.'[6] The attraction of Impulse to Gregg and Dixon lay in its employment agreements, which were much less generous to its staff than Qantas'. Impulse pilots and flight attendants remained employed by Impulse as a subsidiary of Qantas. They did not begin earning the higher salaries of their counterparts at Qantas the moment they transferred to their new company. In essence, Impulse gave Qantas the basis for a low-cost offshoot with a cost base rivalling Virgin Blue's. 'We faced a real battle in losing market share because [Virgin's] cost base was 35 per cent to 45 per cent lower than ours in a two-horse race,' Dixon said later. 'We went very aggressively to get Impulse when we knew it was in trouble. We should buy Gerry McGowan a few beers.'[7]

However, Qantas faced strong countervailing forces in its desire to follow other major airlines in setting up a low-cost carrier to repel Virgin Blue's advances. Some of the deepest reservations came from within Qantas. In 2002, British Airways still had two seats on the Qantas board as a result of the cornerstone stake it had acquired nearly a decade earlier. Under direction from London, Roger Maynard and Nick Tait resisted the push from Dixon and Gregg for Qantas to set up its own low-cost offshoot. The British flag carrier had bad memories of the budget airline phenomenon. It had set up a no-frills offshoot, Go, in 1998, in an attempt to fend off the advances of Ryanair and easyJet.

After the two budget airlines embarked on an intensive lobbying campaign, the United Kingdom's regulator forced British Airways to set up the budget offshoot with a separate management team and board. Before long, Go was eating away at the earnings of its parent. The management of the no-frills offshoot had realised it was far easier to attack British Airways' short-haul business than compete against Ryanair and easyJet. When Rod Eddington began as British Airways chief executive in May 2000, the airline's short-haul business was losing about £300 million a year. Two years later, Eddington sold Go to easyJet for £374 million. 'That stopped us from using Go as an excuse to stop us making the changes we needed to make – some of them painful – to our short-haul business,' Eddington recalled.[8]

British Airways was not alone in failing with no-frills ventures. KLM sold Buzz in early 2003, while Air Canada struggled on with Zip, Delta Air Lines with Song and SAS with Snowflake before they were consigned to history within the space of a few years. The executives running the parent companies realised they had to decide whether they were full-service network airlines or low-cost carriers. The British Airways representatives on Qantas' board feared that a new low-cost airline would end up attacking its parent on routes if Australia's competition watchdog demanded it be kept entirely separate. In the end, the concerns of British Airways representatives were allayed because Qantas was able to maintain control over the low-cost carrier. While the new airline was to have a separate management team, ultimate control would rest with Qantas' chief executive.

In July 2003, Dixon called Alan Joyce, a fresh-faced young Irishman he had hired to Qantas just over two years earlier, into his office in Sydney to ask him to take the job of steering a project to start a low-cost airline. Joyce had just turned thirty-seven, and willingly accepted the chance of a lifetime. Dixon had resisted the urgings of other senior Qantas executives to appoint someone they knew better, instead of the new recruit from Ansett. However, Dixon wanted an executive with out-of-the-box thinking. He did not want someone whose judgements would be clouded by historic aviation practices. Joyce fitted the mould to a tee. It was a bold new venture, and the success or failure of a low-cost subsidiary would play a large part in determining the legacy of both Dixon and Gregg, a key architect of Qantas' overarching strategy.

Gregg was Queensland born, bred and educated. His father had worked for the railways as a train controller, and his son's earliest memories were of Far North Queensland. When Gregg was very young, his father moved his family to a small, remote town for work. It was a hot, barren place to live for Gregg, his three older sisters and younger brother, except when the summer rains arrived, turning the parched landscape into grasslands. The family later returned to Brisbane, where Gregg received a Catholic schooling before studying part-time for an economics degree at university. After working for the Queensland government's Treasury Corporation, where he gained an understanding of public debt markets, he shifted to Melbourne in 1988 to work under James Strong at Australian Airlines. Within a year, he was appointed Australian Airlines' treasurer, working alongside its chief financial officer, Gary Toomey. In 1992, Qantas acquired Australian Airlines and Gregg eventually became its treasurer. After a few years at the enlarged Qantas, he had climbed the ladder to become its deputy chief financial officer, reporting directly to Toomey. Like Dixon, the straight-talking numbers man had become addicted to the adrenaline rush of working in the fast-paced, unpredictable world of aviation.

For Joyce, too, it had been a stellar rise for a young man raised in the working-class suburb of Tallaght, in southwest Dublin. His father, Maurice, had been a postman before he began making cigarettes for Benson & Hedges, and his mother, Colette, was a cleaner. His first home was a government flat, and his family moved into a terrace house in Tallaght when he was six. Alan Joseph Joyce and his three brothers, Anthony, Maurice and Paul, attended a government school.[9] His parents believed it was important for their sons to get an education. After leaving high school, Joyce studied a diploma in mathematics and physics at the Dublin Institute of Technology before enrolling at Trinity College, Ireland's most prestigious university.

In 1988, he graduated from Trinity with a degree in physics and mathematics and a masters in management science, which had involved building mathematical models.

He entered the search for a job in a country that had yet to earn the title Celtic Tiger. The republic's economy remained a laggard among its European peers. A large proportion of its population followed in their forebears' footsteps, immigrating overseas for the chance to put their university education into practice and build a more comfortable life. North of the border, the daily lives of Ireland's citizens were much worse during the decades-long sectarian conflict known as the Troubles; violence continued to blight Northern Ireland.

Joyce gained a job as a computer programmer but after six months left to work at Aer Lingus. One of his first projects as a research analyst at Ireland's flag carrier in 1988 was to run mathematical models on matters such as the overbooking of planes. Before long he was promoted to fleet planning at the airline, and then to market and schedule planning. Later, Joyce spent weeks on the road as he travelled as far afield as Thailand, Ukraine and Albania to sell Aer Lingus' marketing and IT systems to other airlines. In 1994 he returned to Dublin to work on a project under Conor McCarthy to set up Aer Lingus Express, a low-cost offshoot of Ireland's flag carrier. McCarthy would later become part of a group of Irish aviation executives who would have a significant influence on the shape and direction of the world's aviation industry. Within a year, McCarthy had left to become the second-in-charge at Ryanair, and was later credited as the brains behind AirAsia, a low-cost airline in Malaysia that went on to become the Ryanair of Asia. The pair's paths would cross again on a number of occasions in the years ahead. Aer Lingus eventually dropped its plans to set up a budget offshoot, instead reshaping its entire operations as a low-cost airline.[10]

Like many of his countrymen before him, in 1996 Joyce trod the well-worn path from Ireland to Australia, taking a job at Ansett. Just thirty years old, he was hired to the airline by Lyell Strambi to work as its network and schedules planning manager. Like his relationship with McCarthy, Joyce and Strambi's paths would cross in the years ahead. At Ansett, Joyce had responsibility for route network planning while Strambi had a number of senior roles including oversight of a 'business recovery program'. Joyce's efforts to help simplify Ansett's Noah's Ark of a fleet, which ranged from Boeing 767 and 727 aircraft to A320s and Fokker 100s, brought him into regular contact with the chief executive, Rod Eddington. The maths whiz from Dublin had all the route numbers in his head, and knew where Ansett made and lost its money. Like many of his counterparts, Joyce had grown attached to the aviation game.

But Ansett was a failing business. After Air New Zealand gained outright control in early 2000, many of its managers – including Joyce – became increasingly sidelined as the parent stamped its mark. Within months, the New Zealanders were laying off dozens of Ansett's managers as they set about merging the two airlines, and shifting Ansett's centre of gravity to Auckland. By late 2000, Air New Zealand had dismantled the senior echelons at Ansett who had served under Eddington. Strambi followed four other top Ansett executives out the door of its head offices on Melbourne's Swanston Street, including the chief financial officer, David Irvine, and the acting chief executive, Craig Wallace.[11] In January 2001, Gary Toomey arrived at the head office in Auckland with big ideas and an equally big number of lieutenants from Qantas he had convinced to join him. Toomey had long coveted the chance to run an airline. One of the first changes he made in his new role was to alter all of his executives' titles. 'He wanted to be called president and CEO, so we all had title changes,' Trevor Jensen, Ansett's chief pilot at the time, said later. 'We went from the European system to the American system. Titles aren't that serious but to Gary they were very serious things.'[12] It quickly became clear that any hope of implanting an airline model he had learnt at Qantas onto Air New Zealand and Ansett was not going to work. There was no chemistry between Toomey and Air New Zealand's old-school chairman, Selwyn

Cushing. Saddled with a dysfunctional board, the problems were far greater than Toomey had envisaged.

For Qantas, the flood of departures from Ansett gave it a chance to cherrypick executives without having to pay above the odds. Eddington, the Perth-born Rhodes scholar, had left Ansett months earlier to become British Airways' chief executive after he was approached by its chairman, Lord (Colin) Marshall. Despite the challenges of his new role in London, Eddington found himself helping out his former colleagues at Ansett who were leaving the airline in droves. Eddington phoned Dixon to tell him that whatever he did he should hire Alan Joyce, a talented young executive who was still at Ansett. Dixon took his advice and interviewed Joyce in Qantas' Melbourne office, a short distance from Ansett's headquarters. The Qantas chief executive offered Joyce a job and the day Joyce informed his bosses at Ansett he was going to work for its rival he was told to leave, and escorted from its head office by a security guard. By 2001, he was ensconced in a new role in Sydney as the general manager of Qantas' network.

Less than three years later, Ansett was a distant memory as Joyce steered a secret project to set up a budget airline for Qantas. He worked on the project alongside Bruce Buchanan, a then 31-year-old consultant at Boston Consulting Group. As the lead consultant on the project, Buchanan's role was to support Joyce in pulling together the business case for a budget airline. Over the next decade, the pair's lives would become more intertwined than they could have ever imagined in 2003. Buchanan's initial six-month contract was to turn into a near decade at the airline. After gaining financial approval from the Qantas board in October 2003, the project team shifted to an office in North Sydney and began recruiting extra staff. Their plans for what was known internally as the Qantas low-cost carrier were kept under tight wraps. Despite Qantas buying Impulse in 2001, a final decision was yet to be made about whether the shell of its operations would form the basis of a new budget airline. Instead, Impulse's fleet of Boeing 717 planes had been repainted in Qantas livery and flown on domestic routes.

The project team worked to a tight schedule. Qantas was desperate for a weapon to attack Virgin Blue. The Qantas executives knew the industry was on the cusp of a surge in demand from leisure travellers: an annual holiday to far-flung destinations was becoming a ritual for many people. In drawing up the business case, the executives looked overseas to learn lessons from other airlines such as British Airways. Joyce called on Conor McCarthy, his former boss at Aer Lingus who had since set up his own consultancy firm in Dublin, to help draw up the blueprint for Qantas' new airline. Within three months of Joyce's appointment, Qantas revealed plans to launch a low-cost domestic airline by May 2004. The pressure was on to create a new airline in a matter of months. The overarching strategy was to trap Virgin in a pincer movement. The new budget airline would be run more cheaply than Virgin, while Qantas would boast superior products and services. The company would have both ends of the market covered, and Virgin would be stuck in the middle in no-man's-land.

The project team and marketing experts had spent weeks deliberating over a range of names for the new airline, including Jetone, JetBlack and JetX. A brand for an airline was crucial to its identity. Its name would play a big part in whether it was able to convince travellers to fly with it. Consumer research had told Joyce and the rest of his team that 'jet' was a positive word for use in the name of an airline. In the end, they walked into Dixon's office to recommend Qantas adopt JetX as the name for the new airline. 'It sounds like a petrol station,' Dixon retorted. Marketing was Dixon's forte. He had been responsible for building Qantas' brand in the 1990s under the leadership of James Strong. In his office sat model planes sporting the Southern Cross constellation. Turning to them, Dixon said: 'Why don't you call it Jetstar?' Dixon had joined the dots.

The next step was to choose the colour. The team weighted up black, purple and silver before settling on orange. But establishing a brand was not an easy task. A flight simulator business in the US later took the airline to a local court for allegedly trading on its brand name, and Qantas ended up buying it out for about $100 000 rather than endure the costly ordeal of fighting it in a foreign court.

From the outset, Dixon took a close interest in the plans for the new offshoot, knowing it would become a central part of Qantas in the years to come. His right-hand man, Peter Gregg, believed a low-cost airline could grow substantially depending on how far they let it expand without taking passengers from Qantas' premium operations. One of the big debates at the boardroom table was over the choice of planes for the new airline. Many directors wanted to opt for Boeing's 737 workhorses, long a familiar sight in Australian skies. Gregg fought for Airbus' A320 aeroplane, the Europeans' answer to their American rival's Boeing 737. Airbus had yet to deliver its single-aisle planes to low-cost carriers, the new kids on the aviation block. Airbus wanted to make a statement and gave Qantas a deal it could not refuse. Importantly for management, a plane type that the existing Qantas pilots did not fly gave the company a chance to reach new wage deals for those who would eventually be placed in the cockpits of the new A320 passenger jets.

With Joyce ensconced as the CEO of the new low-cost airline in October 2003, Dixon entrusted John Borghetti with the premium brand and its 16 000 staff and fleet of more than 200 planes. Borghetti was obsessed with the finer details and believed in the importance of branding to the extent that he saw himself as a virtual walking billboard. The Qantas brand was upmost in his mind. Earlier in the year, panic about flying due to the outbreak of severe acute respiratory syndrome, or SARS, had buffeted the airline. Overseeing both Qantas' core domestic and international operations, Borghetti set about investing heavily in its brand and product. The split ensured that friction began to develop between the red tails of Qantas under Borghetti and the orange tails of Jetstar under Joyce. 'There was enormous tension between John and Alan, but there was enormous tension between the red tails of Qantas and the orange tails of Jetstar. That was by desire from us,' Gregg recalled. 'We wanted that because we wanted to increase the pace of change among the red-tails to make sure that Qantas could survive in the long term.'[13] The divide between the red and orange tails echoed the tension a decade earlier when the blue team of Australian Airlines, which featured blue kangaroos on the tails of its planes, and the red team of Qantas tussled over who would hold sway in a merged airline flying under the Qantas banner. It took years before the blue and red teams finally settled their differences.

From the outset, Borghetti had made clear that he favoured a budget airline capped at ten planes, and did not want to see Qantas replaced by Jetstar on routes such as those to the Gold Coast. The Jetstar team saw themselves as offering the company a future, and their counterparts at Qantas as dinosaurs who were trying to hold on to old ways of thinking. 'Instead of it being a holistic operation it was like total separation – unless they wanted something, and you were encouraged to cooperate,' recalled Chris Manning, the Qantas chief pilot at the time. 'A lot of people at Qantas found it hard to help them when they would never help the other way. The mistake was not realising that these two airlines needed each other and should have cooperated vastly more than they did. You can't have total separation within a company – it just doesn't work. You have to be working to the same end.'[14] The siege mentality at Jetstar was necessary to get it running, and stem the company's loss of market share in the leisure-travel market to Virgin Blue, which was expanding aggressively. But it created clear battlelines within the company, setting the scene for dust-ups over its overarching direction.

In early December 2003, Dixon, Joyce and Gregg strode before TV cameras at a naming ceremony in Melbourne to detail their plans for a new airline to be badged Jetstar. 'If we are going to be cannibalised, we might as well cannibalise ourselves,' Dixon declared, vowing that Jetstar would be cheaper to run than Virgin.[15] Formed out of the shell of Impulse, Jetstar would be based in Melbourne, away from the head office of its parent in Sydney, and fly a fleet of ageing Boeing 717s before it took delivery of 177-seat Airbus A320 aircraft over the next few years. In the following months Jetstar dangled the carrot of $29 one-way fares to entice passengers and spent $15 million on a marketing campaign featuring Melbourne comic Magda Szubanski.

Just before dawn on May 25, 2004, a Boeing 717 sporting an unfamiliar Jetstar logo on its tail climbed into the skies from Newcastle Airport in New South Wales bound for Melbourne. The flight marked the arrival of a new airline to Australian skies. Waiting for the arrival of Flight JQ371 at Melbourne's Tullamarine Airport was Joyce, sporting an open-neck dark-blue shirt; Dixon; the Victorian premier, Steve Bracks; and the smiling face of Jetstar's marketing campaign, Magda Szubanski. 'Jetstar will take some business off Qantas, they'll take some business off Virgin, but principally . . . this is about growing the market, the lower leisure end of the market,' Dixon told journalists.[16] By the end of the day, Jetstar had flown almost 8000 passengers to thirteen destinations.

Like other budget airlines, Jetstar's focus was on keeping a tight rein on costs in every part of its business. This meant it rolled out online check-in and did not allocate seats to passengers, so that planes could be loaded and unloaded more quickly. The airline flew to airports such as Avalon in Victoria, which had lower charges and used stairs to planes rather than more expensive aerobridges. The industrial agreements for Jetstar staff had the fingerprints of Ian Oldmeadow, a long-time friend of Dixon and his chief adviser on union matters, all over them. The Impulse pilots who had been flying the Boeing 717 aircraft accepted a deal to fly Jetstar's A320s for the same salary, which was significantly less than what their counterparts at Qantas earned. For Qantas unions, the new airline was an attempt to eat away at their hard-won wages and conditions.

In the early days of Jetstar the tight-knit executive team were like a family. The sky was the limit. The airline's Melbourne offices were laid out in an open-plan configuration, and every Friday its senior staff trekked downstairs to a bar next door for drinks. Joyce and Bruce Buchanan were very tight at Jetstar, their focus on growing a business they had led from the drawing board to full operation. In the eyes of some staffers, it was difficult to know whether Joyce influenced Buchanan more or vice versa. The evidence of Joyce's time spent learning the ropes of aviation in Ireland was never far away. In the early days at Jetstar, Joyce frequently recited Ryanair's colourful chief executive, Michael O'Leary. Some of Jetstar's staff hailed from Ryanair. Joyce's former colleague at Aer Lingus, Conor McCarthy, had also influenced the Jetstar chief executive in his thinking about how a low-cost airline should be run. Joyce would also follow Dixon's instructions diligently. 'If Geoff said jump, it would be "How high, sir?" Whatever Geoff wanted, we just delivered,' a former colleague recalled. 'Geoff is a master marketer and he has a terrific read on what the feel of people is. Because of that, Alan was kind of taken by him.'[17]

The thirty-something executives at Jetstar had arrived on the block, elbowing out their older counterparts at Qantas who had served decades there. 'In most of the business there was an undercurrent that we may well see that Jetstar is in fact the sustainable future of the business rather than Qantas, depending on whether Qantas could continue to demand a premium,' Grant Fenn recalled.[18] Dixon saw Jetstar as his baby, and some Qantas executives resented his unbridled support for his new protégé. They termed the airline 'Geoffstar' almost from the beginning. Joyce faced a tough time at executive committee meetings in Sydney, where he was outnumbered by his red-tailed counterparts from Qantas. The Qantas executives, especially Borghetti, did not want to see their airline give ground on routes to the new upstart. Buchanan would not forget a remark from Eddington, who had been on the Qantas board when the airline was approved. Eddington reckoned they should win the Nobel prize for economics and peace if they succeeded with their strategy. It was not far from the truth as they navigated the internal politics and the day-to-day challenges of starting an airline from scratch. 'We were fairly independent – Dixon gave us licence and we followed it,' a former Jetstar executive said. 'It was a good management team – everyone was young.'[19]

Almost from the outset, Qantas' senior pilots harboured deep concerns about the safety standards at Jetstar. They ended up taking their complaints to Dixon, who seconded two senior managers to conduct an internal safety audit of the budget airline's first months of flying in 2004. In November that year, the pair presented their findings to the company's safety committee. The internal audit found Jetstar's operations to be safe and its flight standards high, although it drew attention to differences in procedures between the two airlines. While Jetstar was cleared, the lobbying for an internal investigation highlighted a loathing within a large section of Qantas to the new upstart. Many of Jetstar's senior pilots heralded from Ansett, and a rivalry with their counterparts at Qantas years earlier was rearing its head in another form. The distrust within Qantas towards Jetstar ran all the way from the pilots to the commercial teams.

Jetstar became Qantas' attack dog on Virgin Blue. The question was how big Qantas would allow it to grow, and whether it would eat away at its parent's underbelly. The views differed within the company. 'Jetstar should be going anywhere which is not a business sector,' Chris Manning said. 'Qantas is a full-service carrier whereas Jetstar is an airline for people who want to get from A to B for as little as possible.'[20] Before Jetstar was born, Borghetti had believed a low-cost offshoot's fleet should be capped at ten aircraft, a view not shared by Dixon or Joyce. The three executives sat on a flying committee, which debated whether Jetstar should fly on routes dominated by Qantas. 'Initially Borghetti won a few arguments over routes but as time went on he was losing. Because Alan had the backing of Dixon, he seemed to get most of what he wanted,' Manning said. Borghetti had also objected to Jetstar not allocating seats to passengers before boarding planes. The policy ensured Jetstar planes were on time but Australians did not warm to rushing for seats when they boarded their flights. It culminated in a major argument one day in Dixon's office with Borghetti, Joyce and Gregg. The unallocated seating on Jetstar was eventually scrapped because of customer complaints in October 2006.

The favoured-child status bestowed on Jetstar created resentment throughout Qantas. 'It was as if there were two separate companies fighting,' Manning said. 'The enemy was within. As Jetstar got stronger, I think it got worse. We had nothing to do with them, and yet we had been around eighty-something years. It was as if we didn't exist, and that was silly. It's not using the whole resources of the Qantas community for the betterment of Qantas.'

The scene had been set for showdowns between Borghetti and Joyce in the years to come, and their deep-seated desires to compete with Gregg as Dixon's eventual replacement as Qantas chief executive.

3

TWO TO TANGO

On a brisk early autumn morning, Geoff Dixon was jogging in a park in central London. Dixon paid special attention to his physical fitness, cutting a fine figure for a man in his early sixties. The Qantas chief executive and his right-hand man, Peter Gregg, were in London after spending a few days in New York where they had met analysts from the big credit-rating agencies. Dixon would not learn until he returned to the Sofitel St James, a luxury five-star hotel on the corner of Pall Mall and Waterloo Place where the Qantas pair was staying, that the British Airways chief executive, Rod Eddington, had been trying to get hold of him urgently. Earlier, Gregg's mobile phone had rung with Eddington on the other end of the line asking where Dixon was.

'I think he is probably out jogging at this time of day, Rod,' Gregg replied.

Later on September 8, 2004, Dixon and Gregg trekked out to British Airways' headquarters near Heathrow Airport to meet its top executives. At its large open-plan complex at Waterside, north-west of the airport, Eddington told the pair that British Airways was dumping its cornerstone stake in Qantas on the market, more than a decade after the Keating Government began the march towards privatising the Australian airline. Eddington was letting them know as an act of courtesy that British Airways' bankers would be selling its 18.25 per cent stake in Qantas to institutional investors around the globe. The United Kingdom flag carrier's balance sheet was in need of urgent repair, and the large amount of capital it had tied up in Qantas was better used improving its own fortunes. As it turned out, British Airways' bankers sold the stake to investors for $3.28 a share.

Dixon and Gregg quickly began mulling over what British Airways' decision meant for their airline. The pair was concerned the decision to end an eleven-year management and ownership bond would be perceived as a loss of confidence in Qantas. They had fully expected British Airways to eventually sell, but now it was actually happening. It created a slight dilemma for Gregg. In New York, Moody's and Standard & Poor's had been keen to know whether British Airways was about to sell. Qantas' investment-grade credit rating was crucial to its ability to borrow money more cheaply.

Senior politicians in the Howard Government were also glad to see the end of British Airways' ownership ties. 'That [cornerstone stake] turned out to be a disaster because British Airways just were not good corporate citizens with Qantas. They stymied anything Qantas wanted to do,' Warren Truss, a minister in the Howard Government and later transport minister in the Abbott Government, recalled. 'Their primary loyalty was overwhelmingly to British Airways and British still had, I guess, ideas that it would be the empire airline. That was a bad period for Qantas – there is no two ways about it.'[1]

Despite the sale of the cornerstone stake, Qantas and British Airways retained a close alliance – known as a joint-services agreement – on the so-called 'kangaroo route' to Europe. But for Qantas, the severing of the financial ties with British Airways gave a greater incentive to its top echelons to find a strong partner in the Asia-Pacific region. Singapore Airlines was top of that list. Dixon and Gregg had been fostering a deeper relationship with Singapore Airlines and its majority shareholder, Temasek, since the outbreak of severe acute respiratory syndrome a year earlier. The flying public had avoided Asia in droves during the SARS epidemic, which was devastating for an aviation hub such as Singapore. At the time, Qantas was the second-largest airline at Singapore's Changi Airport. Qantas had built goodwill with Singapore Inc. when it defied calls to avoid flying through the city-state. The stance had opened the door to regular talks with Singapore Airlines' chief executive, Chew Choon Seng, and Temasek, the Singapore Government's investment arm. With the exit of British Airways from its share register, Qantas' destiny now lay firmly in its own hands.

An avid dealmaker, Dixon had long talked about forming a large airline block in the region. A year earlier, competition regulators had halted plans for an alliance between Qantas and Air New Zealand because they believed it would stymie competition. The planned deal had involved Qantas paying $520 million for a 22.5 per cent stake in New Zealand's flag carrier, which was saved by a government bailout following its disastrous foray into Australia with Ansett.

With Jetstar flying routes within Australia by May 2004, Qantas began to step up its focus on where the future of its premium operations lay. As an airline at the end of the world, Qantas struggled to compete against the major international airlines in Asia such as Singapore Airlines and Cathay Pacific, which had their own hubs and lower operating costs. Middle Eastern airlines such as Emirates were a growing force but their impact was yet to be fully felt. Dixon and his senior executives canvassed ways to form a relationship with one of the major Asian airlines. Hong Kong's flag carrier, Cathay Pacific, was a founding member of the oneworld global marketing alliance with Qantas but had rejected every advance from the Australian airline.

The focus increasingly turned to Singapore. Qantas had been giving serious thought to setting up operations in the city-state ranging from ground-handling services to establishing a new airline. In the end, Dixon and Gregg pinned their hopes on the concept of a low-cost airline in Singapore. But in order to get it off the ground, Qantas needed the support of Singapore Inc. or, more precisely, Temasek. During a series of meetings in late 2003, the Qantas executives found the door opened to Ho Ching, the wife of Singapore's prime minister, Lee Hsien Loong. She had been a director of Temasek for more than a year, and was installed as its chief executive at the start of 2004. Over months, Qantas and Temasek built a business case for a budget airline in Singapore. In April that year, Qantas announced plans to set up Jetstar Asia as part of a joint venture with Temasek and two Singaporean businessmen.

Temasek was Qantas' way into Singapore. Singapore Airlines still harboured ill feeling towards Qantas over the way Dixon and Gregg had campaigned against it gaining control of Air New Zealand – and thereby Ansett – in 2001. It was going to take time to repair the damage, and the attempt to get closer to Temasek, the largest shareholder in Singapore Airlines, was a way to achieve it. Four months before Dixon unveiled plans for Jetstar Asia, Singapore Airlines had announced plans to launch a budget airline, Tiger Airways. Tiger's shareholders included both Temasek and Ireland's Ryan family who were behind Ryanair. Now, Qantas and Singapore Airlines were about to butt heads in the low-fares market out of Singapore, linked by a common shareholder in Temasek.

Qantas was mindful of the damage the airlines would inflict on each other, and sought a resolution. Dixon and Gregg again met Ho Ching, the chief executive of Temasek, to point out to her the value that could be created by a merger of Singapore Airlines and the Australian flag carrier. The Qantas executives were gazing into their crystal ball. The world of aviation was undergoing rapid change, the barriers to entry for new airlines dropping significantly. Middle Eastern airlines had begun their upward march. Qantas impressed on their counterparts at Temasek that rather than Singapore Airlines and its budget offshoot, Tiger Airways, competing against Qantas and Jetstar, it made more sense for the two airline groups to cooperate. Singapore was a city-state with a population nudging 4.5 million whose flag carrier had a large network throughout Asia. Australia, one of Singapore Airlines' most important markets, offered a large market of middle-class travellers who could be fed through the Asian nation's hub to destinations around the world.

In early 2005 Qantas' three most senior executives flew to Singapore for secret meetings with their counterparts at Singapore Airlines. On one side of the table sat Dixon, Gregg and John Borghetti; on the other, Singapore Airlines' chief executive, Chew Choon Seng, and longtime airline executive Mak Swee Wah. They met secretly for a reason: the two rival airlines were considering a merger. The executives believed it was a match made in heaven. The airlines began a study that involved data from both being fed to a group of investment bankers who analysed it. Under the arrangement, Qantas could not see Singapore Airlines' commercial data and the Singaporeans could not see the Australians'. The results were mind-blowing for both airline camps. A merged airline group could lead to billions of dollars of extra benefits that neither of them could achieve by flying solo. In business parlance, they termed it 'synergies'.

As the meetings dragged on, both sides became worried that their cover would be blown. The Qantas executives had flown to Singapore several times, and they knew that word would quickly spread in an industry notorious for leaks. Qantas pilots and flight attendants knew the minute one of their senior executives was about to board a flight. Both sides ended up flying to Bangkok, the Thai capital, for a series of talks and believed they could strike a deal. Under the plans, the airlines would form a fifty-fifty joint venture and merge their networks. The airlines could not integrate further because of the Qantas Sale Act, which stopped a single investor from owning more than 25 per cent. The Qantas board backed the plans, as did Singapore Airlines' major shareholder.

The airlines were also greasing the wheels of governments.

Without their buy-in, the plans would sink quickly. Aviation was one of the most highly regulated industries in the world. Out of the blue in early June, Australia's trade minister, Mark Vaile, voiced his support for a merger between Qantas and Singapore Airlines. Days later, the prime minister, John Howard, said the government would examine 'the question of whether Singapore Airlines and Qantas will remain as separate companies for an indefinite period of time' as part of a review of Australia's aviation policy.[2] They were joined two weeks later by Yeo Cheow Tong, Singapore's transport minister, who said his government would encourage Singapore Airlines to pursue the possibility of a merger with Qantas. 'In Asia, we will also have to make sure that we are part of what's happening around the world, the strengthening of airlines,' he said. 'If that means that Qantas and [Singapore Airlines] should also be looking at joining the consolidation process, then I think we will encourage them to actively talk to each other.'[3] The tentative support came at the same time as the Australian government was considering whether to grant Singapore Airlines' pleas to be allowed to fly between Australia and the US, a lucrative route that Qantas had guarded closely for years.

However, several hurdles kept getting in the way. Singapore Airlines' market capitalisation was larger than Qantas'. The Singaporeans felt, quite rightly, that they were getting the rough end of the deal from Qantas, which was pushing for a merger of equals – a fifty-fifty split. The structure of a merged airline also led to the important question of who would become chairman and chief executive. Geoff Dixon wanted to remain CEO. Both sides still had to sell their plans for a merged airline group, which would have dual listings on stock exchanges in Singapore and Australia, to their respective governments. The wider public also had to be won over. Both countries' populations identified strongly with their flag carrier, and would hate to see it fall into the hands of another nation. To win their support, retaining the two airlines' brands was central and the executives toyed with the idea of a dual board, each of which would have its own chairman.

Apart from the difficulty of deciding who would become chief executive, another stumbling block was Jetstar Asia, which Qantas had launched in Singapore in 2004. Singapore Airlines' chief executive, Chew Choon Seng, had begun to back away from the deal as the talks dragged on. Some within Qantas believed Qantas needed to show good faith by shutting Jetstar Asia, while others thought the budget airline was a gun to the head of Singapore Airlines. It could be used as leverage in the negotiations. The idea to scuttle Jetstar Asia was quashed.

The Singaporeans also had long memories. They had missed out on buying a 25 per cent stake in the government-owned Qantas to British Airways for $665 million in December 1992. In the days leading up to the sale, the Singaporeans had thought they had a reasonable chance to buy the cornerstone stake in Australia's flag carrier. Singapore Airlines' then managing director, Cheong Choong Kong, was in Canberra with his advisers when he learnt that they had missed out to their arch rival, British Airways. It gave British Airways three seats on the Qantas board and resulted in the airlines forming an alliance on the kangaroo route to Europe. As part of the sale, the Keating Government had agreed to tart up Qantas' balance sheet by injecting $1.35 billion into the airline. The Singaporeans had failed despite the fact that the Qantas management, then led by John Ward, realised the benefits of aligning the airline with a hub carrier such as Singapore Airlines.

The relationship with Singapore had also hit lows early in the following decade. Dixon and his chief lobbyist, David Hawes, excelled at convincing the Howard Government to block Singapore Airlines from flying between Australia and the US, a route that was becoming one of Qantas' biggest money-spinners. 'On three occasions they had been nixed by Qantas lobbying,' said Peter Stainlay, a former Qantas deputy chief executive and a senior adviser to Singapore Airlines management. 'Qantas at that stage had rights to fly beyond Singapore to twenty-eight destinations in the world, and yet Singapore only had onward rights to fly from Australia to New Zealand. That was how distorted the whole thing was. Three times they got blocked by the Australian government.'[4] The rebuffs went to the heart of feelings of distrust towards the Australians, which surfaced during the negotiations in 2005.

In the end, Qantas and Singapore Airlines fell short of reaching final terms for a deal. The high-level talks in Singapore and Bangkok broke down after less than six months. A deal that would have strengthened Qantas immeasurably had slipped through the hands of its senior executives for a bunch of reasons – too much ego from the Australians topped the list. Neither side could agree on who would become chief executive of a merged airline group. The Singaporeans feared that Dixon, the wily Australian, would end up running one of their best-known companies. 'The moment has probably passed,' Dixon said in October 2005. 'There are moments in time, in all parts of your life, that sometimes things can happen and other times when they can't.'[5]

The failure of the talks with Singapore Airlines increased the pressure to find another partner airline. Airlines with large hubs whose air links fanned out across the globe were in the ascendancy. So-called end-of-the-line carriers such as Qantas were under pressure on international routes and needed to find hub partners quickly or be forced to radically reshape their businesses to compete. In late 2007, Qantas' strategy head, Grant Fenn, spearheaded attempts to reach a deal with Malaysia Airlines. The talks encompassed a number of scenarios, including purchasing a cornerstone stake or forming a deep alliance. However, the benefits to Qantas from a tie-up with Malaysia's flag carrier paled in comparison to those with Singapore Airlines. Their two brands did not match; Malaysia's capital, Kuala Lumpur, was an inferior airport hub for business traffic compared with Singapore; and Malaysia Airlines was a government company mired in bad business practices. The negotiations with the Malaysians went on for longer than those with Singapore Airlines. But their tango ended when

Qantas baulked at the amount of control Malaysia Airlines wanted in the merged entity. 'It just didn't feel right. They kept coming to us. They said the nice things but you knew they couldn't deliver it. In the end, it is a bureaucracy,' a former Qantas executive said.[6]

Despite its non-stop search, Qantas was unable to find a credible dance partner. 'Qantas didn't forge a relationship with a major hub carrier through that period. If you say to me what are some of the problems of today, there you go – that is one of the problems,' Gregg recalled. 'Not only did we dance with Singapore Airlines, we tried to dance with Cathay and were rejected, we tried in the past to dance with Thai and were rejected because of the political instability, and we tried towards the end of the time to dance with Malaysia and British Airways.'[7]

4

BARBARIANS AT THE BOARDING GATE

Lucio's had long been a preferred eating spot for the corporate set, its walls crammed with expensive artwork. On February 2, 2007, the top-notch Italian restaurant in the upmarket Sydney suburb of Paddington played host to the heavy hitters from Airline Partners Australia, a consortium of high-profile investors making an audacious $11 billion takeover bid for Qantas. The corporate high-flyers, who included David Coe, the well-connected founder of Allco Finance Group and a director of the bidding consortium, had taken over the bottom half of the restaurant. Almost everyone was in a party mood amid signs their prize was finally within reach. Many of them knew each other well, their paths having crossed in previous roles.

Earlier on that summer's day in 2007 the board of Airline Partners Australia had made its first major public appearance, releasing a bidder's statement outlining its offer for Qantas. Fronting the press, Coe and other directors of the consortium stressed repeatedly that Qantas shareholders and travellers would benefit in equal measure from their takeover bid. 'A quick-flick opportunity is not on our investment horizon,' Coe insisted.[1] In an attempt to silence critics, the financial engineers vowed not to send aircraft overseas for maintenance, or slash flights to regional towns. They had a simple message for Qantas shareholders: the consortium's offer of $5.60 a share was final. They would not be going higher.

As the senior echelons from the takeover consortium swilled wine at Lucio's before dinner that night in early February, an executive waited in the central city for a printed copy of the bidder's statement. When he eventually turned up with the bound document, everyone toasted each other over glasses of fine wine. The atmosphere at Lucio's was one of euphoria. The deal they had worked and reworked over months was about to make them all much wealthier than they already were. The largesse that night epitomised a golden era when credit was cheap and the money to be made from the scramble for the next debt-fuelled deal was mind-blowing. It seemed as though the party would never end.

Two months earlier, Dixon and the Qantas chairman, Margaret Jackson, had fronted a media conference at Qantas' city offices in Sydney. They announced that the airline's board would recommend shareholders accept the offer of $5.60 a share from the consortium, a 10-cents-a-piece rise on the initial bid. Jackson, who favoured the title chairman over chairwoman, sought to allay fears that the private-equity raiders stalking Qantas would strip the national flag carrier of its assets. 'If you look back in the history of Qantas, in the eighty-six years of Qantas, we've had every ownership structure that you can imagine,' Jackson professed. 'It started off probably as the largest private-equity transaction in Australia, when we began in Longreach, with a group of pastoralists that funded the beginning of Qantas.'[2] Dixon was also eager to emphasise that the bidding consortium's key investors such as Texas Pacific Group could open a new world of opportunities for Qantas. 'In other words, you might be invited to a party you weren't invited to before,' he said.[3]

As they closed the media conference, Dixon, Jackson and the

consortium's public face, Bob Mansfield, threw their arms around each other in a show of unity for the cameras. Dixon, who was about to turn sixty-seven, and Jackson finished with a hug on a day the chairman described as momentous for Qantas. Unbeknown to them, the cosiness of their relationship and the riches awaiting would return to haunt them and the other major players. With David Coe and Macquarie's head of investment banking, Nicholas Moore, standing in the background at the media conference, questions began to be asked about who exactly stood to benefit from this $11 billion takeover to be financed by $10 billion in debt that the Qantas board had embraced.

Macquarie Bank, or the 'Fee Factory' to its detractors, had been the architect of the bid to privatise Qantas. As it scoured the world for targets, Macquarie saw a business ripe for the picking at a time when the phenomenon of private equity was taking off around the world. In the bankers' eyes, Qantas was spinning off loads of cash and was saddled with a highly paid workforce that could be stripped back. Businesses such as its frequent-flyer division seemed to be worth much more on paper than what investors were valuing the airline in its entirety. Almost a decade earlier, Macquarie had masterminded a plan to link with Australian media mogul Kerry Packer and David Bonderman's Texas Pacific Group to launch a hostile bid for Qantas. The plans eventually collapsed when Packer pulled out.[4]

This time, Macquarie had again brought on board Bonderman's Texas Pacific Group, long accustomed to dealing in an industry most investors shunned. Bonderman, a hard-nosed dealmaker from Texas, saw opportunities in distressed airlines. The billionaire had built his reputation on a US$66 million investment in a faltering Continental Airlines in 1993, which he turned into a US$640 million profit years later. The Texas private-equity fund he founded had also invested in budget airlines such as Ireland's Ryanair. It was well versed in the highly unpredictable world of aviation.

On the other side, Qantas' senior executives had become increasingly frustrated that the market had not pushed its share price much higher than $3.50 despite them churning out record profits. Part of the reason was the cap on the airline's foreign ownership. Every time its foreign ownership levels neared the 49 per cent limit, its share price dropped as investors played the stock.

In late 2005, Macquarie began putting out its feelers to the Qantas executives. But it was not until October the following year that the bankers and their counterparts at Texas Pacific returned with something tangible that Dixon and Gregg could take to the Qantas board. Following the advance, the Qantas directors set up a subcommittee to evaluate the possibility of a bid emerging. At this stage, both sides were still sizing each other up. If the consortium was serious, it needed to present a serious proposal. Meanwhile, the structure of the consortium, which included Canadian buyout firm Onex, had changed markedly. Because of foreign-ownership restrictions on the flag carrier, it needed another local investor for the airline to remain at least 51 per cent Australian owned and controlled.

The predators had found their man in David Coe, or 'Coey' to his mates. He was a consummate networker whose links extended well beyond the world of high finance into Australian politics, sport, art and entertainment. The long-time executive chairman of Allco Finance Group had ridden the wave of cheap debt in the noughties and the ensuing share-market boom. Coe had built a $5 billion aircraft leasing, shipping, property and fund-management powerhouse by creating elaborate cross-border finance structures. In the process, Allco's binging on billions of dollars in debt made Coe, the man recognisable for the large gap between his two front teeth, even richer.

As their plans developed, Allco became a bigger part of the syndicate that was about to place a proposal on Margaret Jackson's desk at Qantas. Coe was Allco's loudest proponent of a deal that had been devised by the financial wizards from Macquarie, which also controlled an aircraft leasing business. Under the plans, his fellow Allco directors Bob Mansfield and David Turnbull, the former chief executive of Cathay Pacific, would sit on the board of Qantas. Coe and

Turnbull were very close. For some, it was plain madness mixed with large dollops of hubris. The few people who questioned the takeover deal within Allco quickly recited the oft-quoted remark from Warren Buffett, one of the world's most successful investors, about the first flight by Orville and Wilbur Wright in 1903. 'If a farsighted capitalist had been present at Kitty Hawk, he would have done his successors a huge favour by shooting Orville down,' the Sage of Omaha once told investors in one of his regular newsletters.[5] To critical voices, Allco would need to bundle its stake in Qantas into a separate fund before selling it as quickly as possible. Otherwise, it would become saddled with a large stake in Qantas and subjected to the huge swings in fortunes for which the airline industry was renowned.

The logic to Allco's dance for Qantas lay in the fact that a big part – indeed, the best part – of the finance house's business was the leasing of aircraft to airlines. Qantas was a major client. Allco saw a takeover bid for Qantas as a way to secure its ability to lease planes to Australia's largest airline.[6] In 2006, share markets were hitting records and any thought of a global credit crunch was absurd. The good times were rolling on. Endless riches from the global frenzy in takeovers were there for the taking for the self-appointed masters of the universe. In the domestic market, Virgin Blue was a no-frills airline and Qantas, which had a new weapon in Jetstar, still benefited from its status as the dominant player following the collapse of Ansett five years earlier.

To pull it off, the private-equity suitors required Qantas management to stay on. To guarantee their commitment, the Qantas executives needed skin in the game. The challenge was to convince the executives with reservations about the deal to jump on board. John Borghetti, the third-most senior executive, was the most averse. His reticence towards the deal created tension within Qantas' management ranks. In the end, Borghetti agreed to chip in money. While he had not committed fully, it was enough to deliver the management team to the predators.

Buried in the bidder's statement, which was close to a hundred pages long, several paragraphs confirmed that eleven Qantas executives, including Dixon and Gregg, stood to gain share incentives amounting to as much as 4.5 per cent of the airline. The other top executives on the list included Alan Joyce, the Jetstar chief executive; Simon Hickey, the head of Qantas' frequent-flyer scheme; and the general counsel, Brett Johnson. While they would have to buy the $160 million stake, the consortium would lend the executives the money on interest-free terms and with limited recourse in the event of default.[7]

Private-equity firms – or leveraged buyout firms, as they were known decades earlier – operated on the basis that they needed the senior management of a company they had acquired to become obsessed with making their debt-fuelled deal work. Executives had to be willing to go the extra mile to extract as much as they could from a company for its new shareholders, which required them to cut deeper and drive their staff harder. In order for management to do this, they needed a big incentive. Otherwise, why would they bother?

To keep them on board, the carrot was money – and lots of it. Under the short-term incentives in their contracts from the would-be owners, the 36-strong executive team stood to gain annual bonuses of up to 200 per cent of their base salary. Dixon had attempted to quell concerns about the bounty falling into the hands of management when the deal was unveiled. He pledged to donate as much as $60 million from his long-term incentive plan to Indigenous and medical charities. But he made no mention of the other benefits. Under their existing contracts, Qantas' executives received options for shares each year that would vest when they met certain performance hurdles. In the event of a takeover, the shares would vest automatically. It meant that the share options would be paid out in full to the executives on their final day working for the old owners of Qantas even if they had not met their performance targets. The next day, they would walk back into their same offices to start on generous new contracts under Qantas' new owners. The change-of-control clause in their existing contracts presented a $91 million windfall for Qantas' executive team, including an $8 million gain for Dixon.[8]

It was a bad look. While the Howard Government had declared by early March 2007 that it would not block the deal, shareholders and the wider Australian public still had to be won over. The notion of Qantas' senior executives enriching themselves as the 36 000-strong workforce faced the prospect of wage restraint and job losses under new owners rankled. To the public, management was compromised by a deal that appeared to threaten a brand they had a close attachment to. More importantly, Qantas shareholders were yet to be convinced they were getting a fair deal for their stock in a year that was set to become the most profitable in the airline's history. Although the consortium had upped its offer by ten cents a share in December to gain the approval of Qantas' board, two of Qantas' largest shareholders – Balanced Equity Management and UBS Global Asset Management – believed the bid price undervalued the airline. Within a month, Qantas had issued two profit upgrades, putting it on track to double its earnings within two years. Yet the offer price for the shares remained unchanged.

With the deal in jeopardy, advisers to both Qantas and the consortium were desperate to get the bid back on the rails. Margaret Jackson had picked up a stomach virus in Papua New Guinea, and was awaiting surgery when her advisers arranged for two business journalists from the country's national newspapers to speak to her in late March. Lying in a hospital bed in Melbourne, the chairman told them that Qantas' share price would plummet if shareholders did not accept the bid. Hedge funds controlled about 40 per cent of the airline's register, she warned, and they would dump the stock if the takeover offer did not succeed. 'If anyone thinks this will happen without affecting the [share] price, then they have a mental problem with how the market works,' she exclaimed.[9]

It was a poor choice of words. Her 'mental' remark was perceived as arrogant. It met a hostile reception from shareholders who felt affronted by her demand to accept the bid. She had crossed a line from independent assessor of the offer to actively lobbying shareholders on behalf of the consortium. Days later, the $11 billion bid was teetering on collapse when Andrew Sisson, a fund manager at Balanced Equity, which held a 4.6 per cent stake in Qantas, publicly rejected the offer just two weeks after airing concerns about a lack of information.[10] The consortium faced an open revolt as other large shareholders joined in to voice their opposition. It needed 90 per cent of Qantas' shares or its attempt to gain the keys to the airline would be sunk.

Two weeks later, the consortium breathed life into its bid when it lowered its condition to snare 90 per cent of Qantas to 70 per cent, helping it to sidestep shareholders who had threatened to block the deal. But politicians and unions rebuked the financial engineers when details emerged about their plans to strip $4.5 billion from Qantas in the first year. 'They are not playing with their money. They are playing with everybody else's money and they are playing with our economy,' National Party senator Barnaby Joyce said.[11] The financiers steering the deal had long tried to rebrand themselves as a new breed of financial wizards different from those behind what used to be known as leveraged buyouts. At its simplest, their deals involved piling a target company with high levels of debt, closing unprofitable parts of the business and selling the most attractive assets, before trying to flick what was left onto other buyers as soon as possible. For opponents of the bid for Qantas, it was a case of the barbarians at the boarding gate – a point independent federal senator Nick Xenophon was later keen to stress. The consortium was borrowing $10 billion to fund the deal from a rollcall of the world's largest lending institutions, such as Goldman Sachs, Citigroup and Morgan Stanley.

The financial engineers had been spruiking their grand plan to a wider group of executives within Qantas and its budget offshoot, Jetstar. A presentation to Jetstar managers in Melbourne had left their audience uninspired. The predators had revealed that they had not done their homework. In their briefing, they repeatedly stated that Jetstar did not have a unionised workforce, which was not the case. A large chunk of the budget airline's workforce was employed under enterprise bargaining agreements, albeit on collective contracts less favourable than those of their peers at Qantas. As much as they tried, many of those loyal to the Flying Kangaroo could not warm to the salesmen. They were sceptical of the consortium's prediction that Qantas could boost profits year after year in a notoriously volatile industry. Jetstar lay at the heart of their plans to turn the company into a money-spinner, raising questions about the future of Qantas' full-service operations, especially its international flying business. About a year before the private-equity bid, Qantas had brought in advisers to assess whether it could spin off Jetstar. 'The prediction that profits would continue to rise and the industry wasn't cyclical and you would be able to smooth it out – it's not realistic. Einstein couldn't do that,' a former Qantas executive recalled. 'Basically, we'll wake up one morning, we'll have no money, we'll go to the government and we'll say you take international [operations] for a dollar because we don't want it or we'll shut it down, and domestic [operations] migrates into Jetstar and that's it.'[12]

As the deadline for the deal loomed, the consortium was struggling to get its bid across the line. More large shareholders were baulking at the offer. Hedge funds were making money from rampant trading of Qantas shares as they speculated on the outcome. The Macquarie-backed consortium refused to increase the bid, which was what the hedge funds wanted. It would have closed the deal out. Now, its only option was to buy time.

By late afternoon on May 4 the deal, which just three months earlier had seemed a certainty to its champions at Lucio's, hung by a thread. The consortium had been warning for days that it needed acceptances totalling 50 per cent of Qantas shares to trigger a two-week extension to the offer. Otherwise, the offer was dead. In a high-stakes game of brinkmanship, Macquarie's bankers were desperate to convince Jim Hoffman, the numbers man for American billionaire Samuel Heyman, to sell his firm's shares into the offer. But Hoffman did not believe that his hedge fund was crucial to keeping alive the $11.1 billion bid for Qantas. The US institutional investors believed there was still a high probability the consortium would raise its bid. By surrendering to Macquarie's demands now, there was a chance the consortium would reach the 70 per cent target and succeed in its bid for Qantas without having to dig deeper into its pockets.[13]

That Friday afternoon, Dixon and Gregg had been holed up in Qantas' corporate offices on the eighteenth floor of the Deutsche Bank building, a short stroll from Macquarie's main Sydney bunker in Martin Place. Rather than enduring an anxious wait for the 7.00 p.m. deadline for acceptances to pass in their office, the Qantas duo decided to walk across the street to one of their regular drinking spots at the Sofitel Wentworth. With glasses of red in hand, the pair sat down in the hotel's lounge bar to wait for word to arrive. It had been a tough six months. They had been under attack for the largesse that would flow their way if the bid succeeded. Now, the fruits of their endeavours were in the balance. Shortly after sitting down, Dixon's mobile phone rang. David Coe, who was on a trip to New Zealand, was on the other end of the line. Coe was to the point: the bid had failed to get across the line. The hedge fund in New York that had been counted on to tip its shares into the deal had not faxed through its acceptance of the offer. Dixon and Gregg thought Coe was joking.

He wasn't. The hedge fund's attempts to squeeze more out of the bidders had left acceptances at 46 per cent, just shy of the 50 per cent needed to gain a two-week extension. The consortium and the Qantas executives were snookered. Gregg phoned one of his closest executives, Grant Fenn, to tell him the $11 billion deal had fallen over. Fenn was away at his family farm in regional New South Wales marking calves when the Qantas chief financial officer rang. The significance of the call made Fenn, a former captain of a senior Sydney rugby union team and regarded as an outside chance to one day become Qantas chief executive, sit down on a log for a few minutes to ponder what would happen next. A failed bid would result in endless soul-searching among Qantas' top brass, and questions about what the executive team's plans for the airline would be now. Just before 9.00 p.m., the consortium issued a statement admitting that its offer would not proceed if it was indeed confirmed that the acceptances had fallen short of the threshold.

Later that night, word spread that Hoffman had finally agreed to tip almost half of Heyman Investment Associates' 10 per cent stake in Qantas into the bid. The deal could be saved. Just before midnight, a fax from the US hedge fund arrived, nudging the acceptances across the line. But the deadline had closed almost five hours earlier. Macquarie's investment bankers and the other dealmakers from the consortium had a sleepless night as they weighed their options. Tens of millions of dollars spent on selling their dream were about to go up in smoke if they could not salvage the deal.

The next day, the consortium made an urgent appeal to the Takeovers Panel for the hedge fund's late acceptance to be counted. Its lawyers argued that the deal should not be scuttled just because one shareholder could not get his offer in on time. They also blamed media coverage for leading to 'potentially misleading circumstances'.

But by the Sunday the takeovers umpire had rebuffed the appeal, declaring that the US hedge fund 'should have been well aware of the closing time and date for the offer and of the implications of not meeting that deadline'.[14] After all, Heyman was a 'sophisticated investor'. The panel refuted the consortium's claims that media coverage had resulted in confusion about the deadline. Later that day, the consortium appealed to the corporate regulator to allow it to count the late acceptance from Heyman but their pleas again fell on deaf ears. The deal was as good as dead.

Knives were quickly drawn for the bid's most ardent backers. The federal treasurer, Peter Costello, said he hoped the 'Qantas board would have something to say about their role'.[15] The unbridled support from the Qantas chairman and the rest of the board for a bid that many believed undervalued the airline left a sour taste in shareholders' mouths.

'In our view, [Jackson] must stand down,' the Australian Shareholders' Association's deputy chairman, Stephen Matthews, declared.[16]

On the Monday morning, there were forlorn faces at Qantas' weekly executive committee meeting. The consortium finally accepted defeat the following day, giving up on its frantic attempts to resuscitate the $11 billion bid. Qantas' share price did not collapse as Jackson had warned shareholders two months earlier if the private-equity raiders' offer was not accepted. Instead, the stock rallied with Qantas on track for a near $1 billion annual net profit.

Two weeks later, Jackson fell on her sword following a backlash from large shareholders over her handling of the deal. Her fateful interview from a Melbourne hospital bed had sealed her fate. She would leave her prestigious post later in the year. The same day, James Packer joined her in quitting his directorship after three years on the airline's board. Australia's richest man was loyal to Jackson. She had supported Packer in the aftermath of the high-profile collapse in 2001 of One.Tel, the telecommunications company in which he and fellow media scion Lachlan Murdoch had lost $1 billion invested by their family vehicles PBL and News Corp, by offering him a seat on the Qantas board in 2004.

The takeover tilt for Qantas epitomised the excesses of the first decade of the twenty-first century. It was to be one of the last flares of the era. A year later, the private leasing business David Coe had built into one of Australia's largest structured finance firms collapsed, owing $1.1 billion. The collapse of his one-time share-market darling left retirees and many other Australians who had invested their life savings in the company facing a bleak future. The end of Allco Finance Group in November 2008 was the first of a raft of high-profile failures of large Australian listed companies, such as Babcock & Brown and childcare operator ABC Learning, in the aftermath of the global financial crisis. Had the private-equity raiders succeeded in their tilt at the national airline in 2007, Qantas would have faced a precarious future steering its way through the global credit crunch with a high debt burden. In all likelihood, the airline would have been forced to call on taxpayers to bail it out. Years later, the saga remains a highly sensitive topic for everyone closely involved in the takeover bid.

Qantas' senior executives stayed on and tried to reinvent themselves. In the wake of the failed bid, Dixon unveiled plans for a partial sale of its prized frequent-flyer scheme, the return of money to shareholders by buying back shares and the expansion of its freight business. The board began the search for a replacement for Jackson. It became a three-horse race between James Strong, Qantas' former chief executive, David Morgan, the Westpac chief executive, and Leigh Clifford, the tough mining veteran who months earlier had stepped down as Rio Tinto chief executive. The botched bid ensured that Strong was tainted. His ascension to chairman would have required a change to Qantas' charter because of his previous role as the airline's chief executive. He withdrew from the race and Qantas surprised investors in August 2007 when it named Clifford as its next chairman. He had not been among the names speculated upon in the press as a likely successor to Jackson. Once he was anointed, the directors and management team knew things were about to change in a big way in the senior rungs.

Shortly after Clifford was made chairman, the then president of the pilots' union, Ian Woods, happened to be seated beside Borghetti on a flight from Melbourne to Sydney. During a long conversation on the plane, Woods asked Borghetti what difference he thought the failure of the private-equity bid would make to Qantas' strategy. 'He lent over to me and said, "Nothing",' Woods recalled. 'That told me that the strategy under the next management team would be the two-brand strategy. I didn't realise the significance of the statement when he said it. He was heralding the advent of a much bigger Jetstar. At that point, Jetstar was really only a modest operation.'[17]

Dixon's days were also numbered. As one of its most vocal supporters, he had been tarred by the bungled private-equity bid. A part of Dixon's job in the latter part of his tenure was to work out who was in the frame to succeed him. By August, Qantas had hired head-hunters from executive recruitment firm Heidrick & Struggles to help find a successor. The starter's gun had officially been fired in a race between Gregg, Borghetti and Alan Joyce for the keys to Qantas.

Late 2007 also marked another dark chapter for the airline. In December of that year, Qantas confessed that it had illegally colluded with other airlines to inflate charges for air freight carried on trans-Pacific routes between 2000 and 2006. As part of a plea deal with the US Department of Justice, Qantas paid a US$61 million 'criminal fine' in return for gaining protection for all of its senior management from prosecution. However, lower-level managers such as Bruce McCaffrey, a former military helicopter pilot who had been Qantas' vice-president of freight for the Americas in Los Angeles, were excluded from the deal. While five of his colleagues avoided penalties, McCaffrey was sentenced to six months' jail for his part in the global cartel and fined US$20 000. His sister, Karen McCaffrey, told a court in Washington, DC that his family and friends were 'devastated, knowing he was the one taking the brunt of the blame for this crime'. 'It seems that Qantas could care less about Bruce; he is no longer an employee, so they pinned him in a corner, and now they are hanging their loyal messenger,' she wrote in a character reference. 'They apparently don't care what happens to Bruce, as long as their Australian management are not fined or sentenced.'[18] As a manager four tiers below the chief executive, McCaffrey reported to supervisors in Sydney. Carl Fiel, a former Qantas executive in the US, also wrote in a reference that he was appalled by the 'very unfair treatment' his former workmate received from the airline. McCaffrey's jail term was initially delayed because he was in need of a kidney transplant. In his mid-sixties, he also suffered from the after-effects of a stroke, rheumatoid arthritis, hypertension and an injured knee and broken hip. The 26-year American veteran of Qantas became the first airline manager anywhere in the world to serve jail time for his role in the price-fixing scandal.

The global cartel would haunt Qantas and scores of other airlines such as British Airways, Emirates, Singapore Airlines and Cathay Pacific for years as regulators around the world pursued them. In Australia, Qantas became the Australian Competition and Consumer Commission's biggest scalp from a four-year investigation into the illegal fixing of prices on international routes when it was eventually fined $20 million. The cartel had originated in 1996 when at least seventeen airlines, including Qantas, introduced freight levies on air cargo to counter rising fuel costs. It later widened to security surcharges imposed after the terrorist attacks on September 11, 2001, and war-risk fees arising from the US invasion of Iraq in 2003. In the end, Qantas received fines totalling more than US$100 million in jurisdictions around the world, including Europe, Korea and Canada.

With Qantas scarred, Dixon was also eager in his final days to cement his legacy. Qantas had scoured Asia for years and failed in its search for a dance partner. The less Qantas succeeded in its talks, the more desperate it became. In May 2008, an opportunity opened on the other side of the world when British Airways' chief executive, Willie Walsh, stepped onto the podium at the Royal Aeronautical Society in London to deliver a pivotal speech. Walsh made his case for ridding the industry of regulatory barriers that stopped airlines from merging outside the European Union and the US. 'We need a new world order,' the Irishman declared. 'Governments do not need to run airlines, or bail them out when they run into trouble, or decide who can fly where when.'[19]

For Dixon, the speech was music to his ears. He had envisaged a world of mega-carriers, and wanted to guarantee Qantas a seat at the top table. He seized the opportunity to phone Walsh in an attempt to initiate talks with British Airways about a game-changing deal. The pair had had many dealings over the years, and got on well on a personal level. Walsh had joined Aer Lingus when he was just seventeen as a cadet pilot, and later became one of the few to successfully cross into senior management. Just days after the terrorist attacks in

New York and Washington, DC on September 11, 2001, he had been appointed Aer Lingus' chief executive. Four years later, Walsh had left his hometown of Dublin to succeed Rod Eddington as the chief executive of British Airways at the age of forty-three. Despite his public utterances about the need for a new world order in aviation, Walsh was lukewarm about the initial advances from Qantas.

Dixon was proposing a blockbuster deal: a merger of the two airlines. However, the hurdles to a transcontinental deal in the aviation industry were immense. It had long been a pipe dream because airlines had been unable to dance around stiff foreign-ownership limits on carriers. British Airways had also begun tentative talks about a merger with Spain's flag carrier, Iberia. The barriers to those two teaming up were far less because they operated within Europe's common market. But Dixon was adamant that Qantas had to do a deal to secure its future, and he had alongside him a new chairman in Leigh Clifford who was more than willing to entertain a dance with British Airways.

5

CHANGE OF COURSE

In mid-June 2008, Qantas' directors and senior executives flew to New York in their long-accustomed seats at the pointy end of the plane. They arrived from different parts of the globe for the two-day strategy board meeting. It was an annual ritual: each June the Qantas directors and senior management met for a strategy briefing to chart their long-term plans for the airline. This time, it would serve as a chance to induct two new directors – Barbara Ward and Richard Goodmanson – onto the blue-chip company's board. Meeting in the world's financial capital was also an opportunity for them to catch up with a large number of powerful institutional investors.

Across the Atlantic, Qantas' talks with British Airways about a mega-merger was beginning to show promising signs after a tepid reception. Geoff Dixon and the new chairman, Leigh Clifford, had met their counterparts from British Airways, Willie Walsh and Martin Broughton, at an adviser's office in London.[1] In New York, a bigger game was on the minds of executives as the jostle for power at Qantas was about to reach its climax. The private-equity consortium's botched $11 billion takeover bid was still raw in everyone's minds. Dixon's power and standing had diminished in the aftermath of the bid. The dominant silverback had grudgingly accepted that his time was up. Shortly after the takeover bid failed in May 2007, Qantas hired executive search firm Heidrick & Struggles under the guise of executive development evaluation. Heidrick would assess the strengths and weaknesses of the entire executive team. Its real task was to search for a new CEO. The board wanted to ensure a proper succession plan was enacted. In the months that followed, John Borghetti, Peter Gregg and Alan Joyce each spent long hours in front of the staff from Heidrick. Gregg and Borghetti were the frontrunners for the top job at Qantas due to the reputations they had built over years. They held the second- and third-most powerful executive positions at Qantas. But as the selection process wore on, Joyce's name was mentioned more frequently. He had become closer to Dixon, leaving Borghetti and Gregg feeling as though they were drifting away from their CEO.

Borghetti and Gregg knew each other very well from years spent working closely together at Qantas. They lived and breathed their jobs. They were forever criss-crossing the globe as part of their high-powered positions. They sacrificed time away from their families and the simpler things in life for the intoxicating, adrenaline rush of power, job satisfaction and a bulging hip pocket during the golden days before a tsunami swept through the global financial system. Neither Gregg nor Borghetti was a big supporter of a merger with British Airways. Because the two airlines were at opposite ends of the world, the pair believed the ability to strip out costs and gain other benefits from merging the companies would largely be limited to the kangaroo route to Europe.

Joyce was a rising star as the chief executive of Jetstar, the no-frills airline he had played a central role in building from scratch. He had also built his career outside the Qantas box, which meant he was not perceived as having some of its bad practices. His worth had risen as other airlines approached him. In 2005, Joyce had received an offer from Ireland's flag carrier, Aer Lingus, to take over from Willie Walsh as chief executive.[2] Walsh was leaving to become British Airways' boss in May that year after Rod Eddington stepped down. For Joyce, it was a chance to return home to his family and friends – and to the airline where his career had begun. Before the Jetstar chief executive left for a trip to Ireland, Dixon had given him a letter to open on the plane. In it, Dixon made him a counter offer, increasing his salary, in a bid to keep him at Jetstar. It worked.

Clifford, the ultimate manager of the succession process as chairman, had called the three candidates in one day in late 2007 and told them he would run a proper process. Each of them would be asked to present their pitch for the CEO's job to the board. Clifford later told the *Financial Review*: 'I said to the internal candidates we were going to make an assessment over time and I would make sure everyone got exposure to the board. I said I'd treat people with dignity and have a fair process.'[3]

On those early summer days in Manhattan in 2008, the Qantas directors and executives were to canvass a list of strategic matters confronting the airline. These included the potential blockbuster deal with British Airways. But turmoil back home was never far away. A dispute with its licensed aircraft engineers was forcing Qantas to cancel scores of domestic flights and ruining its on-time performance, a key metric that airlines used to judge how they rated against each other. The stalemate over a new collective labour agreement was leading to a growing backlog of planes in need of maintenance. It was causing many sleepless nights and long hours for the operational managers tasked with keeping the network running as smoothly as possible, and threw into jeopardy the airline's hard-won reputation for safety. The Qantas brand was suffering from the inconvenience caused to customers. The engineering dispute was also straining the relationship between Dixon and Gregg over the way it should be handled.

The Sofitel in Midtown Manhattan offered a temporary refuge from the daily operational dilemmas at home – and prying eyes. The plush hotel on West 44th Street had been a regular place for Dixon and Gregg to stay whenever they visited New York. They could peer out of its windows to marvel at landmarks such as the Chrysler Building's distinctive silver crown. Opened at the turn of the twenty-first century, the thirty-floor Sofitel was a short walk from landmarks such as the Rockefeller Center, Grand Central Station and Times Square.

Dixon and Gregg had been joined in New York for the board meeting and strategy briefings on June 18 and 19 by other executives, including Joyce, Borghetti and the strategy chief, Grant Fenn. Years earlier, Gregg had hired Fenn from KPMG, one of the big-four accounting firms. The pair was close, and Fenn was still an outside chance at replacing Dixon. Nearing a pivotal moment in their own lives, the Qantas executives and their board were at ground zero of the unfolding financial crisis. It was to climax a few blocks away from the Sofitel three months later when Lehman Brothers, the fourth-largest investment bank in the United States, was declared bankrupt. When the Qantas board met, the former masters of the universe had yet to file out of Lehman's 36-storey headquarters near Times Square for the final time, carrying boxes full of their personal belongings.

Qantas was at a crossroads. It had ridden on the coat-tails of a once-in-a-generation mining boom, a financial system awash with cash and the collapse of Ansett. But the airline's wheels were starting to creak amid signs of an end to the golden run. The rapidly deteriorating state of the global financial system in mid-2008 threatened to play havoc on a business that relied on high-yielding passengers to turn a profit. Airlines are among the first to feel the impact of consumers tightening their belts. After a day of detailed discussions about strategy, the board and executives retired to the Sofitel's art-deco-themed French restaurant, Gaby, for dinner. The hotel staff had blocked off the restaurant in an L-shape and assembled a long table where its high-powered guests could sit to eat and chat. The Qantas executives were scattered among the directors as they consumed their entrees and main courses. The strategy briefings were over but the CEO succession at Qantas was still on people's minds. After dinner, they mingled with others in the group. Borghetti, who had been locked in a conversation, saw what appeared to be celebrations in the corner of the restaurant between Dixon and Joyce. From that moment in Midtown Manhattan, Borghetti had a gut feeling that his fate had been sealed. His long-held dream for the top job at Qantas appeared to have been dashed.

Just over a month after the meetings in New York, Joyce officially made his pitch to the board at Heidrick & Struggles offices over two hours on July 22.[4] Out at Qantas' main offices near Sydney Airport, Gregg and Borghetti were in meetings with Airbus executives about the delivery of the first of the airline's brand-new double-decker A380 planes. They had no idea what was occurring in town, and would not get a chance to make their own pitch to the board.

Three days later, Qantas' luck was to be sorely tested. On the morning of July 25, the four engines of a Qantas Boeing 747-400 roared as it climbed to its cruising altitude of 29 000 feet after taking off from Hong Kong's Chek Lap Kok Airport. Qantas flight QF30 had stopped off in the Chinese territory on its way from London to Melbourne. Aboard the jumbo were 350 passengers and nineteen crew members. Tara Kynnersley was flipping through a bridal magazine as she settled into her economy-class seat on her way home to celebrate her thirty-first birthday. She had just endured a teary farewell with her boyfriend, who was staying on in Hong Kong briefly to attend a friend's party. They were young lovers: he had just proposed to her on Italy's Amalfi Coast. David Saunders, a 34-year-old Melbourne architect, was another passenger in the glow of romance. He was heading home after proposing to his girlfriend in Israel.[5]

Just fifty-five minutes into the flight, the crew and passengers heard a loud bang, quickly followed by a sharp jolt. In the cabin, curtains swayed as a sudden rush of cold air swept down the aisles. Oxygen masks fell from the overhead compartments as the jumbo's interior began to depressurise rapidly. The passengers on QF30 frantically began donning their masks. Some masks didn't work. 'There was a bit of panic with the oxygen masks not working,' Kynnersley recalled later. 'I just thought, I'm really happy with life. I have a beautiful fiancé, family, friends – I have had a wonderful life. And I thought, I'm on a plane, there's nothing much I can really do about it.'[6]

The thought of dying rushed through the mind of Rachael Angley, an eighteen-year-old who was seated in 48C in the economy cabin next to her younger brother, Ben Wallace. She panicked as the jumbo tilted to one side and cold air whistled through the cabin. 'I thought there must be a hole in the plane of some sort and wondered what if people got sucked out like some kind of horror film,' she said. 'I feared we would suffocate, or that the plane would crack in half and we would fall to our death.'[7]

In the cockpit, the first officer, Bernd Werninghaus, took manual control of the plane as the autopilot disconnected after the pilots heard a 'loud bang or cracking sound'. Multiple warning lights lit up the array of panels in front of the crew in the cockpit, alerting them to the loss of cabin pressure and problems with a cabin door. Just twenty seconds after the bang, the pilots reduced the thrust on the plane's four Rolls-Royce engines. With the cabin depressurising, the pilots donned their oxygen masks and scrambled to put the plane into a rapid descent to 10 000 feet. Captain John Bartels, a former Skyhawk pilot in the navy, made a MAYDAY radio call, the international distress signal, alerting authorities to the fact that the lives of the 369 people on board were in imminent danger. As the plane plunged in a controlled manoeuvre, passengers clutched their heads as they endured headaches, ringing ears and a temporary loss of hearing. Within six and a half minutes, the plane had dived 19 000 feet to an altitude where passengers and crew could remove their oxygen masks.

Back at Qantas' headquarters in Sydney, the crisis centre had been activated upon receiving the MAYDAY. Neither those on QF30 nor those on the ground who were trying to manage the unfolding crisis knew what had caused the explosion in the jumbo jet's hold. The force of the blast had punctured the cabin floor, damaging a cabin door and overhead panels before piercing the lower fuselage of the plane, creating a two-metre-long hole. Cargo protruded through the gaping hole.[8]

In the crisis centre watching over the midair emergency was Borghetti, the senior executive charged with operational oversight of Qantas' domestic and international operations. The centre was in contact with the pilots but all they knew was that their plane had a large hole in its fuselage. The immediate thought of those in the crisis centre was that a bomb had exploded in an act of terrorism. Borghetti was trying to hold his nerve in front of a growing number of executives, such as Chris Manning and Peter Wilson, who were gathering in the crisis centre. It was a scary place to be. Hundreds of lives were on the line. Borghetti was not about to tell his staff what he was thinking. The situation looked bleak for the Qantas jumbo and the 369 people on board. As the badly damaged plane limped towards Manila less than 500 kilometres away to make an emergency landing at Ninoy Aquino International Airport, Borghetti got an urgent call from Dixon who was in Qantas' city office. The CEO wanted him to travel into the centre of Sydney straight away.

'Geoff, I've got this aircraft,' Borghetti said.

Putting down the phone, Borghetti turned to one of his senior staff, telling him he needed to take over in the crisis centre. 'Are you serious?' the executive replied. Qantas' enviable record of never having lost a jet airliner since it began eighty-seven years' earlier in the Queensland outback town of Winton was in serious jeopardy. Borghetti rushed to the basement, climbed into his car and dialled into the crisis centre as he drove to Sydney's CBD. He wanted to keep abreast of what was happening to the stricken jumbo. His phone dropped out when he parked in the basement of the Deutsche Bank building on Phillip Street where the airline's executive offices were located.

After taking the lift to the eighteenth floor, Borghetti rushed to the CEO's corner office where Dixon was at his desk. With the midair emergency top of his mind, Borghetti began rattling off his concerns that the plane was in serious trouble. It quickly became clear that he had not been summoned to talk about the midair emergency. Instead, Dixon had called him in to tell him that he had missed out on the CEO's job. He wouldn't be replacing the man he had answered to for the last seven years. The board had chosen Alan Joyce. Before he was told, Borghetti had a strong hunch that he had missed out. But it was still a shock when the final decision was delivered. It was a role he had aspired to for years. Dixon told Borghetti that he had also just informed Peter Gregg, who was in his office next door, which looked out to Sydney Harbour.

After receiving the news from Dixon, Borghetti walked into Gregg's office. Up until Dixon had delivered the verdict, Gregg had believed he stood a fair chance of claiming the coveted role. Perhaps the outcome should have been obvious. He felt that no one had engaged him in a meaningful conversation about succession. Nor did he know whether Heidrick & Struggles, the firm hired to help in the selection of the next chief executive, had made a recommendation on the preferred candidate. Gregg – or 'Greggie' to his friends – was tarred with the old management tag and the hangover from the botched private-equity bid a year earlier. Then aged fifty-three the rugby-league devotee had a tendency to speak his mind, which did not always go down well with the board on which he had sat as an executive director for seven years. But after dealing with multiple crises from nearly two decades spent in the senior echelons, Gregg had become emotionally attached to the airline.

In Gregg's office, Borghetti talked through the decision with his longtime colleague. With the thought of QF30 still running through his mind, Borghetti left Gregg and walked next door to his own office. He still had to speak to the Qantas chairman before he could head back to the crisis centre. Once on the line, Clifford told him that he believed Dixon had spoken to him before outlining his reasons why he believed Joyce was the right man for the top job. Borghetti put down the phone before taking the lift back down to the car park and making the twenty-minute drive to the main offices near Sydney Airport. The midair emergency was still under way.

Before it could land at Manila's international airport, QF30 jettisoned 50 tonnes of fuel over the South China Sea to ensure the jumbo's weight was within safe limits for a touchdown. Almost two hours after it had taken off from Hong Kong, the plane landed smoothly in Manila. Emergency vehicles surrounded the Qantas jet as it pulled to a halt on runway six. A near disaster had been narrowly averted. QF30's passengers and crew were shaken and traumatised but had escaped physical injury. As its passengers and crew were soon to learn, one of thirteen alloy-steel oxygen bottles in the plane's hold had been turned into a deadly projectile after rupturing. 'It was luck that no one was sitting in the seat above it when it went off,' Chris Manning, the Qantas chief pilot at the time, recalled.[9] Captain John Bartels, a sanguine character, quickly realised how badly damaged the jumbo was when he walked around the outside of it shortly after landing. The pilots were lucky the weather had been favourable at Manila, because the oxygen bottle had cut wiring to the instrument landing system when it exploded. Air-safety investigators would spend the next two years piecing together the events but were never able to rule conclusively why the cylinder had burst. It was the only oxygen bottle ever to have ruptured in a civilian or military plane. They would eventually close the case on QF30 by ruling that the risk of oxygen cylinders exploding on aircraft remained very low.

A day after the midair emergency, Dixon fronted a media conference in Sydney where he talked of his shock at learning about the emergency, and apologised to passengers. 'I was horrified. I think that this is a very, very serious incident. We are not downplaying it,' he told the journalists.[10] He gave no inkling of the events that had played out in Qantas' city offices on the same day that QF30's passengers and crew diced with death.

Borghetti and Gregg, the two most senior executives at Qantas after Dixon, had been told to keep quiet about the succession until it was announced on the Monday morning. Both were left to stew over the weekend about the way they had been treated. The announcement was slated for late morning. Borghetti had to attend a breakfast function for a client at 7.30 a.m. on the Monday. One of his major roles was to keep the large corporate clients, who controlled travel accounts worth tens of millions of dollars, flying with Qantas. He thought Qantas would release a statement about the new chief executive to the market at 10.00 or 11.00 a.m. But the airline had lodged it at 8.36 a.m. After the client meeting Borghetti returned to the city office, and as he walked in he was confronted with junior staffers telling him they were sorry he had missed out on the top job. Borghetti had been denied the chance to sit down with his team to tell them personally. Instead, they had learnt about who had won the race from a press release. He would not forget.

Later that morning, Clifford walked into a conference room in the city offices flanked by Dixon and Joyce to officially deliver the verdict to journalists. Clifford, a big-framed man who towered over Joyce and Dixon, appeared to bear the scars of battle. He sported a bandage over his left ear and markings across his nose and face. 'I didn't expect to look like this. I hope you're going to airbrush this out of your photograph,' he said, pointing out that he had had surgery to remove sunspots the week before. Unlike during the events three days earlier in the very same offices, the playmakers engaged in banter to present a united front. Joyce regaled journalists with his past at Jetstar and Ireland's flag carrier, Aer Lingus: 'Three people used to share a tea bag at Aer Lingus . . . I used to be the last one to get a dip, as the youngest.' Dixon, too, was left under no illusion that his time as kingmaker had ended as journalists peppered Joyce and Clifford with questions, trying to gain an insight into their plans for Qantas. 'I was getting worried that I wouldn't get a question,' he said, when he was finally asked how he felt to be leaving. 'Then I would have really known it was time to go. The king is dead, long live the king.'[11] Joyce and Clifford later left the room, leaving Dixon to deal with more questions about QF30's midair emergency.

Under the terms of his departure, Dixon was to officially step down as CEO four months later at the annual meeting in Brisbane. As part of his deal, he would remain as a consultant to Qantas until March 2009, working out of its city offices in central Sydney. The man who had steered Qantas for seven years would eventually walk out with cash, shares and entitlements totalling almost $23 million for his final eighteen months, making him one of the highest-paid executives in Australia.[12] His reign was over and now the spotlight fell on a diminutive Irishman who had his own plans for Qantas. Having just turned forty-two, Joyce had gained the keys to the national carrier from a man almost three decades his senior – and the large burden of responsibility it carried.

Within days of his confirmation as Qantas CEO, Joyce walked into Gregg's office and took a seat. After a brief chat, he asked Gregg when he would be leaving. Within the next few days, Clifford also arrived to talk to Gregg and said he understood he was departing. The purge had begun.

For Gregg, the rejection was a bitter pill to swallow after he had played a critical role in charting Qantas' path for years. He had lost out to a man who looked many years his junior. But his fate was sealed. The decision had been made and there was no longer a place for him at Qantas. At the time, Clifford told the *Financial Review*: 'People who miss out have to face it like a man.'[13] The blunt words from the hard-nosed former Rio Tinto chief executive would not be erased from Gregg's memory. 'They had taken a decision and dressed it up in a certain way. The fact that we subsequently found out that Alan was given an opportunity to present his wares and others weren't – that was what rankled,' Gregg recalled later. 'From my perspective, I had worked a long time in that business. I had given it a fair bit of my own personal time and effort and I didn't get the gig, and that hurt. But shit, you have to get up and keep moving. It is a bit like playing sport – once the referee blows the whistle you are not going to reverse the decision. You have got to take your disappointment and manage it as best you can. It opened up other opportunities for me to go and do a multitude of things, including being involved in one of the largest construction and mining companies in the world. And the experiences I had at Qantas put me in good stead to handle the pressures of those roles.'[14]

The formalities were dealt with three weeks later. Gregg, a key architect of the Dixon era at Qantas, officially resigned on August 19, 2008, after eight years as chief financial officer. As the strategy overlord, Gregg had played a major role in shaping Jetstar's growing operations in Asia. Investors worried that a mass exodus of experienced executives was under way. 'It is disappointing to see him go, as he made a big contribution to the group over a long period of time. There is a lot going on at Qantas . . . so it would have been good to see the company retain his services a bit longer,' said Paul Fiani, one of the large investors who had opposed the private-equity bid a year earlier.[15] After sixteen years at Qantas, Gregg walked out with almost $5 million in pay for his final six months, and aggrieved about the way he had been treated.

In the fast-paced world of aviation, Joyce had little time to savour his climb to the top. The talks with British Airways were gaining momentum. Just weeks after Qantas had anointed him the heir, Joyce and Dixon met Willie Walsh at the Sofitel St James, a short stroll from Buckingham Palace. The Sofitel chain of hotels was Qantas' choice. For Joyce, it was a reconnection with his past. Like Joyce, Walsh was an alumnus of Dublin's Trinity College, and the pair's paths had crossed at Aer Lingus in the 1990s. Walsh had been subdued when he was first approached about the prospect of a merger but had become increasingly keen as the negotiations wore on.

The high-level talks were just the tip of the iceberg. A whole raft of Qantas staffers were assigned to the project, spearheaded by its head of strategy, Grant Fenn. His team was negotiating a deal with British Airways executives such as Roger Maynard, who had garnered a deep knowledge of Qantas from a long stint on its board. Both sides knew each other well because of the airlines' long-term alliance on the kangaroo route to Europe. Under the proposed deal Dixon had masterminded, the two companies would be listed on stock exchanges in Australia and London. Walsh would become the chief executive of the merged airline group and Clifford its chairman, while Joyce would oversee the Qantas-branded airline. Martin Broughton, British Airways' chairman and a former CEO of British American Tobacco, was willing to step down.

Four days after the collapse of US investment bank Lehman Brothers was to push global financial systems to the edge, a party was thrown on the other side of the Atlantic in the southern French city of Toulouse. Two years late, Airbus' boss, Thomas Enders, handed over the keys to Qantas' first A380 superjumbo. Amid a dazzling light display beamed against the plane's white fuselage, Dixon and his heir glided between tables at a dinner for several hundred guests to celebrate the occasion at Airbus' large manufacturing base. The showroom arced in a semicircle around the double-decker plane, whose freshly painted white fuselage and red tail gleamed under the lights. It was a car-sales room on steroids. After a tough eighteen months, it marked a high-note for Dixon, who revelled in the moment. Standing in front of the new flagship of the Qantas fleet, Joyce joked to the press that he was related to Willie Walsh because the British Airways CEO's wife was his mother's second cousin. 'It's a long-distance relationship,' he quipped. Unbeknown to the journalists, the Qantas top brass had much hanging on building a stronger relationship with Walsh.

Behind the glitzy scenes at the handover of the Nancy-Bird Walton, named after the pioneering Australian aviatrix, a more serious game was at play. For more than two weeks Dixon and Joyce had been criss-crossing Europe to meet investors. At the delivery ceremony in Toulouse, Dixon and Joyce did not join the Qantas staffers and the large press contingent in boarding the A380 superjumbo on the thirty-hour inaugural trip to Sydney. Instead, they flew to London the next day to meet Walsh to nut out plans for a tie-up between the two airlines.[16] The wheels were spinning ever faster in a deal that proposed to create the world's first transcontinental mega-merger.

In the unpredictable world of aviation, the Qantas executives knew another crisis was never far away. On a perfectly clear day in early October 2008, a Qantas A330-300 passenger jet was cruising at 37 000 feet above the Indian Ocean on its way to Perth from Singapore. It had been a smooth ride for the 303 passengers and nine flight attendants on Qantas Flight 72. They had not encountered any turbulence as they neared their final destination. At 12.33 p.m. local time captain Kevin Sullivan, a former Mirage fighter pilot in the Royal Australian Air Force, returned to the cockpit from a scheduled rest break.[17] Six minutes later, first officer Peter Lipsett, a former navy seahawk pilot, left the flight deck for a break, and the second officer took his seat beside Captain Sullivan. On this spring day, the pilots were rostered to fly back to Singapore after landing in Perth to offload passengers. In the cabin, flight attendants had finished a meal service and passengers were settling back into their seats for the final part of the trip. Some were queuing up for the toilets.

At 12.40 p.m., one of the plane's three air-data units began feeding incorrect figures to other systems on the plane.[18] Several seconds later, the autopilot disconnected and the highly experienced captain, who had also served as a US Navy pilot, took manual control of the plane. A series of warnings began appearing on the computer monitor that kept watch over the plane's systems. The airspeed and altitude readings on Sullivan's primary flight display were fluctuating based on what appeared to be unreliable information. The pilots could not see any other indications that the plane was about to stall. Concerned about the information from the plane's system, the captain told the second officer to call the first officer back from the nearby crew rest to the cockpit to help them find the problems.

The A330 lurched into a nosedive just as the second officer was telling a flight attendant via an intercom to send the first officer back to the flight deck. As it did, Sullivan pulled back on his sidestick to halt the plunge. For a spine-chilling moment, the plane would not respond to his command. In the cabin, any passengers or flight attendants not buckled into their seats were catapulted into the aircraft's ceiling, overhead lockers or walls. One of the flight attendants, Fuzzy Maiava, was in the rear galley when the floor disappeared beneath his feet and his head smashed into the cabin roof as the plane plunged 690 feet.[19] Thoughts of dying rushed through the minds of both passengers and crew. 'It was horrendous, absolutely gruesome, terrible – the worst experience of my life,' Jim Ford, a passenger from Perth, said later.[20] The first officer in the crew rest area was thrown into the ceiling, breaking his nose. After several seconds, the captain was able to halt the plunge and return the plane to its assigned altitude over the Indian Ocean, about 150 kilometres west of the small town of Exmouth in Western Australia.

The pilots began dealing with multiple warning messages on the computer system. While they were sorting through the alerts, the plane plunged again but in a less severe jolt than the first nose-dive. The captain again pulled back on his sidestick to arrest the rapid descent. But the flight control system again did not respond to his command for several seconds. Within fifteen seconds, the plane had plunged 400 feet before the pilots were eventually able to return to its flight path.

Minutes later, the first officer rushed into the cockpit, telling the captain about scores of injuries to passengers and cabin crew. Realising the severity of their predicament, the pilots quickly decided they would need to make an emergency landing as soon as possible. They feared the plane would plunge towards the earth again at any time. An air-force base at Learmouth was nearby and large enough to handle a plane the size of an A330. Seven minutes after the first dive, the captain made a PAN-PAN call to air-traffic controllers, a warning one step down from a MAYDAY. Sullivan told them about the injuries to passengers and the problems with the flight-control computer, and asked for clearance to make an emergency landing at

Learmouth. Seconds afterwards, he told the second officer to see how badly injured the passengers and cabin crew were. After he was told about several serious cases, Sulllivan declared a MAYDAY and warned air-traffic control that they had multiple injuries to passengers and crew on the plane.

The plane finally made an emergency landing at Learmouth, just over three-quarters of an hour after the first nosedive above the Indian Ocean. Eleven passengers and a flight attendant were seriously injured with broken bones, fractured vertebrae and lacerations, while another thirty-nine people needed hospital treatment. More than a hundred passengers and crew suffered minor injuries. Some of them, such as Maiava, spent weeks in hospital, and years later still suffered physical and psychological injuries from the midair accident. The accident seriously dented the pilots' confidence in flying Airbus planes. Captain Sullivan was one of a number on QF72 to suffer post-traumatic stress disorder. A report by air-safety investigators later pointed to an unknown software design limitation in the flight-control computer and a fault with an air-data unit as the reason for the plane to be sent into two sudden nosedives.

Less than two months later, Dixon filed onto the stage in a large hall at Brisbane's Convention Centre with the Qantas chairman, Leigh Clifford, and the rest of the board for his final act as the face of the Flying Kangaroo. The attempted dealmaking with British Airways was still a secret. 'I leave Qantas very confident indeed of its soundness as a business,' Dixon told the shareholders at Qantas' annual meeting. 'The next step for Qantas will be to participate in consolidation of the aviation industry. But that is a task that awaits Alan and his team.'[21] Standing on the podium, Clifford sought to allay concerns about the two recent midair plane incidents and to put to bed rumblings about the selection process for the new chief executive. 'Over the course of almost twelve months, the Qantas board managed a thorough process to select a new CEO and to provide for an orderly transition,' he said. 'Alan Joyce has already been a highly successful leader at Jetstar and the board is convinced he has the talent, the skills and the vision to lead the Qantas Group.'[22]

Dixon did not get the farewell he would have wanted. Shareholders were outraged at his $12 million pay for the year to the end of June 2008, which dwarfed his $6.5 million package of a year earlier. His cash-based payments for the year made him the highest-paid aviation executive in the world, overshadowing by a wide margin Gerard Arpey, the boss of the world's largest commercial carrier, American Airlines. 'Paying top dollar for top talent is a load of baloney,' a shareholder responded after Clifford sought to justify the pay packets.[23] Unbeknown to shareholders at the time, Dixon would receive the following year another $10.7 million for his final months at Qantas. As a chapter closed in his career, more than two-fifths of shareholder votes were cast against the largesse heaped on him and the rest of his senior management team.

Within days of Dixon's departure, news about Qantas' talks with British Airways leaked, resulting in a firestorm of newspaper headlines about the creation of an $8 billion global airline. In Hong Kong, Grant Fenn and his team from Qantas, which included its long-serving general counsel, Brett Johnson, and finance executive Richard Richards, had been scheduled to hold secret talks at the Grand Hyatt with their counterparts from British Airways. 'It will create the first genuinely global airline, which will help us cover the world and give us the ability to further grow,' British Airways' chief financial officer, Keith Williams, gushed in the days after their plans were leaked. 'Qantas would benefit from that as well.'[24] Despite slashing its profit forecasts two weeks earlier, Qantas was still one of the most profitable airlines in the world. In contrast, British Airways was staring at a loss.

Years earlier, Dixon, Gregg and Qantas' then chairman, Margaret Jackson, had arrived at British Airways' headquarters near Heathrow Airport in London to present an audacious plan. Their offer in the early noughties to British Airways' chairman, Lord (Colin) Marshall, was to merge the two airlines to the extent allowed under each country's aviation laws. In the British Airways boardroom at Waterside, the three Australians had walked Marshall through their plan to create a dual-listed global airline to connect to twenty common destinations around the world. At the time, British Airways still had a cornerstone stake in Qantas, and their plans were based on creating a cross-shareholding structure. The Australians were met by stony silence from Marshall, who promptly told them they had the opportunity to buy into British Airways on-market like every other investor. That was it – their plans were dashed. Although British Airways was in a world of pain at the time, its top brass never thought such proposals would fly because they believed it was almost impossible aero-politically. Foreign ownership and control limits in bilateral air-rights agreements were too large a barrier.

Less than a decade later, the impossible seemed as though it could become a reality. Walsh was eager to turn the talks with Spain's Iberia and Qantas into a three-way proposition aimed at creating a global airline superpower. He also had hopes of one day reaching out to American Airlines and Cathay Pacific. But after meeting Walsh in Hong Kong in early December, Joyce returned to Sydney and dampened expectations that a deal could be reached. Qantas and British Airways had struggled to find common ground on the split of ownership between the two, and Joyce harboured concerns about the UK flag carrier's large pension liabilities. 'There is a reasonable chance that this might not go ahead,' he said in a high-rise tower overlooking Sydney Harbour. 'We need to get to a stage where we're comfortable with the merger ratio.'[25] A week later, Joyce torpedoed the negotiations. With them sank Dixon's hopes of cementing a partner for Qantas and his own legacy. The abrupt end to the flirtation with British Airways severely strained relations between the two airlines and their executives. Walsh had become a major proponent of a merger despite his initial reluctance to entertain Qantas. He had come so close to brokering a deal, only for the door to be slammed shut.

Within months of Joyce officially taking the reins, a coterie of executives who had served under Dixon began walking out the door for the last time. The dismantling of the so-called Qantas club raised concerns about the loss of experience at the upper echelons. Gregg was followed by the industrial-relations boss, Kevin Brown; Qantas' veteran head of engineering, David Cox; the chief of services, Curtis Davies; and Grant Fenn. After Joyce was anointed in July 2008, Borghetti had surprised him by telling him he was keen to stay on at Qantas. It had been his life since he started in the mailroom thirty-six years earlier. But in March 2009, Borghetti walked into the new chief executive's office to tell him he was quitting. With his role diminishing, he felt like a kebab spit in a takeaway shop: every time he looked, there was another slice missing. He walked out of Qantas for the last time several weeks later clutching a half-full container the size of an A4 paper box. In it was a Cartier pen he had been gifted to mark his thirty-six years at the airline. In the following years, he would use the pen only for special occasions.

In the aftermath of the global financial crisis, a former federal transport minister, John Sharp, echoed sentiments many aviation diehards shared but few would express publicly about the clean-out of the top tier of Qantas' management. 'My only concern with Alan is that he has got rid of the entire management team that was there under Geoff Dixon, and there is no one with long-standing corporate experience at the company,' said Sharp, the deputy chairman of airline Regional Express. 'The value of that shines through when you get difficult times like now.'[26] Joyce was a surprise choice to almost everyone except Leigh Clifford and his inner circle. 'He was different from previous managements. He really had to earn respect,' Warren Truss recalled. 'Normally someone comes in as CEO and they have got immediate recognition for the position.'[27]

Neither Gregg nor Borghetti could turn back the clock. But they would not forget. Nor would Dixon let go, especially as he later began to question the trajectory of Qantas under the bloke he had guided to the top job. The die had been cast. 'Alan had a moment to capture Qantas – instead, he took them on,' Chris Manning, the Qantas chief pilot between 2003 and 2008, said later. 'What Qantas needed was a healer. It needed someone to come in and say, "I can only win if I have people with me. Let's get this great Australian brand going."'[28] The way Dixon's successor was selected and the handover of power was managed left a sour taste in many people's mouths, setting the scene for what was to follow.

6

BEHIND THE BAMBOO CURTAIN

With the British Airways deal dead, Alan Joyce stepped up the search for other avenues of growth for Qantas. Asia was top of his list, and Qantas' no-frills offshoot, Jetstar, the vehicle for tapping the fastest-growing economies on the planet. However, the path to unlocking what appeared to be endless opportunities was fraught with hidden dangers for Joyce and his inner sanctum. Six days before Christmas 2009, they faced their first major crisis at Jetstar Pacific, the Vietnamese budget airline that Qantas part-owned. At Vietnam's largest airport, Tan Son Nhat, Jetstar Pacific's chief financial officer, Tristan Freeman, his wife and two young daughters joined the departures queue at the customs desk. The new international terminal, located just 6 kilometres from the centre of Ho Chi Minh City, hid the airport's traumatic past. During the Vietnam War, Tan Son Nhat was one of the busiest military air bases in the world. For many desperate South Vietnamese, the airport was one of the last avenues of escape from advancing communist forces in the final days of the war in April 1975.

More than thirty-four years after the fall of Saigon, Freeman and his family were on their way home to Australia for Christmas. At the customs desk Freeman was pulled aside and his passport confiscated. Customs officers eventually returned his passport but told the Australian he would not be boarding his flight home. His family was free to leave for Australia but had been barred from leaving Vietnam. Worse still, Freeman was informed that Vietnamese police wanted to interview him about the operations of Jetstar Pacific. This in a country where the rights of the individual held little sway.

Jetstar Pacific's chief operations officer, Daniela Marsilli, was also booked to depart Ho Chi Minh City on December 19 with her family to spend Christmas back in Australia. After receiving advice warning her to stay put, the 43-year-old decided against attempting to get out of the country with her husband, John Brinkley, and their four-year-old daughter, Amelia. A short time later, Marsilli was told Vietnamese police wanted to interview her, too.[1]

In an instant the pair found themselves living a nightmare, snared in a high-stakes game of political brinkmanship in a foreign land. They were wanted for questioning over tens of millions of dollars of losses on a fuel-hedging contract at their fledgling budget airline, Jetstar Pacific. Vietnam had slowly opened its economy but behind the facade, the Communist Party's iron first ruled with impunity. The detention of a Rio Tinto executive, Stern Hu, in neighbouring China on bribery charges six months earlier was never far from their minds. Like Hu, Freeman and Marsilli worked in a country where the state could intervene at will to crimimalise an ordinary business activity. Vietnam had a history of detaining foreigners for loss of state funds. The Dutch bank ABN AMRO paid US$4.5 million for the release of four employees jailed or under house arrest in 2006 over alleged illegal foreign-currency trades on behalf of a state-owned bank.[2]

Jetstar's chief executive Bruce Buchanan, crowned Joyce's successor at Jetstar the year before at just thirty-seven years of age, was on holiday in Bali when he received an urgent call about the ban slapped on his two Jetstar executives in Vietnam. Buchanan had flown to Bali with his wife and children for his sister-in-law's wedding. It was supposed to be a week-long break from the frenetic, non-stop world of aviation. Instead, he was dealing with a full-blown crisis that was yet to become public. Clutching his phone, he spent hours pacing around the pool at the Balinese resort where he was staying with his family, talking to senior staff in Australia and Vietnam about what could be done to get the two Australians out. 'That week leading up to Christmas, all of us were on the phone non-stop to do everything we could to get them out of the country,' Buchanan recalled.[3] The highly sensitive case would become one of the biggest challenges of his career. The treatment of the two executives quickly raised questions about whether Qantas and Jetstar could continue to run a business in Vietnam.

The matter at the heart of the investigation ran to the top of Qantas. Joyce was one of two Australian executives on the six-member board of Jetstar Pacific that had approved the fuel-hedging contract in February 2008. With fuel prices near record levels, Freeman had struck a one-year deal with a state-owned fuel company to cap about 75 per cent of the airline's fuel at US$135 a barrel. Fuel-hedging contracts were a common tool airlines around the world used to help stabilise the volatile price of jet fuel over the long term. But to the Vietnamese, fuel hedging was a form of Western alchemy – a world away from the centralised planned economy to which they had been long accustomed.

Within months, the spot price for jet fuel had fallen sharply to just US$50 a barrel as the global financial crisis spread panic through markets. It left Jetstar Pacific staring at US$31 million in losses on the contract. Marsilli was inadvertently caught up in the dispute because her signature was on the fuel-hedging contract. She had stepped in for Luong Hoai Nam, the Jetstar Pacific chief executive, who was on holiday when the deal to lock in the fuel price was signed. In Vietnam, it was not a trivial matter. The loss or misuse of money at a state-owned enterprise – even what was considered a small amount to foreigners – could carry the death penalty. The losses were ammunition for a part of the Vietnamese political hierarchy linked closely to Jetstar Pacific's arch rival, Vietnam Airlines, and opposed to Qantas' investment.

Vietnam represented the frontier of Qantas' overseas investments. The Australians' entrapment just before Christmas did not surprise some of their colleagues in Vietnam more attuned to the darker side of its political and judicial system. They had feared that Australians sent to Vietnam to help run Qantas' part-owned budget offshoot could be detained because of the multimillion-dollar losses on the fuel-hedging contract early in 2008. Months later, Qantas commissioned its chief risk officer, Rob Kella, to begin a risk assessment of Jetstar Pacific.

It proved too late for Marsilli and Freeman. Their foreign postings had turned from an adventure into a high-stakes dispute more akin to a spy thriller. 'It was surreal, not believable,' Marsilli said shortly after the travel ban was slapped on her.[4] The initial shock quickly turned to uncertainty and despair. The fear of being charged for the losses at Jetstar Pacific loomed large. In the months that followed, the pair would endure interrogations at the hands of the Economic Police and, worse still, be forced to appear in front of the feared secret police. Neither executive spoke Vietnamese, and on occasions were denied access to lawyers.

Months passed without any sign of a breakthrough. They had not been charged. Marsilli was a strong woman, long accustomed to the brutal world of big business, but friends worried for her morale. Her state of mind deteriorated as the weeks passed with no indication of when she would be allowed to leave Vietnam. Her plight was in marked contrast to two years earlier when she had moved to Vietnam's bustling financial capital of Ho Chi Minh City. An ambitious former boss of Adelaide charter airline National Jet, she had been sent to the wild frontier of Qantas' empire. Her job as chief operations officer was to help turn the small, loss-making airline in Vietnam into a profitable offshoot of Jetstar.

A year later she had been joined by Freeman, a young executive who had toiled at Jetstar since its inception in a small office in North Sydney. He had worked closely with both Joyce and Buchanan for almost a decade at Jetstar. Freeman moved into a large upmarket apartment with his young family in District 1, in the centre of Ho Chi Minh City. It was a part of the city expatriates flocked to because it offered the best of Vietnam's burgeoning financial capital. Nearby, the Saigon River snaked its way through the bustling city where streets were packed with noisy motor scooters from early morning until late at night.

More than two years before the two Australians' ordeal, Qantas had begun splashing out US$50 million in a deal that would eventually lead to it building a 30 per cent stake in the state-owned Pacific Airlines. What was later to be rebadged Jetstar Pacific had been bleeding cash and was in need of a capital injection as it faced a bigger and tougher competitor in Vietnam Airlines. Most of the remainder of Pacific Airlines was in the hands of the Vietnamese government's investment arm, the State Capital Investment Corporation. It was a major deal in Vietnam because it was part of the first wave of part-privatisations of state-owned companies. But it was small fry in comparison with the deal under way in Australia. In early 2007, the $11 billion private-equity bid for Qantas was reaching its end game.

Vietnam was part of a wider push by Qantas into Asia. The stellar growth in other markets in the region, such as Singapore, was beginning to slow, forcing Qantas to look to countries tagged as emerging economies. Qantas eyed Ho Chi Minh City as an eventual low-cost hub for long-haul Jetstar flights to Europe using Boeing 787 Dreamliner planes. The rationale was simple: the southern Vietnamese city was a cheaper alternative to Singapore or Bangkok. Qantas had not been the only airline eyeing Vietnam as its economy was prised open, much to the disdain of elements of the country's political establishment. Both the Singapore government's investment arm, Temasek, and Malaysia's fast-growing budget airline, AirAsia, entered talks about buying a stake in Pacific Airlines, the second-largest airline in Vietnam, but eventually walked away.[5]

Less than a year after the initial purchase, Joyce and Geoff Dixon flew to Ho Chi Minh City to unveil the rebranding of the Vietnamese airline as Jetstar Pacific. In their minds, the country offered enormous opportunity. They emphasised that the main trunk route from Ho Chi Minh City to Hanoi was potentially larger than one of the busiest air routes in the world between Sydney and Melbourne. They were the days of unbridled optimism about the riches in Asia there for the picking. The pair planned to boost the size of Jetstar Pacific's fleet from four planes to as many as thirty by 2014.[6]

It was to prove wishful thinking. By the end of 2014, Jetstar Pacific's fleet had grown by six planes. The airline's losses continued to mount as it faced a fast-growing rival in privately owned low-cost carrier VietJet. The hard hand of the Vietnamese government was never far away. A cap on what airlines could charge for domestic flights made it difficult to realise the market's potential. The dream of Jetstar flying to Europe was to remain just that.

Almost from the outset of Qantas' foray, the state-owned Vietnam Airlines worked to squeeze the life out of its smaller rival. Jetstar Pacific also faced its own internal challenges. It was lumbered with a large workforce of almost a thousand staff welded to the way of working for a state enterprise. The Australians sent to Vietnam to keep watch over Qantas' new investment were stunned at the operational practices at the airline. In Australia, Jetstar could turn around a plane at the airport for its next flight with about seven people. In Vietnam, it took as many as thirty. To some Vietnamese, the rebranding of the airline as Jetstar Pacific was evidence of Qantas riding roughshod over a small operator and its local workforce. Australians now occupied many of the top executive ranks, creating animosity among their Vietnamese counterparts who could only dream of earning their high salaries and perks. While often justified, the Australians' attempt to impose their cost-conscious model dreamt up in a foreign land was bound to spark a response from the local workforce. It was a clash of cultures, and a tin ear on the part of the Australians to their new colleagues.

Jetstar Pacific was becoming a threat to Vietnam Airlines, especially as Qantas injected much-needed capital to kickstart its planned expansion and lent its management expertise. The rebranded airline was advertised aggressively, and threatened to eat into Vietnam Airlines' market share. Qantas was caught between two camps in Vietnam. One wanted it to bolster Vietnam's second-largest airline; the other saw it as a menace and wanted it out. The budget airline was subjected to underhanded tactics. Shortly before the rebranding in April 2008, Vietnam Airlines stopped tankers from refuelling its rival's planes at Ho Chi Minh City's airport.[7]

One of Buchanan's first challenges after taking over from Joyce as Jetstar chief executive in late 2008 had been to fix the growing list of problems in Vietnam. He quickly found himself flying into a perfect storm. Later the following year, the airline's safety record came under siege from whistleblowers. After failing to get an airing internally, two expatriate aircraft engineers raised concerns about maintenance standards at Jetstar Pacific, sparking an investigation by Vietnamese authorities. One of them, New Zealand engineer Digger King, weathered intimidation from his colleagues for taking his concerns with Australian colleague Bernard McCune to authorities. 'This guy came around to my place on a motorcycle and rammed it into my door. He then started to kick it down,' King said. 'There was a lot of hatred there for me. People were telling me, "You're going to bring us down." I told them if they did something when we first complained about it, it never would have come to this.'[8] Jetstar sacked the engineers several months before a report from the Civil Aviation Administration of Vietnam found safety practices at Jetstar Pacific to be 'very poor and ineffective', and defects hidden from supervisors.[9] Jetstar Pacific was encountering hurdles at every turn. The same month the engineers blew the whistle, Vietnam's powerful Ministry of Transport demanded the airline dump its logo. It claimed the bright-orange star was a corruption of the star on the Vietnamese flag.

But the safety probe and the storm about the use of the star logo were sideshows to the main event. Less than three weeks after Freeman and Marsilli were stopped from leaving the country, events escalated when police arrested Luong Hoai Nam for 'causing serious losses'.[10] Two months earlier, on November 9, Nam had quit as Jetstar Pacific chief executive without explanation. The 47-year-old had a small stake in Jetstar Pacific and a tense relationship with his counterparts at Vietnam Airlines, where he had worked for nine years. When he was arrested in January 2010 for losses on the fuel-hedging contract, Nam was thrown in jail where he was to languish for months without charge. Suspicions of political motivation were never far away in a case that went to the highest levels of Qantas, Vietnam Airlines, and the Australian and Vietnamese governments.

Early on in the investigation, Marsilli and Freeman were called to the capital, Hanoi, and interviewed separately. The interviews in Hanoi and Ho Chi Minh City were harrowing experiences for the two Australians. At least one interrogation was in front of a two-star general. The case prompted the Department of Foreign Affairs and Trade to warn other Australians with links to Jetstar Pacific to stay out of the country. Some did not take the advice because their families remained in Vietnam.[11] At first, Buchanan had been advised not to travel to the country because of fears he, too, would be detained – after all, he was on the board of Jetstar Pacific. Such was the level of concern that a Jetstar Pacific board meeting scheduled to be held at its base in Ho Chi Minh City was shifted to Singapore.

The investigation into the losses at Jetstar Pacific was the job of Vietnam's economic police. Before long, the stakes rose immeasurably when the secret police stepped in. Their very presence instilled fear and intimidation. The Ministry of Public Security invoked terror in the minds of ordinary Vietnamese. A law unto itself, the internal spy agency was a secretive part of the communist machinery in a country where the buck stopped with the military and the party president and prime minister. Freeman endured a series of interviews by high-ranking staff at the Ministry of Public Security – the country's equivalent of the Australian Security Intelligence Organisation – in Ho Chi Minh City and Hanoi. They were conducted in poorly lit rooms with austere tiled floors, wooden chairs and ceiling fans.

From the start, the operation to free the pair was conducted behind a veil of secrecy, highlighting the sensitivity of the negotiations under way in Ho Chi Minh City and Hanoi. The case brought into play the highest levels of government in both Vietnam and Australia. Qantas set up a high-powered taskforce that included Steve Jackson, its security chief and a veteran of the Australian Federal Police; its general counsel, Brett Johnson; its government relations head and chief spin doctor, David Epstein; and Jetstar's commercial chief, David Koczkar. After the initial warning against travelling to Vietnam, Buchanan eventually flew in to help steer the negotiations for his executives' release. Over the following months, he and the other executives spent countless hours in meetings in Vietnam. Like something from a bygone era, the meetings with senior government officials were often held in grand halls with high ceilings. The two most senior members from either side sat in chairs akin to large thrones, facing out to their teams of advisers who sat in front of them. It was not the usual Western way of sitting around a large meeting table to nut out a deal. As in other parts of Asia, face time was crucial in Vietnam. Trust was not easily won.

For both Jetstar and Qantas, the attempt to free their executives was a major distraction from the core job of running the two airlines. Jetstar was trying to extend its reach in Asia beyond Singapore and Vietnam to Japan and Hong Kong. The Australian business, the engine room of its earnings, could not be ignored. For Jetstar's parent, Qantas, the saga was also demanding an all-out focus from a large number of senior executives. After years of record profits, Qantas' golden run had come to an abrupt end. For Joyce and his new executives, luck was not on their side as the global financial crisis threw up major challenges. Airlines are vulnerable to the whims of consumers and, with an economic downturn gripping Europe and the US, they suddenly stopped waving their credit cards and began saving or paying off their high levels of debt. As a result, demand for first- and business-class seats on international routes dropped. In 2009, Qantas sank to its first half-year loss in six years as Joyce axed 1750 jobs, grounded aircraft, delayed the delivery of new A380 and Boeing 737 planes and tapped investors for $500 million. The unfolding dramas in Vietnam were the last thing he needed.

Rather than summonsing the Vietnamese ambassador in Canberra for a dressing-down about the Australian executives, the government chose to work on the case behind the scenes. Australia's consul-general in Ho Chi Minh City, Graeme Swift, became heavily involved as most of the interrogations of the two executives were carried out in Vietnam's financial capital. The career diplomat reported directly to Canberra. Further north in Hanoi, Australia's ambassador to Vietnam, Allaster Cox, dealt with the top levels of Vietnam's government.

The executives' plight was shrouded in mystery. A crucial part of the investment agreement between Jetstar Pacific's two shareholders – Qantas and Vietnam's State Capital Investment Corporation – was due for renewal shortly after Freeman and Marsilli were banned from leaving the country. As part of the deal, Qantas held what is known as a put option. It acts as a form of safety net. Put options are used to attract investors by giving them the right to recall their investment if the company they have injected money into fails to live up to expectations. With its put option coming up for renewal, Qantas could exercise its right to pull its investment out of Vietnam. As much as some wanted to see the back of the Australians, an exercising of the put option would require Jetstar Pacific's controlling Vietnamese shareholder to pay about $43 million to Qantas. It was an enormous sum in Vietnam, and likely to require the State Capital Investment Corporation to seek financial help from its political masters in Hanoi.[12] Qantas was seen as effectively being held to ransom by the Vietnamese authorities – with Marsilli and Freeman used as collateral – to ensure it would not exercise the put option.

The efforts behind the scenes to release Marsilli and Freeman ground on. Qantas and the Department of Foreign Affairs and Trade sought to keep a tight lid on any information about the case. A two-year battle for the release of documents from the department about the case later helped to finally shed light on what happened behind the veil of secrecy. The documents showed that in June, the department's diplomats churned out eighteen secret cables, email conversations and so-called 'consular media talking points' about the pair's plight. One from the Australian embassy in Hanoi was stamped AUSTEO, which stood for Australian eyes only. A top-secret classification on a document from the embassy was regarded as rare. One of the cables, on June 4, 2010, was marked 'commercial in confidence' and detailed an email conversation about a letter from the investment arm of the Vietnamese government, which owned the majority stake in Jetstar Pacific. The same day, Allaster Cox met Vietnam's finance minister, Vu Van Ninh. The government's investment arm answered to the finance minister.

Then, on June 26, 2010, Qantas and the State Capital Investment Corporation struck a deal on a 'commercial package'.[13] Three days after the deal was struck, Freeman and Marsilli fronted a meeting before a two-star general, Tran Trung Dung, and a colonel, both from Vietnam's feared secret police. They told the pair they were free to leave the country. The next day, they were whisked by car with Australia's consul general to Ho Chi Minh City's airport and put on an 11.30 a.m. flight out of the country bound for home. Their traumatic experience was over. They had been barred from leaving Vietnam for more than six months, subjected to intimidation and interrogation, denied legal representation in some interviews, never charged and not told when they would be free to leave for home until the very end. 'They are just downright relieved to be home – it was pretty ugly,' a friend said. 'It is like someone being released from jail. There are all sorts of emotions that go through one's mind.'[14]

Qantas later refused to release the actual details of the deal it struck with the State Capital Investment Corporation, citing 'commercial in confidence'. It would say only that the 'commercial package' was a heads of agreement that set out the expectations of the two main shareholders and their continuing interest in Jetstar Pacific. Qantas denied it had done a deal to get its executives out of Vietnam but did admit that it had extended the put option – the security over its investment in Jetstar Pacific – shortly before the two executives were eventually released.[15] It also insisted that the police investigation into the fuel-hedging losses was 'quite separate to any commercial relationship' between it and its major shareholder in Jetstar Pacific. Yet heavily censored cables later released to the *Sydney Morning Herald* under freedom-of-information laws stated categorically that Qantas and the State Capital Investment Corporation had 'reached agreement on a commercial package that would also count as mitigation under Vietnamese law, so allowing the travel restrictions' on the two Australians to be lifted.[16]

Keeping the case out of the public eye was always a top priority for Qantas and the Australian government. A classified cable from one of the top diplomats at the Department of Foreign Affairs and Trade's South-East Asia bilateral branch revealed how it sought to manage public perceptions of the case. Stamped 'consular media talking points', the cable, from Bassim Blazey, a former head of the Howard Government's Iraq Task Force, told diplomats how to respond to questions from journalists. The cable sent on the day Marsilli and Freeman flew out of Vietnam revealed that the department wanted to avoid questions about whether a deal had been reached to free the pair.

If asked what conditions were set on the Australians' release, diplomats were told to tell journalists that 'they are entitled to their privacy and we don't intend to provide further comment on this matter'. They were also prepped for the key question of whether Qantas was forced to 'provide any commercial concessions' to set them free. The advice to diplomats was to avoid directly answering the question by stating that 'the Australian Government has focused on the consular welfare of the two Australians'. The cable stated that Qantas was also 'keen to manage media interest downwards' when its two top-ranked executives eventually arrived home.[17]

At the very least, the Australian pair's harrowing ordeal shone a light on the trouble Jetstar faced in Vietnam. It was an insight Qantas did not want revealed. Until then, its performance in the one-party state had slipped below the radar. It was operating in a country where the media was merely a mouthpiece for the government, and far from the prying eyes of Australian investors and journalists. Contrary to the early hype from Qantas, the airline it had rebadged Jetstar Pacific had become a liability. But with Qantas determined to forge on with plans to set up budget airlines in Japan and Hong Kong, Vietnam was not to be the last of the pitfalls in Asia for Qantas and its new chief executive, Alan Joyce.

7

MOMENTS FROM DISASTER

Just before 10.00 a.m. on November 4, 2010, a Qantas A380 passenger jet soared into the skies on a clear, sunny tropical day from Singapore's Changi Airport. The double-decker plane named after the Australian pioneer aviator Nancy-Bird Walton was the first A380 aircraft that Qantas had taken the keys to two years earlier at a lavish ceremony in Toulouse in the south of France. The world's largest commercial passenger jet and new flagship of Qantas' fleet was 72 metres long with a wingspan of 79 metres and capable of holding 310 000 litres of jet fuel. The *Nancy-Bird Walton* dwarfed every other passenger plane around it. A large crowd of plane spotters had woken early on a Sunday in late September 2008 to find spots along Sydney Airport's fenced perimeter to catch a glimpse of the first Qantas superjumbo to touch down in Australia. The plane's size gave it a wow factor.

Two years on, the plane plied the kangaroo route to Europe. After a two-hour stopover in Singapore and a crew change, the *Nancy-Bird Walton* was on the final leg of its journey to Sydney from London's Heathrow Airport in early November carrying 440 passengers and twenty-four flight attendants. It was also the last leg of a nine-day return trip for the cabin crew, and they were eager to return home. Richard de Crespigny was sitting in the captain's chair for Qantas Flight 32 to Sydney. To his right in the first officer's seat was Matt Hicks, a pilot with more than 11 000 hours of flying experience under his belt. Behind the pair sat Mark Johnson, the second officer, Harry Wubben, a pilot training to become a check captain, and Dave Evans, a supervising check captain. Usually three pilots would fly an A380 from Singapore. On this occasion the cockpit was full. Wubben was carrying out a route check of de Crespigny, while Evans was supervising Wubben because he was still in training as a check captain. Between them, the five pilots had more than 72 000 hours of flying experience to their names. Before they left Singapore, the crew had asked for an extra two tonnes of fuel to be pumped into the passenger jet's tanks to allow them to divert around an active volcano, Merapi, in Indonesia. Despite this, the conditions in Singapore were ideal for flying.

Following a smooth take-off, the pilots settled into the journey as they retracted the plane's landing gear and flaps and continued on a steady path towards cruising altitude. 'We departed normally, the aeroplane was relatively light and consequently used a relatively low thrust setting for departure,' Evans said later.[1] Weighing 464 tonnes on take-off, the *Nancy-Bird Walton* was a marvel of modern technology. Qantas' distinctive red livery adorned the rear of each of the plane's four Rolls-Royce engines. QF32 was almost full on the flight from Singapore to Sydney. It had just ten spare seats on its two decks across first, business, premium economy and economy. Among the 440 passengers on the flight were Judith and Donald Friederich, a Sydney couple on their way home after a holiday in Spain. Judith had discovered *The Good Wife* on the in-flight entertainment system on the first leg of their flight from London, and was settling into another episode in her window seat in economy class on the A380's bottom deck. Out the window, she had a bird's-eye view of the long, arcing left wing and the rear end of its two massive engines.

As the A380 accelerated in its climb through 7000 feet, the pilots and passengers heard two loud booms, followed by shudders. They came one after another in quick succession. They were like metallic bangs that the passengers and crew felt as much as they heard. Passengers looked at each other, stunned, and wondered aloud what on earth it could be. 'I heard the first bang and, oh great, an engine blew. I heard a second bang and I saw a flash of light go off and I knew something was wrong,' Emma Teres, a flight attendant in economy class, recalled. 'We just told all the passengers everything was fine. We knew it wasn't, but we were on duty.'[2] Just four minutes after take-off, warning lights lit up the instrument panels in the cockpit of QF32. Almost immediately, de Crespigny selected altitude hold on the autopilot control panel. The A380 instantly levelled off. De Crespigny expected the auto-thrust system to reduce power on the engines to maintain 250 knots as the plane levelled off. It quickly became clear that the auto-thrust had failed. The captain manually took control of the thrust levels to control QF32's speed.[3]

In the cabin, startled passengers peered out of the plane's windows to see the left wing dotted with holes and fuel escaping. Openings had appeared in the wing like holes punctured in a sardine can. 'We heard this big bang. The next minute we looked out the window and we could see fuel coming out of the engine next to our window,' Judith Friederich recalled. 'You could just hear this murmuring going on with the flight attendants and we knew something had happened, but we just weren't sure how severe it was.'[4] The A380's cabin service manager, Michael von Reth, and other flight attendants dialled the emergency button on the plane's interphone system to alert the pilots to the gaping hole in the wing they could see.[5] 'What shot through my head straight away is you have one choice only and there's no way back,' von Reth later told the ABC. 'Either you get an uncontrollable cabin with panic, fear and aggression, or they sit back and just trust you and follow your instructions and go with you.'[6] On the upper deck, Sheena Fenton peered out the window from her business-class seat at the holes in the left wing. 'I was feeling very anxious and frightened. And I looked around at everybody and their faces were a bit worried that something drastic had happened,' the Sydneysider said. 'You do have that moment of your life flashing in front of you but then you pull back. They reassured me I was okay. They said we could fly on three engines.'[7]

In the plane's cockpit, a barrage of alarms signalling system failures elsewhere on the A380 went off. The normal procedure following a warning about an engine overheating was to move the thrust lever for the engine to idle, and monitor it for thirty seconds. As they did, the pilots sent a PAN-PAN, a state-of-urgency call one step down from the worst-case MAYDAY, to air-traffic control at Changi Airport. At that moment, the first officer looked down at the control panel to see a warning light indicating a fire in the number-two engine. A moment later, it changed to an overheat warning. With their predicament deteriorating by the second, the pilots decided to shut down the Rolls-Royce Trent 900 engine. After selecting the master switch, the electronic centralised aircraft monitor, or ECAM, displayed a message that the engine had failed. The ECAM keeps watch over the plane's systems, alerting pilots to faults and listing ways to fix them. QF32's pilots quickly realised that the engine was seriously damaged. They discharged one of two fire-extinguisher bottles into the engine. To their shock, the system did not confirm whether the extinguisher had worked. They pushed the discharge button again. But the pilots still did not know whether it had gone off. They tried the engine's second extinguisher. The pilots discharged it twice but again had no idea whether it had worked.

To reduce the risk, they began shifting fuel from the large tanks in the plane's outer wings to the inner tanks on the A380. As they did, the pilots noticed that the display for the number-two engine now showed a fail, while the number-one and number-four engines were indicating a degraded mode. By this stage, the control panel resembled a Christmas tree, alerting the crew to multiple system failures.

It was a pilot's worst nightmare. The list grew by the second. The wing slats had failed. The pilots' control over the spoilers was reduced while the left wing had pneumatic bleed leaks. The avionics system was overheating. They would not be able to jettison fuel due to a fault. The auto-thrust and auto-land systems were out.

The pilots were forever weighing up their options. They decided it would be best to hold the plane's altitude while they worked systematically through the warning messages rather than make an emergency dash for Singapore. They radioed Singapore's air-traffic control again to tell them that they would need thirty minutes to process the warning messages. They wanted to remain within 56 kilometres of Changi Airport in case they needed to land quickly.

After the loud boom from one of QF32's engines, debris from the plane had rained down on a 1.5-square-kilometre area on the Indonesian island of Batam, just south of Singapore. Pieces of metal struck houses and the roof of a school, injuring a student and teacher. It was obvious that the debris had fallen from a plane. Residents picked up pieces covered in Qantas' distinctive red livery emblazoned with a kangaroo. Mohammed Yani, forty-five, was at home when he heard a loud noise overhead. He rushed outside to find metal debris had smashed through the front window of his car. 'I looked up and saw an aeroplane that was flying low and it has white and red colours but I don't know which airline was it,' he said in broken English.[8]

Shortly after plane debris landed on Batam, residents began to tweet about what they had seen. Within minutes, the world was awakening to a crisis before Qantas' operations centre in Sydney knew the full extent of what it was dealing with. Wire services and global TV networks followed the tweets with news flashes that a plane had crashed. Reuters reported that 'Qantas told CNBC Television that a plane that crashed near Singapore was an Airbus A380'. A China-based senior officer at United States private intelligence company Strategic Forecasting sent urgent emails to his office. 'There are reports all over the wires that the plane hit the deck in Indo,' he wrote.[9] Qantas' security department paid for the firm's intelligence to help it assess threats. On the Australian Stock Exchange, the airline's share price fell sharply as investors traded on the speculation.

The *Sydney Morning Herald*'s Indonesian correspondent, Tom Allard, phoned the newsroom in Sydney after spotting the messages on Twitter, the instant-messaging service that in 2010 was still untried by many people, including myself. The pressure to report sketchy information that had yet to be confirmed as correct was immense. I could not report that a plane had crashed when I had no reliable evidence beyond posts on Twitter. No longer did print journalists work to a deadline in the evening for the next day's newspaper. Now, readers expected to learn about events as they were happening – even if the information was unreliable. As the newspaper's aviation reporter, I phoned Olivia Wirth, Qantas' chief PR who was at her Sydney office, to confirm that a plane had indeed crashed. She was surprised at what I was telling her. She had not heard anything but said she would put in calls to Qantas' operational managers. By the time she phoned back, the incident had become a global event playing out on TV screens and news websites as it happened. The tweets were wrong: she told me a Qantas plane had not crashed but that an A380 was returning to Singapore after its pilots had been forced to shut down one of its four engines. The severity of the incident seemed to fall a notch or two – it was not uncommon for pilots to shut down aircraft engines in mid-flight.

But the plane was still in peril. Circling in a holding pattern near Singapore, the *Nancy-Bird Walton* was in danger of becoming the worst aviation disaster in Australia's history. The airline was dealing with an urgent demand for information.[10] Unlike the emergency landing of a 747 jumbo jet at Manila two years earlier, the media was alive to what was happening to QF32 while it was still in the air, and speculating on what was happening with the limited information available. The era of social media had arrived with a vengeance. A major event had become widely known before the authorities had formally been made aware of it.

In Sydney, Qantas' crisis-management centre was grappling to understand what was happening to the pride of its fleet. The level of concern within Qantas was high from the outset. The first words many operations managers heard about the incident were that a Qantas plane had crashed. 'If you weren't nervous before, as soon as you heard that, you turned white. I think most of us did,' a Qantas manager said later.[11] The staff could not speak to the pilots because the plane's satellite phone had been knocked out. In the minutes after the loud booms on QF32, the engineers in maintenance watch, which was a floor below the operations centre in a building at Qantas' main offices in Sydney, watched their screens show system after system fail on the A380. As per protocol, Qantas managers phoned air-safety investigators in Canberra as soon as they got word about the full-scale emergency under way in the skies near Singapore.

With QF32's pilots battling to remain in control, the second officer, Mark Johnson, raced into the cabin to peer through windows to see for himself the damage to the number-two engine. Another Qantas pilot sitting in a passenger seat quickly gained his attention. He pointed Johnson to the plane's in-flight entertainment system. It showed fuel leaking from the left wing. Johnson ran downstairs to the bottom deck to get a better view of the engine. To his shock, he saw fuel flowing from underneath the damaged left wing near the number-two engine. The trail of fuel was about half a metre wide. The engine had exploded, sending shrapnel flying in all directions and piercing the wing. 'One was more like a gash mark and the other one was quite a largish hole where, you know, clearly a projectile had just been punched up through the wing,' Johnson told the ABC.[12]

The protective sheeting encasing the rear of the engine had been blown away. The explosion had sent debris flying through the wing, severing crucial wiring to vital systems and puncturing structural spars. It had ruptured a fuel pipe, narrowly missing the wing's fuel tank. A small fire had begun in the lower part of the Rolls-Royce engine. The jet engine's outer layer was designed to prevent dislodged parts from escaping. The flagship of Qantas' fleet had suffered what the industry termed an uncontained engine failure. It spelt severe danger.

After Johnson returned to the cockpit, the pilots decided against transferring more fuel to the A380's inner tanks. They did not know how badly damaged the system was. At about that moment, they received an electronic message known as an ACARS from Qantas' operations centre in Sydney indicating that it had received multiple failure messages. The in-flight broadcasting system was akin to a fax and sent a message that appeared on a screen in the cockpit and could be printed. The pilots were frantically responding to their plane's system warnings. They knew first-hand about the multiple system failures, and had time only to acknowledge the message.

De Crespigny and the supervising check captain, Dave Evans, began a series of announcements over the PA to the passengers shortly after the explosion. With a calm demeanour, considering the circumstances, they told them they were dealing with a technical issue with the number-two engine but emphasised that everything was secure and the A380 was flying safely. In the cabin, passengers were hoping that the pilots would turn the plane back to Singapore as quickly as possible. 'We kept thinking, just please turn around and go back. We really wanted to go back to Singapore. We didn't want to stay up there,' Judith Friederich said. 'All those things go through your mind that we are not going to make it back. I just thought, we are this little tiny spot up in the air in this great, big universe.'[13] Hon Mok, the owner of a travel agency in Sydney, was sitting nearby in seat 69C in the economy-class cabin. 'I was thinking they should do an emergency landing when I saw the metal protruding from the wing. I knew that jet fuel was in the tank of the wing,' he recalled. 'It could just explode and blow us to pieces.' Immediately after the explosion, he began praying to himself and made a wish list of the things he wanted to do if he survived. 'I said to myself, after this I better search for some sort of religion or God, or go for some Buddhism. I did a mental checklist of what I had done in the past and what I should do after this. I was afraid.'[14]

The pilots' repeated attempts to calm passengers masked the seriousness of the situation. In all, the crew spent fifty minutes dealing with more than fifty warning messages. They had to deduce which systems were still working. Each had the potential to affect the calculation required for the approach and landing at Changi. The pilots worried that the number-one engine may also have been damaged. They alerted air-traffic control that fuel was leaking from the left wing and called for emergency services to be prepared for their landing.

Before their attempt to land, the pilots had to work out whether they could do so safely at Changi. Evans and Hicks began punching numbers into the plane's computer. They could not dump fuel because the system had failed. It meant the plane was about 50 tonnes over its maximum landing weight. The computer could not calculate the length of runway the plane would need because of the high number of system failures. After discussing their dilemma, the pilots decided to re-run the calculation on the computer by eliminating data relevant to landing on a wet runway. It was a sunny day in Singapore, so the crew knew the runway would be dry. After running the numbers, the computer spat out a response that gave them hope: they would stop just 100 metres short of the end of the 4-kilometre-long runway. It was a fine margin for a plane full of highly explosive jet fuel.

As they readied for an emergency landing, the precariousness of their situation became clearer. The list of obstacles was immense: only the number-three engine had reverse thrust; the leading-edge slats were out; control of the ailerons and spoilers was limited; the anti-skid braking was restricted; and the nose-wheel had limited steering. Adding to their woes, the pilots discovered that they would not be able to apply maximum brakes until the nose-wheel was on the runway. The captain knew that accurate speed control on the final approach to Changi would be crucial to avoiding an aerodynamic stall of the superjumbo or it overshooting the runway. De Crespigny phoned von

Reth to tell him about the possibility the A380 could run off the end of the runway. The flight attendants had to be prepared for an evacuation of the plane if it did.

The lives of 440 passengers and twenty-nine crew members hung in the balance. Lining up for the approach into Changi's centre runway, the autopilot disconnected and the captain tried to reconnect. When it kicked out again at 1000 feet, de Crespigny made the split-second decision to land the A380 manually. Because the margin for error was so small, Harry Wubben reminded de Crespigny that the landing would have to be made with a final nose-up pitch to reduce the rate of descent at touchdown. They did not want to overshoot the runway.

Some passengers adopted the brace position, even though the crew had not asked them to. Judith Friederich had been watching *The Good Wife* to try to divert her mind from thoughts that her life was in jeopardy. Her husband, Donald, had switched on the footage on his in-flight entertainment system from the camera mounted high on the tail of the A380. He quickly became transfixed to the screen on the back of the seat in front. But he soon wished he wasn't as the plane looked as though it would ditch into the water as it approached the runway at Changi.

Nearly two hours after the engine exploded, QF32's wheels struck the runway, de Crespigny slamming on the brakes and the reverse thrust on the number-three engine. As it shot down the runway, it seemed that the plane would not slow. 'I was actually telling Rich, telling him to brake. You know, I called it a couple of times, I said "Brakes!" You know, "Brakes!" And he said, "I am!" And I said, "No, get into it!" And he said, "I am!"' Hicks, who was sitting beside the captain, told the ABC.[15] With the braking and the reverse thrust working to slow its speed, QF32 eventually ground to a halt just 150 metres from the end of the runway. Passengers burst into applause as it stopped. They had survived.

In the 24-hour operations centre in Sydney, the landing was

greeted with a sense of relief – not an almighty cheer, as you would expect. The team had to remain focused on getting the passengers off QF32 and back to Sydney, as well as running the rest of Qantas' fleet. At the same time, the managers were receiving details such as photographs of the plane debris that had fallen on the Indonesian island. The world was already demanding answers to what had nearly claimed the *Nancy-Bird Walton* and the lives of those on board.

Parked near the end of Changi Airport's centre runway, QF32's pilots began shutting the A380 down. As they flicked off the final engine master switch, the plane's electrical system went into an emergency mode. Many of the displays in the cockpit switched off. Just before they did, the pilots noticed a display showing the temperature of the landing gear had hit 900 degrees Celsius. Hicks used the only high-frequency radio still operating to contact the airport's fire commander. To his alarm, the fire chief asked for the number-one engine to be shut down. It had been. But the commander told him one was still running. The pilots tried to use an emergency off-switch and fire-extinguisher bottles to again shut down the engine. It didn't work. To make matters worse, the fire chief radioed to warn that fuel appeared to be leaking from the plane's left wing. Hicks told him about the hot brakes and demanded he get his crews to quickly spray foam over the fuel. 'I remember thinking okay, we made it. Good, you know – job done. But it wasn't. It just changed,' Hicks told the ABC.[16]

It quickly dawned on the cabin crew and passengers that the emergency was far from over. 'We've got a situation where there is fuel, hot brakes and an engine we can't shut down. And really the safest place was on board the aircraft until such time as things changed,' Dave Evans said.[17] The captain told the passengers over the PA to stand by for an evacuation. The fire crews were dealing with a leak from the plane's left-hand side. Even passengers with little knowledge of aviation knew a fuel leak in an emergency situation was bad news. A spark could blow the plane to smithereens. 'There was no sign of the fire brigade and there were just bucketloads of fuel belching out of the engine,' Donald Friederich recalled. 'At some point, I just imagined seeing walls of flames coming up the window. I was really pretty sure then that we were just a whisker away from the whole thing going sky-high.'[18] To make matters worse, the firefighters had seen smoke rise from the plane's landing gear shortly after it had come to a halt. They unleashed tens of thousands of litres of water from their cannons onto the number-one engine in a frantic effort to shut it down. The anxiety levels rose again among staff glued to their screens back in Qantas' crisis centre in Sydney.

In the economy cabin, Emma Teres and her colleague Claire Beynon became anxious about a fire signal. Teres ran to check whether there was indeed a fire under a crew rest area. It was a false alarm but she could not disable the warning signal. Beynon tried to call the captain but couldn't get through. She tried again without luck. The flight attendants tried an emergency call but that did not work either. Thinking that the captain could be out cold, Teres ran to find the cabin-crew manager, who also had been unable to get hold of the captain. As they considered charging into the cockpit, the captain called. Everything was okay but the internal communications were playing up.

The passengers became increasingly anxious as the minutes ticked by. Without air-conditioning, the cabin was turning into a sauna. 'I was shocked because I could see jet fuel spewing onto the tarmac,' Hon Mok said later. 'There was happiness when we landed and suddenly there is this anticlimax that you have to face another huge danger. You could see fumes rising from the tarmac because it was such a hot day. I was wondering that the first thing that they should have done when we landed was to give us emergency instructions to run from the plane because of potential for fire. But they didn't. They said they couldn't let us out because they had to wait for the fire engine to come to stop one of the engines.'[19] Finally, about fifty minutes after QF32 made its emergency landing, the first of the 440 passengers began hurriedly filing off the A380 row by row, without bags. The elderly, women and children were first. The passengers had endured almost an hour in the cabin without air-conditioning in Singapore's sweltering heat. The pilots had decided to use just one door to evacuate the plane. They wanted the rest of its right side to be kept clear in case escape slides were needed. Flight attendants stood at the doors on the right side of the plane in case the slides were inflated for an evacuation. If the call was made, they would have just ninety seconds to evacuate the aircraft. Within about ten minutes, the last of the passengers and flight attendants had rushed off the *Nancy-Bird Walton*. The pilots were still battling to shut the number-one engine down. They tried to starve the engine of fuel, as well as attempting to shut it down by pulling out circuit-breakers. The engine's blades finally fell silent after firefighters doused them in foam. Walking into the terminal at Changi Airport, the magnitude of the midair explosion dawned on passengers and crew as they strode past television screens showing the full extent of the damage to the plane. 'It was such a long, draining, daunting experience,' Teres said. 'It wasn't until we were in the terminal that we finally felt secure.'

About three hours after QF32 landed at Changi Airport, the emergency was over. Qantas' highly experienced pilots had saved 469 lives. Luck had also been on their side. The plane had five, not the usual three, pilots on board. QF32 had flown within an inch of becoming one of the world's worst air disasters. 'It could have been much, much worse,' said Richard Woodward, a Qantas A380 captain and a vice-president of the Australian and International Pilots Association. 'It could probably be termed a one-in-a-100-million event with bits and pieces going everywhere.'[20]

In a heartbeat, the near disaster sent shockwaves through the world's aviation industry. That afternoon in Sydney, a clearly shaken Alan Joyce fronted a media conference to announce that Qantas' A380 fleet would not be returning to the skies until he was assured they were safe to fly. The airline had everything riding on its safety record. 'We are not going to take any risks with passenger safety,' Joyce said. 'We're talking about new aircraft and new engines. It looks like an uncontained engine failure but it's too early to speculate and it will involve us leading a detailed investigation with the manufacturer, Airbus, and . . . Rolls-Royce.'[21] Emails between officers at US private intelligence firm Strategic Intelligence in the wake of Joyce's decision highlighted the immediate fears for other airlines. 'This is the big double-decker plane with the showers and bar in business and first class. I have flown in it from Toronto to Dubai. Never had a more comfortable flight,' one wrote after he was asked what type of plane had been involved in the near disaster. 'But if there is a problem with the aircraft then this has implications for Dubai's Emirates airlines [sic], which has the largest fleet and has a few dozen on order.'[22]

Before QF32's wheels had scraped the runway at Changi Airport, Qantas had scrambled to ready a relief plane to fly to Singapore within hours. It would bring QF32's passengers home the next day. On board the flight to Singapore was a six-strong team of engineers, pilots and other specialists from the Australian Transport Safety Bureau. 'We were able to use a special flight up there to get our preliminary team on the ground in Singapore, where the aircraft eventually landed,' the bureau's chief commissioner, Martin Dolan, said later.[23] Because the midair explosion happened above Batam Island, responsibility for an investigation fell on Indonesian shoulders. 'I rang my Indonesian counterpart and asked if we could have QF32. He said, "Go for it",' Dolan said. The Australian air-safety bureau began steering a multinational team that included experts from its French and British equivalents.

The next night, QF32's pilots and cabin crew boarded a Qantas Boeing 747-400 bound for Sydney. Drained after their ordeal, they were eager to get home to family and friends. Their plane home had stopped in Singapore on its way from Frankfurt, and had a large contingent of German passengers. Within minutes of QF6 taking off from Changi Airport, passengers heard a loud bang and saw sparks fly from an engine as they felt a slight jolt in their seats. 'We just lost any sense of control. What the hell, is this all happening again?' Teres recalled.[24]

Her fears worsened when one of QF6's cabin crew screamed, 'Brace, brace!' Anxious after the events of the day before, the flight attendant on QF6 had misread the situation. A blade in the engine had failed but it was not a grave situation, and it was quickly shut down. However, their plane would be forced to dump fuel before returning to Singapore for repairs. 'By the time we got back into Singapore and into the terminal, quite a few of us had just lost the plot,' Teres said. 'That is when we lost the plot at Qantas as well, because we got back to the hotel and they were like, "Yes, off you go". Everyone had just had enough. We ended up staying in Singapore for four or five days before we were brought back.' Their manager, Michael von Reth, insisted on trauma counselling from Qantas for his crew.

In the following days, the number of air-safety investigators sent to Changi Airport to search for clues to the midair explosion quickly rose to about a hundred. It included experts from Airbus, Qantas, Singapore and Rolls-Royce. The British company synonymous with engineering excellence had as many as 200 engineers working around the clock on the case at its headquarters in Derby, England, the birthplace of the industrial revolution. They were under pressure to find the exact cause of the engine explosion and fix it. They needed to allay mounting concerns from the flying public and airlines. After all, A380 superjumbos powered by the same engines bolted onto QF32 were still criss-crossing the world, potentially placing the safety of passengers and air crews at risk. Rolls-Royce's reputation and those of airlines that used its engines were on the line.

Almost immediately, Joyce had pointed the finger of blame at Rolls-Royce. The investigation into the midair explosion focused on an oil fire that had caused a heavy turbine disc to break up and burst at high velocity through the engine's protective shell. The fire was the result of an oil stub pipe that had cracked and leaked oil. QF32's near disaster had been the first catastrophic failure of the British company's Trent 900 engines, which powered twenty of the thirty-seven superjumbos in service in late 2010. Other airlines that flew A380 superjumbos using Rolls-Royce's Trent 900 engines had to decide quickly whether to follow Qantas' lead. Germany's flag carrier, Lufthansa, kept them flying while Singapore Airlines, the first to buy the double-decker planes, briefly delayed flights as it carried out precautionary checks of the engines in its fleet of eleven superjumbos in less than a day. Singapore Airlines was quick to point out that its inspections found 'absolutely no findings of concern'.[25] Days later, the airline was forced to change engines on three A380s after Rolls-Royce advised it to make further inspections because of 'oil staining' around turbine blades.

Qantas' decision to ground the five other A380s in its fleet created headaches for staff running its international network. To many passengers, airlines seem rather simple. But behind the sense of orderliness lie insanely complex organisations. Qantas was no different to its rivals. On the night of November 4, 2010, the indefinite grounding of its A380 fleet forced Qantas to cancel flights out of Los Angeles and Sydney and accommodate hundreds of passengers in hotels. Its operations centre and network-planning team had to quickly decide how they were going to plug the gap left by six large planes that flew long-haul routes. It had to press into greater service its ageing fleet of Boeing 747 jumbos to maintain flights on its international network in the weeks to follow.

Rolls-Royce also faced a growing list of questions about what it knew and when. Three months before QF32's midair emergency, European air-safety regulators had issued an alert about abnormal wear inside the Trent 900 engines installed on the A380s. This raised questions about whether, in the most extreme case, a recall of the engines should have been made or more extensive checks carried out. Qantas, too, had quickly shifted the blame for the midair explosion onto the world's second-largest maker of jet engines. Joyce had been on the phone to the Rolls-Royce chief executive, Sir John Rose, almost daily since the explosion in the skies above Indonesia.

Apart from occasional short statements, the engine-maker's

PR strategy was to simply not respond to questions about QF32. Its approach frustrated journalists and Qantas, whose own reputation was on the line, and allowed others to fill the news vacuum, leading to speculation that Rolls-Royce had something to hide. Airbus's head salesman, John Leahy, fuelled the speculation when he told journalists during a whistlestop visit to Sydney in mid-November 2010 that Rolls-Royce had begun making changes to engines bolted onto A380 planes before the midair explosion on QF32. 'I know that they are constantly updating their manufacturing standard,' Leahy said. The big-talking American let slip that Alan Joyce and Qantas' operations boss, Lyell Strambi, were 'more than a little upset by a lack of statements from Rolls' when he met them a day earlier.[26] Hours after Leahy stirred the pot, Rolls-Royce released a statement admitting it was responsible for QF32's engine failure.

Qantas' lawyers were also ready to hand Rolls-Royce a hefty compensation claim. They were not going to take any chances. To prevent the engine-maker from trying to stop Qantas pursuing a compensation claim in Australia, its lawyers launched a pre-emptive strike against Rolls-Royce in the Federal Court in Sydney a month after QF32's lucky escape. Qantas feared Rolls-Royce would go straight to British courts for an 'anti-suit injunction' had it known about the airline's plans to make a large claim.[27] The legal action was a safeguard while the two companies fought over a settlement behind closed doors.

The same day that Qantas filed legal papers, the Australian Transport Safety Bureau released its preliminary report into QF32, which pointed the blame at a faulty oil tube in the two-year-old jet engine. 'Essentially, it was a manufacturing defect, or a potential manufacturing defect, in oil pipes in a number of Trent 900 series engines,' the bureau's chief commissioner, Martin Dolan, said.[28] It would be another two-and-a-half years before the investigators laid to rest the cause of QF32. In its final report, the ATSB concluded that the walls of the oil-feed stub pipes had been bored thinner than their design specifications. The pipes that funnelled oil to lubricate bearings in the engine were ticking time bombs for those A380s flown at maximum thrust on take-off on long-haul routes. The thin walls reduced the life of the oil pipes, allowing a crack to develop in one in the number-two engine on QF32. In turn, oil seeped through the crack into an area that was hot enough for a fire to start. The fire led to the separation of a 200-kilogram turbine disc from the drive shaft. Free from the shaft, the disc quickly accelerated before breaking in three, flying at such velocity that it tore through the engine's casing. A large part of the disc pierced the left wing's leading edge before flying through a spar and an inner fuel tank and exiting through the top of the wing.[29] How QF32 did not end in tragedy, just twelve days shy of Qantas' ninetieth anniversary, was a miracle.

The near disaster also shone a spotlight on the airline's choice of aircraft and engines. Airlines are forced to make big bets on their future when they buy aircraft. New planes they take the keys to years after they have been ordered from manufacturers play a large role in determining an airline's ability to compete against other airlines. The lawsuit against Roll-Royce offered a glimpse into the Qantas hierarchy's decision-making years earlier. The case triggered the release of hundreds of pages of confidential documents, including top-level advice to the Qantas board and contracts with Rolls-Royce. The grounding of Qantas' A380s in the wake of QF32 raised questions about whether Qantas was paying the price for betting on two new aircraft types – the A380 superjumbo and Boeing's yet-to-be delivered 787 Dreamliners – for the bulk of its fleet. At the turn of the century, Qantas chose the higher-risk strategy of leapfrogging from the dependable workhorse of its international fleet – the 747 jumbo – to a completely new model in the A380. Before then, the airline had a history of buying later versions of aircraft to avoid teething problems that often beset new models.

Documents filed in the case against Rolls-Royce revealed unease from some quarters of the Qantas board in 2000 about buying the world's largest passenger jet from Airbus. Qantas was weighing up its choice of 500-seat aircraft – the A380 or the stretched version of Boeing's 747 aircraft – to replace its older long-haul planes. In November 2000, a 'request for approval' to buy twelve superjumbos from Airbus went before the Qantas board. 'Both manufacturers have priced their aircraft aggressively in an attempt to secure a launch customer base,' an internal paper from two Qantas executives, Grant Fenn and David Cox, stated. Confidential minutes of a top-level meeting revealed that Qantas directors talked at length about the significant discounts Airbus and Boeing were offering for their aircraft. They also highlighted that Roger Maynard, a Qantas director and one of British Airways' representatives on the board, 'expressed reservations on whether acquiring a very large aircraft fleet is the correct long-term decision for Qantas'.[30] In the end, the Qantas board approved the purchase of twelve A380s and an option to buy twelve more.

To the chagrin of pilots, Boeing's much lauded 777 was not on the list of planes to be purchased. The aircraft was a centrepiece of the fleets of Cathay Pacific, Emirates and Singapore Airlines. Factions within Qantas wanted the Boeing 777 to fly on long-haul routes to destinations such as Los Angeles and Frankfurt. While it was ideal for a so-called 'hub carrier' such as Singapore Airlines or Emirates, Qantas executives who opposed the purchase of 777s believed the aircraft type was suitable for only a handful of routes for their airline. Instead, they believed Airbus' A330 was the best plane for Qantas because it was ideal for flying scores of medium-haul routes to destinations in Asia and within Australia. They also reasoned that buying another aircraft type would make the fleet more complex to operate and maintain. However, many Qantas pilots would not forgive successive management teams for overlooking the Boeing 777.

Seven months after QF32's midair explosion, Qantas reached a $95 million damages settlement with Rolls-Royce. The grounding of Qantas' A380 fleet had created a logistical nightmare in the lead-up to Christmas in 2010, forcing it to chew through at a rapid rate the allowable flying hours of pilots who flew its Boeing 747 jumbos on long-haul routes. At one stage, Qantas came close to running out of 747 pilots it could legally allow to fly.[31] For some of QF32's passengers and flight attendants, their nightmare would not end. Years later, they would still suffer from the trauma of a flight that had begun in such an ordinary fashion. Passengers such as Donald and Judith Friederich developed a fear of flying, suffered nightmares and increased levels of anxiety, and found they could not handle stressful jobs. Several flight attendants, including Emma Teres, decided they could no longer fly for a living and quit Qantas. 'I had such anxiety and such hate for Qantas. I didn't even want to put on the uniform,' Teres said. 'I just lost complete respect for them. There was no care factor. It was fake – even if they did attempt to speak with me.' Teres later joined other flight attendants and passengers in a class-action lawsuit against Rolls-Royce, claiming psychological harm from the midair emergency.[32]

Yet from the depths of despair, the pilots and cabin crew of QF32 had emerged to deliver Qantas one of its finest moments. It was a rare glimmer of light in the year ahead, which was to become one of the most chaotic and damaging in the airline's long history.

8

REDQ

Like most secret projects, Project Darwin started as an idea Qantas executives knocked around a table at the airline's head offices in Sydney. Its aim was to solve a dilemma: that the costs of Qantas' international flying business were as much as 20 per cent higher than competitors', such as Emirates, Singapore Airlines and Cathay Pacific. While Qantas had similar costs to other airlines that flew on routes to the US, it was blown out of the water on runs to Asia and Europe. For Qantas' strategists, it boiled down to two options: ask the workforce to take a wage cut to slash costs, or set up a new airline in Asia that employed staff on cheaper wages.

Qantas had experience starting new airlines. Almost a decade earlier, it had created the building blocks for Jetstar out of Impulse Airlines, which later morphed beyond its initial intentions. Qantas established Jetstar Asia in Singapore, Jetstar Pacific in Vietnam and a labour-hire company in New Zealand that supplied crews for Qantas-branded flights on trans-Tasman routes. Jetconnect employed pilots and flight attendants on cheaper wages and conditions than those in Australia. It also had on the drawing board plans to set up Jetstar offshoots in Japan and Hong Kong. It was a well-worn business strategy not unique to Qantas: shift jobs to countries where they could be done much cheaper.

Project Darwin began in utmost secrecy in late 2010. Qantas knew it risked a political firestorm if word leaked of the project's goal of starting a new premium airline in Asia. Unions would portray it as further evidence of a company sending Australian jobs overseas. The task of turning the idea into a viable concept fell on the shoulders of consultants from Boston Consulting Group. Over the following months, the plans for establishing a premium airline took many shapes as they were passed back and forth between the external consultants. In the end, they delivered a plan to Qantas executives to set up an ultra-premium airline in Singapore. Asia's premium travel market ran in a diamond shape from Tokyo and Hong Kong to Taipei and Singapore. The new airline needed on-board products to set it apart because the plans were for it to fly single-aisle A320 aircraft. Passengers needed to be able to forget that they were sitting in cabins smaller than Singapore Airlines and Cathay Pacific's twin-aisle aircraft – namely their Boeing 777 and A330 planes.

For Alan Joyce, 2011 was shaping up as a pivotal year. Three labour agreements covering influential parts of the Qantas workforce were up for renegotiation. The hoped-for recovery in demand in the international market following the global financial crisis in 2008 had failed to materialise. At a speech at the Melbourne Press Club in early February, Joyce outlined the challenges ahead for the airline, singling out one part of the business in need of an urgent shake-up. Making the case for radical change, he questioned the long-term future of Qantas' full-service international operations without a change in direction. He apportioned part of the blame on airlines from the Middle East and Asia for flooding the market with extra flights. 'If we continue on our current path, there will be a real question mark over the viability of Qantas International,' he declared. 'I have no intention of letting our flagship business decay through inaction.'[1] His speech was both a signal to the federal government to stop foreign airlines dumping capacity on routes to Australia, and a warning to Qantas' workforce that it would have to stomach further cost-cutting to slash its labour bill.

Joyce also emphasised Jetstar's 'aggressive pan-Asian strategy' aimed at tapping into the world's fastest-growing travel market. He noted that 'we think premium airlines will also have a role to play'. Qantas wanted a seat at the table in Asia to prepare for when the market was freed of its regulatory shackles. Little did his audience know that behind the scenes, Qantas was feverishly working away on a top-secret plan for Asia. Weeks earlier, Joyce had given Lesley Grant, Qantas' head of marketing and customer experience, the job of leading a special project team to 'explore options' for Qantas' international operations.

Top of the list was a new airline. Grant's job in early 2011 to set it up ran in parallel with work under way by the Boston consultants and Qantas' strategy team headed by Jayne Hrdlicka. Born and raised in the American Midwest state of Kansas, Hrdlicka heralded from the world of management consultancy, working for Bain & Company in both the US and Australia. One of Bain's most famous alumni was the Republican Party's nominee for US president in the 2012 election, Mitt Romney. In Australia in the late 1990s, Hrdlicka's first client for Bain had been none other than a thirty-something Alan Joyce, then in charge of Ansett's route network and scheduling for its domestic network. Joyce and Hrdlicka clicked. 'Alan and Jayne got on really, really well,' a former Ansett staffer recalled. Ansett had hired Hrdlicka to work on its business recovery program, which Lyell Strambi was overseeing. When Hrdlick's consultancy gig for Ansett ended, she and Joyce stayed in touch and, more than a decade later, Joyce hired the no-nonsense executive to Qantas. In August 2010 she began running the strategy team and IT for the entire company, including Jetstar.

Until then, Qantas had for years been a happy hunting ground for guns for hire, who extracted large fees along the way for their advice.

Consultants from Bain, Boston Consulting and McKinsey regularly passed through Qantas' Sydney headquarters, much to the disdain of large swathes of the airline's workforce. Under Hrdlicka, Qantas sought to reverse the tendency to hire external consultants. She quickly built its strategy team from four to more than twenty staff.[2]

The plan for a new airline was aimed at fixing a growing problem for Qantas on routes from Australia to Asia. With airlines such as Singapore Airlines, Cathay and Malaysia Airlines boosting the number of flights to Australia, Qantas faced bigger losses on routes to destinations in the region. Demand was not keeping pace with the extra flights despite a rapidly growing middle class in Asia. Ticket prices struck record lows, making it near impossible to earn a buck. It equalled a never-ending sea of red ink for Qantas, which had a higher cost base. Its other option was to form a deep alliance with a premium Asian airline. Qantas' previous management had tried time and again to cement deals with Singapore Airlines, Cathay and Malaysia Airlines without success.

Grant's team included senior staff from across the group who were regarded as experts in setting up an airline. They would form the management team for the new airline. Her team had staff in charge of everything a new airline needed, from engineering, commercial relationships and IT to aircraft planning and seat design. They worked on the project on the basis that the new airline would get off the ground in 2012. RedQ was the preferred name for the new airline, which in the eyes of brand experts borrowed heavily on Qantas' heritage but was distinct enough to signal the arrival of a new entrant in the global aviation market. While the colour red retained the links to Qantas, it also symbolised good fortune and joy in Chinese culture. Qantas kept its options open as it later sought to register RedQ, RedQ Executive Flyer, OneAsia and RedSky as trade names for the new offshoot.[3]

The livery designed for RedQ's A320 planes resembled a killer whale with black and white licks of paint on the fuselage and a 'Q' on a red tail. Their interior would seat about twenty passengers in business class and ninety in economy. For Qantas, its executives believed it was not a shot in the dark: its research indicated that it would be attractive to passengers. It had advertisements ready to go to spruik the new airline to customers in Asia. With its focus on corporate travellers, RedQ would fly to key destinations such as Beijing that Qantas did not serve. It would help solve Qantas' flight frequency disadvantage and the lack of an aviation hub in Asia.

In the heavily regulated world of aviation, setting up a new airline was no easy feat. The biggest obstacle lay in convincing the Singapore government to grant it an air operator's certificate – a licence to run a commercial airline. Singapore had opened its doors to foreign airlines setting up offshoots in the city-state years earlier. Qantas had done it with Jetstar Asia, a joint venture with Singaporean investors. But for the new airline to gain access to air routes between Singapore and other destinations in Asia, local investors needed to own at least 51 per cent of the holding company. This would allow it to be tagged a Singaporean airline, giving it access to the country's air rights with other nations. Negotiations to gain access meant repeated trips to Singapore for Tony Wheelens, one of Qantas' government lobbyists and an expert in bilateral air rights.

In mid-May 2011, Qantas' secret was outed. *The Australian*'s business columnist, John Durie, revealed Qantas' plans for a new airline based in Asia to target the business market.[4] The revelation coincided with a rise in brinkmanship between Qantas management and three key unions representing its long-haul pilots, aircraft engineers and ground staff over labour agreements. The airline's 1600 licensed engineers had flagged the start of nationwide strike action ranging from one- to 48-hour work stoppages. 'We will wind it up slowly,' warned Steve Purvinas, the national secretary of the Australian Licenced Aircraft Engineers Association. 'It might be some time before there's much impact on Qantas' flight schedule but it might be wise for passengers to consider all their options when travelling.'[5] The unions had long railed against the company setting up offshoots of Jetstar in Asia, and plans for a premium airline only raised their fears that management planned the same for Qantas. The disclosure aided them in their public campaign for job-security clauses to be inserted into collective contracts.

To the Qantas unions, Joyce had revealed his stripes at Jetstar. In 2006, the then president of the pilots' union, Ian Woods, had flown to Brisbane to hear Joyce address Jetstar pilots at the Riverview Hotel about his plans to fly A330 aircraft on long-haul routes to destinations in Asia. 'The first thing he said to the audience was, "While he is here, I can't remain here". I left the meeting and waited for the pilots to come to the hotel bar,' Woods recalled. 'It was a very confrontational approach and not one any previous executive had exhibited. If you are not willing to sell your strategy to your critics, how capable are you of leading change? Dixon or any of the others wouldn't have done that. It was simply that he started with a belief that he thought he could not have anything to do with Qantas pilots because they would poison his culture.'[6]

While from a working-class family and a Labor voter, Joyce had been surrounded in his early working life with Irish executives who espoused new ways of running airlines. The loose-lipped Michael O'Leary, Willie Walsh and Conor McCarthy had a large influence on him. Like Joyce, they were graduates of Dublin's prestigious Trinity College. They would go on to reshape and build airlines such as Ryanair, Aer Lingus and British Airways by stripping out costs and tackling unions head on. Their influence on aviation spread far beyond Ireland's borders. A tight focus on expenses was central to their business philosophy. In a speech to the Wings Club in Dublin four months after he took the reins at Qantas, Joyce had paid tribute to the far-reaching influence of his countrymen on global aviation. 'There must be something in the water – or the Guinness – here because there's certainly a very special Irish connection with aviation. Even our writers look skyward. After all, Oscar Wilde thought we were all in the gutter, but the best of us are "looking at the stars",' Joyce had declared. 'The global aviation business is crowded – though not, I think, overcrowded – with Irish aviation executives like Willie Walsh, Dermot Mannion, Michael O'Leary and Conor McCarthy.'[7] After his formative years in Ireland, Joyce discovered first hand at Ansett the consequences of so-called legacy airlines not responding to changing circumstances. Rod Eddington, the chief executive at Ansett in the late 1990s, often reminded his executives – who included Joyce – not to forget that the once-mighty Pan Am had gone broke. Less than a decade after the Ansett collapse, Joyce had been appointed Qantas chief executive by the son of a banker who had earned a reputation at Rio Tinto for union busting. Born in South Australia, Leigh Clifford began his 37-year career in the mining industry on King Island in Bass Strait before finding his way to Broken Hill in western New South Wales.[8] At Rio, Clifford had successfully taken on the unions representing coalminers in the Hunter Valley in New South Wales in the 1990s. He was responsible for Rio's energy division and had oversight of its strategy in the Hunter to change work practices and put in place individual contracts for staff.[9] Clifford was an imposing figure who dwarfed Joyce. At Rio, he had shown that he would not shirk from a fight. At Qantas, he would be no different.

As a welter of speculation about the details of Qantas' plans for a new airline in Asia ensued in mid-2011, Joyce made clear he would not bow in the fight with the unions. He accused them of making ridiculous wage claims and copying the playbook of the US labour movement by attacking the airline's brand and undermining management. 'When we have these outrageous claims on the table we have nowhere to go,' Joyce said. 'They have actually had American union leaders down talking to them about tactics.'[10] The Transport Workers Union, which represented baggage handlers and other Qantas ground staff, had well-established links with US trade union the International Brotherhood of Teamsters. As for a new airline in Asia, Joyce would neither confirm nor deny the plans. Instead, he declared that Qantas needed options to stem the mounting losses in its international business. But it was too late. Qantas had its cards revealed to the world before the Singapore government had signed off on its bold plan.

With Qantas focused on Asia and a worsening dispute with three unions, its arch rival had been working away on its own long-term plan. One of Qantas management's worst fears had become a reality in March 2010 when Virgin's chairman, Neil Chatfield, strode into a room in the Establishment Hotel in central Sydney, with John Borghetti and Brett Godfrey in tow, to announce that the former Qantas executive general manager would become the next chief executive of Australia's second-largest airline. A year earlier, Borghetti had told Joyce he was quitting. Now, he was about to take the Qantas chief executive head on. At the media conference, Borghetti was characteristically tight-lipped about his plans for Virgin. As his former colleagues at Qantas knew well, he liked to play his cards close to his chest on most matters. In this case, there was no way he was about to give the man he lost out to for the top job at Qantas any inkling of his plans for the airline. However, Virgin's largest shareholder, Richard Branson, was more forthcoming about what was in store. 'I suspect he will . . . go after the business market in a big way,' he declared over the phone from his home on Necker Island in the Caribbean.[11]

One of Borghetti's first priorities as chief executive was to rejuvenate the airline's brand. In early May 2011, Branson jetted into Sydney to help showcase a rebranding of Virgin Blue as Virgin Australia. On cue, the English businessman delivered his typical theatrics on the tarmac at Sydney Airport for the relaunch ceremony. Until then, the airline had been blocked from using the Virgin moniker on its international operations. A licensing agreement between Singapore Airlines and Branson – the two shareholders in British long-haul airline Virgin Atlantic – had given both the right to veto the use of the Virgin brand on the Australian airline's international flights. One of the challenges for the Australian airline had been to emphasise to travellers that its four brands – Virgin Blue, Pacific Blue, V Australia and Polynesian Blue – were one and the same airline. Royalties from the use of the Virgin brands were a valuable revenue stream for Branson's Virgin Group, and he protected them vehemently. But Borghetti had been able to convince Branson and Singapore Airlines to agree to allow him to rebrand its long-haul airline, V Australia, and Pacific Blue. His well-established relationship with Singapore Airlines had finally overcome a decade-long roadblock to Virgin's wider ambitions. While Qantas faced challenges with its international operations, Virgin was in a world of pain of its own as it stared at a second-half loss of as much as $150 million. But the rebranding was a step towards extracting itself from the no-man's-land between Qantas and budget airlines Jetstar and Tiger Airways, which had begun flying domestic routes in Australia in 2007.

As with everything in aviation, Qantas' plan for a new airline in Asia was also a big gamble. But Qantas' strategy team believed RedQ would fly. The strategists' role was to think longer term. While investors often focused on short-term earnings, their task was to identify problems Qantas would face in five years, and set about trying to avoid them. RedQ was intended to solve the fact that Qantas did not have a hub in Asia. Unlike Singapore Airlines' and Cathay Pacific's hub-and-spoke models, Qantas was an end-of-the-line carrier due to Australia's geographic isolation. A way of overcoming this was to form a relationship with an airline that operated a hub model, or set up a new airline in a country such as Singapore. RedQ had parallels to the two-brand strategy the company had created in Australia with Qantas and Jetstar. In Singapore, Jetstar Asia would serve the low-fare end of the market and RedQ the premium. It was a bold but high-risk move. Qantas' strategy team also had to keep in mind the overall long-term plan for the airline group, which encompassed Qantas, its regional offshoot QantasLink, Jetstar, the frequent-flyer division and freight. RedQ was one part of an overarching strategy for the company's flying operations in Asia. The strategists reminded themselves that the new airline could not be seen in isolation as they worked to a timeline to unveil a company-wide strategy to investors in August 2011.

In early June that year, Joyce and his senior executives flew to Singapore. At the Marina Bay Sands, the city-state's answer to Dubai's luxurious Burj Al Arab hotel, they joined airline executives from around the world for the annual meeting of the International Air Transport Association. Besides watching the usual public jousting between airline CEOs, it was a chance to press the flesh and cultivate relationships that could cement deals later. The memory of Qantas' close brush with disaster was just a short distance away. About twenty minutes' drive from the resort, the *Nancy-Bird Walton* remained locked in a hangar at Changi Airport. Seven months after narrowly avoiding disaster shortly after take-off from Singapore, the Qantas A380 super-jumbo was still awaiting repairs costing tens of millions of dollars.

On the first day of the conference, Joyce talked up the opportunity to build a closer relationship with Malaysia Airlines. Qantas was helping Malaysia's flag carrier to become a member of the one-world marketing alliance, and he hoped this would lead to something more substantial. Forming deep alliances with airlines in Asia such as Malaysia Airlines was a means of fixing the growing problems of Qantas International. But any meaningful deal was not an easily won thing. With the public slanging match between management and unions intensifying, Joyce refused to pour more money into Qantas' international operations until they returned their cost of capital. After a long day of back-to-back meetings, Joyce and his executives joined other airline bosses and journalists atop the Marina Bay Sands in a bar next to an infinity pool perched on the rooftop. It was a chance to unwind and savour the spectacle of Singapore's glittering skyline at night.

The Dubliner would need a stiff drink the next day. His worst nightmare was realised when Borghetti strolled onto the stage early in the morning with his counterpart from Singapore Airlines, Goh Choon Phong. In one of the rooms at the sprawling conference centre adjoining the Marina Bay Sands, Borghetti announced that the newly rebranded Virgin Australia and Singapore Airlines would enter into a long-term alliance. 'This completes our Asian puzzle,' Borghetti told journalists. 'We want more of the international market, and this will give us that.'[12] Qantas had for years wanted to form a deep alliance with Singapore Airlines. Now Borghetti had trumped his adversary at Qantas by securing a deal in super-fast time with one of Asia's premium airlines.

It capped off a frantic year for Borghetti since he had taken the reins at Virgin. For Joyce, Virgin's deal with Singapore Airlines piled on more pressure. Qantas' share price had lost more than a third of its market value – or $2.26 billion – in seven months amid the stand-off with unions, high jet-fuel prices and airlines boosting flights on routes to Australia. Jetstar was also facing a tougher fight, with Singapore Airlines unveiling plans weeks earlier for a new budget airline, Scoot.

This increased pressure to make RedQ a reality in Singapore. Over the next few months, the negotiations with the Singapore government to gain the right to set up an airline took priority. In early August, the Qantas board signed off on RedQ as part of an all-encompassing strategy for the group. It would not sign off on RedQ on its own. Project Darwin needed to be part of a comprehensive package, which included capital for a large order of new A320 planes, some of which would be flown by RedQ. The new airline was ready to go because it had to be. If the Singapore government gave approval, it had to be ready to fly. Airlines have long lead times. Aeroplane orders are made years in advance. For a new airline to launch services by a set date, an awful lot of work has to be carried out well ahead of time, ranging from aircraft orders to designs for cabin interiors.

Following the board's tick of approval, Joyce launched on August 16 his long-term vision for Qantas. Its centrepiece was two new airlines in Asia to save its international flying division: Jetstar Japan and an ultra-premium airline. Under his four-pillar strategy – a term coined by Qantas' PR team, to the chagrin of its strategists – Joyce wanted to point Qantas and Jetstar northwards in what had been dubbed the Asian century. 'To do nothing, or tinker around the edges, would only guarantee the end of Qantas International in our home Australian market,' Joyce told journalists at the Westin hotel in central Sydney. 'That would be a tragedy. So we must change. We have a five-year plan and it must start today.'[13] The new premium airline would launch services with a fleet of eleven A320 planes before increasing the fleet to twenty-four. Their interiors would feature the latest seats and in-flight entertainment. They would boast the best of everything. Joyce's four-pillar plan included ambitious targets, including Qantas' international flying operations to become profitable within three years. Within five years, he wanted both Qantas' domestic and international businesses to exceed their cost of capital on a sustainable basis.[14] The chance of the international business achieving its goal would become tougher as its predicament worsened over the following years.

Joyce's plan to expand aggressively into Asia was a step in the right direction for some of Qantas' large shareholders. But many others did not share their optimism about RedQ, a key plank of Qantas' plans to turn around the fortunes of its international operations. 'Any attempt to recreate the Qantas brand and intercontinental network from an offshore base is doomed to failure,' said Hubert Horan, an American aviation consultant who had worked on a merger proposal between Qantas and Air New Zealand in the 1980s. 'Even if there were net cost savings, brave new Qantas would still not close the competitive gap against Singapore Airlines, Emirates and others.'[15] AirAsia X's chief executive, Azran Osman-Rani, accepted the rationale for Qantas wanting to tap into the fast-growing travel market in Asia but pointed out that building a brand from scratch in a region with different languages, cultures and politics was a huge challenge. 'What we have learnt is that ideas are worth nothing – it is how you execute them,' he warned.[16]

For Joyce, Qantas had no choice. His mantra was that the Flying Kangaroo could go the way of Ansett, TWA and Pan Am if it did not turn around its international business. 'We could kick the can down the street. [But] eventually this great brand will disappear if we keep kicking the can down the street. We need to fix it now,' he said.[17] It would be a catchcry he would repeat over the coming months as he sold his plan to investors and the Australian public while he battled the unions.

However, Qantas' plan to set up a new airline in Singapore was becoming increasingly fraught. Project Orca was born when the airline began to seriously consider an alternative base to Singapore for RedQ. The name for the new project was inspired by the paint job on the planes for RedQ. Under Project Orca, Qantas turned its focus 300 kilometres north-westwards to Malaysia's capital, Kuala Lumpur. The door to an alternative home for RedQ was opened when attempts were made to shore up Malaysia Airlines via a share-swap deal with the country's fast-growing budget airline, AirAsia. The deal put AirAsia's founder, Tony Fernandes, and his close associates in the box seat with a stake of almost 21 per cent in Malaysia Airlines. Fernandes, a former employee of Richard Branson with an ego as big, had had many dealings over the years with both Joyce and Bruce Buchanan, the Jetstar chief executive. In early 2010, the trio had formed an operational alliance that never lived up to its hype. Now, Joyce's ambitions relied on buy-in from Fernandes, who had built AirAsia from two planes and a pile of debt into Asia's largest low-cost carrier. He was crucial to steering a deal to set up a new airline as part of a joint venture with the majority-government-owned Malaysia Airlines. Under the plans, the new airline, to be based in Kuala Lumpur, would fly fifteen A330 planes that Malaysia Airlines had been due to take the keys to.

But the plans were a stretch from the outset. While Fernandes was receptive, Malaysia Airlines' financial position was precarious, relying on the country's government to keep it afloat. Within Qantas, senior staff harboured serious reservations about setting up an airline in Kuala Lumpur. To them, it was Singapore or nothing. Even Conor McCarthy, the mate of Joyce's who had co-founded AirAsia, expressed reservations about Qantas' ability to set up a new premium airline in Asia. 'There is a sizeable market but the problem is that it's a pretty fragmented market. It is all over Asia, and Asia is a big place,' he said. 'The problem with the airline business is that there are some great ideas running out of capital before they get a chance to establish themselves.'[18] McCarthy was well attuned to the challenges of running airlines in Asia, and had previously been a linchpin for Qantas in helping to open doors in the region.

By October, Qantas' application for a licence to operate a commercial airline had landed in the hands of the Singapore government's cabinet for consideration. The Australian flag carrier had lobbied hard about the benefits a new airline would bring to the city's economy, whose main strategic assets were its port and airport. Singapore's Changi Airport was in Qantas' camp because it would benefit directly from a new airline, and the country's Economic Development Board had cleared Qantas' proposal for a new airline.[19] But after a concerted campaign against RedQ by Singapore Airlines, the government refused to grant Qantas an air-operator's certificate. RedQ had come within a whisker of gaining approval to base its operations in Singapore but in the end its efforts amounted to nought. 'We put all the arguments to them but in the end Singapore Airlines made a more compelling argument,' a former Qantas executive said.[20]

Project Darwin was thrown into the bottom drawer to gather dust, and just months afterwards Project Orca met the same fate. Qantas' competitors were not going to deliver a part of their hard-won market on a platter. They would fight hard against a new entrant, as Jetstar knew well from setting up joint ventures in Singapore and Vietnam. The international business was a huge distraction for Qantas executives. The focus on attempts to set up a new airline meant less time to spend on the operations in its home market, where Qantas made the lion's share of its profits. In the meantime, Virgin Australia was working away on its own strategy of gaining a bigger share of the lucrative corporate market from Qantas. The door had been left ajar.

9

VEIL OF SECRECY

As early spring breezes wafted across Sydney in late August 2011, a small group of senior managers strolled into a meeting room at Qantas' corporate bolthole in central Sydney. The executives did not know why they had been called in from Qantas' headquarters on the outskirts of Sydney Airport. They were loyal lieutenants of Lyell Strambi, one of Alan Joyce's long-time colleagues and, at that time, the third-highest-ranking Qantas executive. Strambi oversaw the airline's domestic and international flying operations. He and Joyce went way back. He had first met the fresh-faced Irishman in the mid-1990s and was so impressed he recruited Joyce to Ansett in 1996. Almost a decade later, Joyce hired Strambi from Richard Branson's Virgin Atlantic to become Qantas' operations chief.

Strambi's senior managers sat in a windowless meeting room on the eighteenth floor of a building that also served as the home for Deutsche Bank's traders and investment bankers. Qantas' senior executives regularly worked at the Norman Foster-designed city offices because they were close to client meetings at the so-called big end of town in Sydney's CBD. The new offices were a step up from Qantas' drab main offices, which were full of nooks and crannies, near the airport. In the CBD tower, they had views north-east out over the Botanic Gardens, Fort Denison and beyond to the entrance to Sydney Harbour. On a blue-sky day, it was one of the most spectacular sights in the world.

On this day in late winter, Strambi's team did not have a chance to soak up the view. By late August, the relationship between Qantas management and three powerful unions had become acrimonious. The warring parties were at the business end of negotiations over new three-year wage agreements. But the talks showed little sign of headway. For Joyce and his executives, the damage to Qantas from a ten-week dispute with its 1600 licensed aircraft engineers in 2008 was still raw in their minds. The airline had put the cost of that dust up at $130 million. This time, Qantas and the three unions had become embroiled in a Mexican stand-off that was threatening to become even more costly.

Three months earlier, the engineers had begun notifying Qantas of their plans for strike action. At the eleventh hour, they aborted their one-hour stoppages and other tactics such as overtime bans, painting it as a willingness to engage Qantas in meaningful talks.[1] But the engineers' on-off actions were damaging to Qantas' operations because the airline still had to plan for potential disruptions even if they did not eventuate. A few weeks later, Qantas' long-haul pilots sought the right from the industrial umpire, Fair Work, to take strike action for the first time in forty-five years.

With the brinkmanship intensifying, Strambi's executives were about to get their first hint that something else was up. Qantas was considering a radical option to stop the unions' attack in its tracks. Meetings at the CBD offices were well away from the prying eyes of other Qantas staff at the operational headquarters. Strambi's team included Qantas' engineering manager, Chris Nassenstein; the head of customer experience, Alison Webster; the boss of cabin crew,

Samantha Taranto; the executive manager of ground operations, Matt Lee; and Qantas' chief pilot, Peter Wilson. At first, they talked about whether Qantas could circumvent the unions by taking pay deals directly to the workforce. Strambi quickly gained their attention. 'The direction and advice that Lyell gave is that we may need to bring this to a head,' one executive said.[2] Qantas might have to consider locking out its staff. Every other option just prolonged the dispute. Strambi's executives were told to be ready. If a lockout was to take place, it would happen quickly and without much notice. The possibility of a lockout shocked the executives.

As they walked out of the meeting room, few of the executives comprehended what a lockout really meant. 'To be honest, it didn't dawn on me what a lockout really meant because at this stage there was always a bit of bravado – let's take it on; we have to protect the business,' one recalled.[3] With three unions refusing to budge from their claims, they accepted that a radical option had to be considered to break the impasse. They believed they had to protect a business whose profitability – and future – was under assault. Forward bookings had begun to collapse. Consumers were turning to other airlines for fear of being caught up in the dispute. Yet on this day in August they still believed they had a good chance of reaching a deal.[4]

Even so, the wheels had been set in motion. The option of a lockout had already been discussed at the highest levels of Qantas, and now Strambi had filled in his closest executives. The circle had widened. With it came a greater risk of word getting out. Qantas always feared leaks. With a heavily unionised workforce and an insatiable public appetite for news about the airline, the company was forever battling to keep a lid on what was happening internally. But this was a big one. If it leaked, Qantas would lose the key element of surprise. A bigger risk was the federal Labor government using a section of the Fair Work Act to stop Qantas from locking out its workforce.

The planning was covert. There was an atmosphere of who knew and who didn't – and all but a handful didn't know. The executives and managers involved in planning, which had begun as early as July, were led to believe that there were only about a dozen individuals in the loop in the entire organisation. However, several groups were now in the know: those who reported to Strambi, and those answerable to Olivia Wirth, Qantas' ambitious chief spin doctor and government lobbyist. She had risen to national prominence in the days after QF32's midair emergency, becoming the face of Qantas as she appeared on TV news bulletins around the nation. She was also a bridge between Qantas and government ministers and the opposition. Within Qantas, the two groups worked in near isolation from one another at the beginning. It had been made clear to some of them that Joyce would not hesitate to ground the airline if the stand-off with unions was not resolved.

Management wanted to reach a deal. But the top brass believed that the history of previous negotiations – and the personalities involved, such as union firebrands Tony Sheldon and Steve Purvinas – made the chance of a negotiated settlement slim. Qantas' industrial relations team of Sue Bussell, Ian Oldmeadow and his wife, Justine, led the negotiations, and regularly briefed Joyce and his executives. Oldmeadow was a former assistant secretary of the Australian Council of Trade Unions, and had long been the go-to man for Qantas in how to deal with the unions. 'Oldie' had been close to Dixon and was now Joyce's right-hand man on industrial relations. Under them, Qantas' operational executives met their counterparts from the Transport Workers Union, and the two unions representing the licenced aircraft engineers and the long-haul pilots, as part of a never-ending round of negotiations. Qantas feared that three of its most powerful unions would act in unison to bring the airline to its knees. While there was cooperation between the three unions, they trusted each other only so far.

Several weeks before Strambi's team was called into the secret meeting in the city, Joyce unveiled his five-year plan for Qantas to investors hungry for a vision for a company mired in difficulties. The strategy included the bold move to establish an ultra-premium airline to ferry corporate high-flyers around Asia, as well as a new offshoot of Jetstar in Japan. Joyce wanted to point Qantas and Jetstar northwards in what had been coined the Asian century. But with Joyce's long-term plan came short-term pain: 1000 jobs to be axed from Qantas. The unions condemned the cuts. What alarmed them most were the plans to establish the ultra-premium airline, RedQ, in Singapore. It went to the heart of their claims in the industrial dispute for job security. They argued that the new subsidiary airlines in Asia would undermine Qantas' and Jetstar's Australian workforce. In short, they believed Qantas was on a crusade to send their members' jobs offshore and bust the unions. 'We will be doing everything we can to stop this destructive strategy for Qantas' future,' said Barry Jackson, the Australian and International Pilots Association president.[5] But it was a step in the right direction for Andrew Sisson, the founder of Qantas' second-largest shareholder, Balanced Equity Management, who had blocked the $11 billion private-equity bid four years earlier. 'These international operations either have to make a profit or be closed – that is not a very palatable message,' Sisson said.[6] The battle lines were drawn in the public arena.

More than a month after Joyce's new vision was unveiled, a number of executives were called into Qantas' main offices near Sydney Airport. Joining them for the weekend meeting were heavy-hitters from Qantas' industrial relations team. Lawyers from a large city law firm were there to meet them on the ninth floor of Building A. Model planes were scattered throughout the executive floor. The Qantas staff in the loop about the planning for a lockout had not given their work a codename but some of the lawyers had dubbed it 'Project Purple'.

The meeting was a chance for the highly paid lawyers to brief the executives on what a lockout would mean in the eyes of the law, and what they would have to do to comply. 'That is when we started finding out that if you lock out, you lock out everybody,' an insider said. One of their major concerns was that a wrong step would result in Qantas losing its element of surprise. They feared an injunction could stop a lockout dead in its tracks. The Fair Work Act allowed the federal government to intervene to terminate protected industrial action if it threatened the national economy. It applied as much to a company locking out its staff as it did to workers striking.

The national-interest test could also work in Qantas' favour. 'In the strategising and the planning with lawyers, they obviously had identified that Qantas' running of the operations was in the national interest, and if a lockout got to that point it would force the government to intervene,' the insider said. 'The lawyers who briefed us clearly hadn't been retained the week before.' In a clever bit of thinking, the lawyers had honed in on a clause in legislation passed by a Labor government that, ironically, relied on the support of trade unions such as the Transport Workers Union.

The complexity of the work ahead soon dawned on the executives in the meeting room on the ninth floor. The more they talked, the more even simple tasks became burdensome. If workers were to be locked out, Qantas had to be able to prove in the eyes of the law that it had taken every step to officially inform them about what was happening. At first blush, it seemed easy for Qantas to write letters to staff. But it quickly dawned on the executives that they did not know if all workers' addresses were stored in the computer system. Some staff may have moved house and not notified the airline of the change in their details. Other legal tasks became more difficult than first thought. As the questions piled up, the executives realised that they would have to widen the circle of managers in the know. It was a proposition resisted by their superiors because of the fear that their big secret would leak.

But the executives got their way. They left the meeting and set about briefing in the week that followed a small coterie of their direct reports in different parts of Qantas operations. They told their closest managers to prepare for a range of scenarios. The secret was slowly working its way down the chain of command. No one could easily predict what would happen if the ultimate decision was made to lock out Qantas workers. In the age of social media, passengers checking in for flights were likely to learn before check-in staff or flight attendants that the entire Qantas fleet had just been grounded. It was an unnerving time for those in the know as scenario after scenario was played out behind closed doors.

Until this moment, the executives who oversaw the day-to-day operations of the Qantas network had been readying for a lockout of staff. They had not seriously thought that this would require a grounding of the fleet. Now it was becoming a serious part of the thinking. The more they talked and planned, the more questions they had about the ramifications. How will staff react? Will they be distracted from their jobs at crucial moments? Will passengers grudgingly accept that they have no choice but to disembark the plane? What is the risk of sabotage? What is the wider risk for the nation? 'We had to do this planning relatively discreetly. We were trying to build up scenarios of what would happen, and to be honest, we were overthinking it and trying to be too cute,' one insider recalled. 'Right up to the time beforehand, we were struggling and under a veil of secrecy. The big issue is what are you going to do with all these customers? Then it was, shit, how many hotels are we going to need?'[7]

Strambi was also chairing weekly meetings with his direct reports, some of whom were in the negotiations with the unions about labour agreements. Joyce attended some of the meetings, as did human resources boss Jon Scriven, senior executive Rob Gurney and members of the PR and industrial relations teams. The meetings were a forum to share information about where the company was at in the union negotiations. They were running in parallel to the secret meetings to plan for a possible grounding of the airline and staff lockout if the industrial disputes could not be resolved.

Qantas had long put a ring around 2011. Its executives knew it would be a pivotal year. Labour agreements covering the three key unions were up for negotiation. Keeping a lid on costs was top priority for a business that burned through cash like few others. If one union received an above-inflation 4 per cent annual wage increase, it would set a benchmark for the others. Management was determined to keep pay rises to no more than 3 per cent – about the rate of inflation. The unions' members worked in some of the most vital roles in Qantas' flying operations, and some were among the highest paid. They included long-haul pilots, aircraft engineers and ground staff. In 2008, the aircraft engineers had caught the airline on the hop with their industrial action. This time, the company worked to ensure the health of its fleet was as high as possible in the lead-up to the labour talks. Qantas did not want to allow its 1600 licensed engineers to use the need for aircraft maintenance as leverage in the negotiations.

Early in the year, Qantas had dusted off other contingency plans. Highly conscious of the prospect of industrial action ranging from stop-work meetings to work-to-rule action and strikes, it began preparing managers and non-unionised staff to step in at a moment's notice if ground staff walked. They needed to be able to fill in for key roles at airports such as the 'push back' of aircraft from terminal gates. The measures involved flying managers to Los Angeles to learn first hand from private contractors how to drive tows and perform other jobs. They needed to know the basic legal requirements of hands-on work in restricted parts of airports, including driving trucks onto the tarmac to load and unload baggage from aircraft. The trip to LA for staff had been part of contingency planning for strikes over the last decade but the urgency was greater this time.[8] In mid-2011, the company also put feelers out to aircraft maintenance companies in Asia to ensure it could send planes to engineering facilities abroad if the dispute turned ugly. 'It was not about strike-breaking but keeping planes flying,' an insider recalled. 'We didn't know what these guys would do – we needed to be prepared for any eventuality. It happened back in 2008, and back then they were very much on the back foot. It was just a backstop in case these guys got crazy and put 24-hour stoppages in.'[9]

Qantas did not have the same ability to make contingency plans for the pilots. An airline could keep flying with its engineers and

RIGHT: Qantas founders Hudson Fysh (left) and Paul 'Ginty' McGinness served at Gallipoli and later flew together in No.1 Squadron in the Australian Flying Corps. *Fairfax Media*

BELOW: Hudson Fysh (left) beside the cockpit of a BE2e biplane, which made up half the fleet of the Queensland and Northern Territory Aerial Services in 1921. *National Library of Australia*

ABOVE: Hollywood actor and Qantas ambassador-at-large John Travolta, flanked by the then Jetstar chief executive, Alan Joyce, and comedian Magda Szubanski, at the unveiling in Sydney of the Jetstar livery and flight-attendant uniforms in May 2004.
William West/AFP

LEFT: With a penchant for dealmaking and political lobbying, Geoff Dixon foreshadows at a briefing in August 2005 plans to shift thousands of jobs overseas despite Qantas posting a record profit.
Steven Siewert/Fairfax Media

ABOVE: The Qantas chief executive, Geoff Dixon, and the airline's chairman, Margaret Jackson, embrace at a media conference in Sydney in December 2006, where they announced the board's recommendation that shareholders accept a $5.60 per share takeover bid for the national carrier. *Tamara Voninski/Fairfax Media*

BELOW: Qantas' chief financial officer, Peter Gregg (left), and the third-in-charge, John Borghetti, were firm favourites in 2007 to eventually replace Geoff Dixon. *Louie Douvis/Fairfax Media*

ABOVE: The Qantas chairman, Leigh Clifford (centre), takes questions from journalists on July 28, 2008, about the surprise selection of Alan Joyce to succeed Geoff Dixon as the airline's chief executive.
Ben Rushton/Fairfax Media

BELOW: Firefighters douse one of the engines on QF32 following the Qantas A380's emergency landing at Singapore's Changi Airport on November 4, 2010.
Vivek Prakash/Reuters

RIGHT: Technicians inspect the extensive damage to QF32's number-two engine.
David Loh/Reuters

ABOVE: Jetstar executives Daniela Marsilli (left) and Tristan Freeman found themselves living a nightmare in Vietnam where they were interrogated by secret police and barred from leaving the country for six months. *Wakako Iguchi/Fairfax*

BELOW: Geoff Dixon, Brett Godfrey, then chief executive of Virgin Blue, and Alan Joyce lock arms at a glitzy farewell for Godfrey in May 2010. The public display would be almost unthinkable for Dixon and Joyce two years later when they fell out in spectacular fashion. *James Morgan*

ABOVE: Protesters from the Occupy Sydney movement show their support for Qantas workers outside the airline's annual meeting in Sydney on October 28, 2011 – a day before Alan Joyce grounded the fleet.
Rob Homer/Fairfax Media

LEFT: Alan Joyce at his desk the day after his shock decision on October 29, 2011, to ground the Qantas fleet and lock out thousands of staff.
Lee Besford/Fairfax Media

BELOW: Hundreds of Qantas passengers are left stranded at Los Angeles International Airport following the unprecedented grounding.
Justin Bodey

ABOVE: Ensconced as Virgin Australia's chief executive, John Borghetti set about removing the brash edges that had been synonymous with the airline's co-founder, Richard Branson, in favour of a more refined style.
Glenn Hunt/Fairfax Media

RIGHT: Qantas executive Olivia Wirth and her partner Paul Howes, one of Australia's highest-profile union leaders, often courted attention.
Alex Ellinghausen/Fairfax Media

BELOW: Alan Joyce and Geoff Dixon chat over drinks at a plush hotel in The Rocks in Sydney in March 2012 before their very public falling-out later that year.
James Brickwood/Fairfax Media

LEFT: The Emirates chief executive, Tim Clark, and Alan Joyce spruik their new alliance in Sydney in September 2012. *Nic Walker/Fairfax Media*

BELOW: Six years on from his appointment as chief executive, Alan Joyce reflects at Qantas' annual meeting in November 2014 on a year that saw the airline sink to one of the largest losses in global aviation history. *Quinn Rooney/Fairfax Media*

ground staff on strike for a certain amount of time. Planes could be sent overseas for maintenance and strike-breakers brought in to load and unload baggage onto planes. But if pilots walked off the job they could ground an airline – something Australia had learnt from the damaging pilots' strike in 1989. The reality was that there was little Qantas could do if its pilots went on strike. However, it knew that they were the least likely of the three unions to walk. The last time Qantas pilots had taken action was in 1966.

In public, the rhetoric from the unions and Qantas management began reaching fever pitch as the annual meeting of shareholders in Sydney in late November neared. It was quickly becoming an ideological battle over the place of trade unionism in Australia. Qantas had gifted the unions a large and easy target in the form of a $2 million pay rise for Joyce that year. No matter how Qantas tried to explain how the figure was calculated, the airline's annual report was clear: the CEO's pay had risen from $2.92 million to $5 million. The largesse for the top brass aided the unions in their public campaign for job-security clauses to be inserted into the collective employment contracts. 'They are taking huge pay rises when they are offshoring jobs to reduce people's pay and get around Australian workplace laws,' said Richard Woodward, the vice-president of the Australian and International Pilots Association. 'There is one rule for them and one for the airline's workers.'[10]

As the slanging match intensified, Qantas' head of security, Steve Jackson, made the call for security guards to be stationed outside the homes of the airline's executives he believed most at risk. Jackson was a veteran of the Australian Federal Police and had been operational commander for the Sydney Olympics in 2000. He had won accolades for his part in helping to track down the perpetrators of the Bali bombings in 2002. Qantas assigned security to keep watch over Joyce, Wirth, Strambi, Nassenstein and a number of others. They were in the firing line in this increasingly hostile contest. Security guards made occasional sweeps past the homes of other executives believed to be less at risk. While this helped allay fears, it added to the growing divide between management and the highly unionised staff. It fostered a feeling of a management under attack, whether real or perceived.

In early October, Qantas decided to go public about personal threats made to Joyce and other Qantas executives. They included a letter that had been sent to Joyce's apartment in The Rocks in central Sydney using terms such as 'foreign filth'.[11] But the leak to Sydney's *Daily Telegraph* newspaper about the alleged threats left Qantas open to criticism from unions that it was a PR stunt aimed at winning public support in its battle with them. Complaints from Qantas about threatening letters and emails led police to set up Strike Force Barrine. The police investigation was dropped without explanation a month later.[12]

The damaging game of cat and mouse between Qantas and the Transport Workers Union and the engineers' union was beginning to cause major operational headaches. The airline sent extra staff to airports around the country that were about to be hit by work stoppages, often putting them up for the night in hotels. The stoppages by ground staff lasted for only one to four hours. The guerilla-style campaign was the reality of industrial relations warfare in the twenty-first century. The days of strikes lasting for weeks on end were over. Now, it was a game fought on the front pages of newspapers, TV news bulletins and, increasingly, social media. Few union members had the appetite to stand on picket lines week after week without pay. They had hefty mortgages, credit-card bills, childcare and school fees to pay.

In the midst of this, the Transport Workers Union's national secretary, Tony Sheldon, was running for the national presidency of the Australian Labor Party. In the eyes of Qantas management, he was using the high public profile that a stoush with Australia's national airline attracted to further his own political interests. Qantas workers who were members of the Transport Workers Union walked off the job for four hours at Melbourne and Sydney airports on October 13, forcing at least fourteen flights to be cancelled. The airline also had to reschedule services to parts of the day when ground staff were not on strike. The following day – a Friday – hundreds of aircraft engineers went on strike for four hours, which prompted the federal tourism minister, Martin Ferguson, to warn that the government would intervene if a resolution was not reached because of the damage it was inflicting on the tourism industry. 'It is about time the parties sat in a room and sorted these issues out,' he said. 'They have a responsibility to think about the broader public interest.' Ferguson, a former president of the Australian Council of Trade Unions, condemned as 'un-Australian' the head of the aircraft engineers' union, Steve Purvinas, for urging travellers to shun Qantas and fly with its rivals in the lead-up to Christmas.[13]

Later that day, the team led by Olivia Wirth met others who had been in the loop for months on Level 18 of Qantas' building in central Sydney. The negotiations with the unions were going nowhere. The fall in Qantas' forward bookings had accelerated. The backlog of planes needing maintenance was growing. To the shock of some, they began discussing the possibility that a grounding would have to happen the very next day – a Saturday. In the strategising, Saturday had been identified as the best day to ground the fleet because it would have the least impact on passengers. The smallest number of people were flying. 'We were all discussing the possibility – if this happens tomorrow, are we ready?' an insider said. They had to decide whether to tell pilots sitting in planes on the ground the same as they told those in the air. How would they offload passengers from grounded planes? What would be the likely legal outcome of grounding the fleet and locking out staff? There was just so much to run through.

As they kept going over a growing list of what needed to be done, Joyce strode into the room and sat down to hear how preparations were going. A short time later, it was decided that they were not ready. There were holes in the strategy. They walked out of the room, and that was it. A grounding of the national airline the next day had been averted – for now.

The next question was when? If it wasn't to be the next day, what date was best? The shareholder annual meeting in Sydney was in two weeks. The feeling in the room on that Friday in mid-October was that once the AGM was out of the way, they could choose to ground the airline if necessary the following day – a Saturday. Importantly, a delay in deciding whether to ground the fleet would give them breathing space, and time to prepare. They had mapped out an ideal situation whereby the prime minister, Julia Gillard, would be phoned on the day to give her notice of a grounding of the fleet at 5.00 p.m. She would step in, terminate the industrial action immediately and thereby avert the grounding. The delay would also keep open the possibility, however slim, of a settlement with the unions. 'It was with military-like precision that this had to be executed: the timing, the coordinating, making sure they had the maximum number of people on the road to manage the impact but the minimum number of passengers to affect,' another insider said. 'Thus, Saturday afternoon at five o'clock was deemed to be the right one.'[14] Apart from advertising guru Neil Lawrence – who had coined the 'Kevin 07' catchcry in Kevin Rudd's successful campaign to become prime minister in 2007 – Qantas drew on expertise from Rod Cameron, the silver-haired former pollster for the Labor Party. Qantas needed to be able to measure the public mood, as well as that of its prized frequent-flyer members lauded with gold and platinum status, towards the airline during the dispute. 'The golds and the plats', as they were known internally, were customers Qantas could not afford to lose.

Over the next two weeks, meetings were held regularly late in the afternoon in the boardroom for the Qantas executive committee (or 'ex-co' as it is known in corporate parlance) on Level 9 of Building A at the Qantas head office near Sydney Airport. The Qantas campus encompassed seven office blocks, including Building A, in which management was housed. There, Wirth's trusted team was updated on the negotiations as they continued to strategise. Were they prepared for key messages if the fleet was grounded? What would the media releases say? How would they handle the calls? What would they tell the prime minister and her ministers, and when? Where would they hold media conferences? How would they encourage journalists to drive out to the head office on a Saturday afternoon when most were on their day off work, without letting word slip? One of the biggest speeches of Joyce's life still had to be written. A major advertising campaign would also have to be rolled out quickly to win back customers once the grounding and lockout were over.

They set about laying the groundwork for winning over public opinion. If the thermo-nuclear option was chosen, they needed a damn good reason for convincing the public that they had no alternative. They were about to disrupt the travel plans of 100 000 people, and not just domestic travellers. 'A lot of it was about messages, nuance and the narrative that would take them towards a particular outcome justifying the impact of the industrial action that was being taken,' an insider recalled. Central to the PR campaign was leaking stories to the media about the impact on Qantas of the unions' campaign. News Limited's tabloid newspapers, the *Daily Telegraph* in Sydney and the *Herald Sun* in Melbourne, topped the list of outlets to target because they had what is known in the PR trade as 'cut through'. If they splashed stories about Qantas on their front page or printed them in the first few pages, they would catch the biggest readership in the country, and radio and TV networks would pick them up for follow-up stories. Expectations of fiery encounters at the AGM helped create a scene of impending chaos. It would be a dust-up between Qantas' board and management and the unions, separated by police, security guards and airport metal detectors.

The unions were also battling for public support. The Transport Workers Union and the engineers' union never shied away from attacking the company via the press, but their PR teams were outgunned. Qantas' PR machine dwarfed those of the individual unions. The engineers jumped on any signs of maintenance shortcomings as evidence of what would happen if more work was sent overseas.

But their chest-thumping aided their corporate enemy by fostering an impending sense of chaos. Steve Purvinas, the federal secretary of the Australian Licensed Aircraft Engineers Association, who had long been a thorn in the side of successive Qantas management teams, had handed the airline the ammunition it needed to return fire. His warning in mid-October that travellers should 'probably be looking at airlines other than Qantas' in the lead-up to Christmas played right into Qantas' hands.[15] The remark came two months after his threat to Qantas to 'bake them slowly' in a post on a website for pilots, PPRuNe.[16] If Joyce was going to ground the Qantas fleet and lock out staff, he needed justification for doing so. Qantas needed to convince the public that the unions had given Joyce no option.

On about October 20, internal risk assessments were highlighting the danger to safety from a lockout of staff due to human factors. 'Lockout with immediate grounding appears to involve significantly less risk,' Qantas' head of safety, Susan D'Ath-Weston, wrote in a detailed assessment for Strambi.[17] The need for a lockout and grounding to run in tandem became a near certainty. The strain on those who had been briefed about the likely course of action was immense. They carried a telling secret that troubled some of them. Others were focused on carrying out a job that needed to be done. Qantas was a business that could not easily be stopped without directly affecting tens of thousands of lives beyond those involved in the stand-off between management and the unions.

Secrecy had been paramount from the start. While there was no edict, those in the loop knew they had to keep emails about their planning to a minimum. An email sent to the wrong address, or worse, that was leaked to journalists, could undo the closely guarded plans and derail the entire campaign. The efforts to conceal the level of planning going on behind the scenes were nearly undone on October 20 when *The Age*'s aviation reporter, Andrew Heasley, sought a response from Qantas to speculation that it was prepared to ground its international fleet. 'I've not heard that – that's just a rumour,' Wirth told the journalist.[18] The idea that Qantas was prepared to ground its fleet seemed so far-fetched at the time that the newspaper decided not to take it any further. But clearly, speculation, in some quarters at least, was beginning to grow.

Throughout the entire period Wirth was glued to Joyce's side. She had had a meteoric rise at Qantas. In April, she had been officially elevated at the age of thirty-five to become a direct report to Joyce as the head of government and corporate affairs. She had been acting in the role since David Epstein, a former adviser to Kevin Rudd, had departed Qantas in December 2010 to become BHP Billiton's chief spin doctor. By now, she was Joyce's closest confidant. No other senior executive was as close to him. She seemed to know almost everything about him – his whereabouts and, in the eyes of some of her colleagues, almost what he was thinking. She earned praise even from some of her rivals for the way she had made herself indispensable to Joyce. At the executive offices in Sydney's CBD, her office was close to the CEO's. Wirth could be charming, and was pragmatic about the way she operated in the lofty world of big business and politics. She was a former adviser to Liberal MP Joe Hockey, a rising star in the Coalition, and had worked at the Tourism & Transport Forum – a lobby group chaired by former Liberal MP Bruce Baird – and Tourism Australia. Wirth lived in the inner-city Sydney suburb of Surry Hills, which had changed over the decades from a working-class neighbourhood to a trendy, affluent part of the city. Her home was metres away from an old-style inner-city pub her brother, Jaime, and a business partner had turned into a fashionable bar and Spanish restaurant, and one where she occasionally drank.

While Wirth's inner circle crafted and recrafted the scripts, the executives charged with the actual running of Qantas met to assess how preparations were progressing. Again, the level of detail kept piling up. If Jetstar and the regional subsidiary QantasLink were not grounded, would they be able to operate on their own? What about airlines such as Air New Zealand, with which Qantas had a baggage-handling agreement in Australia? Who would notify the Civil Aviation Safety Authority, and when? If an aircraft was taxiing when a decision was made to ground Qantas, would it be allowed to continue on its journey?

With the hostility growing, the federal transport minister, Anthony Albanese, sought to bring Joyce and Sheldon together to broker a deal on neutral ground in his electorate office in the inner-west suburb of Marrickville in Sydney. Albanese's electorate of Grayndler sat under the main flight path from Sydney Airport; the roar of passenger jets was part of living in this part of the city. With memorabilia from Albanese's time as transport minister hanging on the office walls, Joyce and Sheldon sat down to talk on October 21. Albanese knew both men well. He had met Joyce to talk about the dispute just a week earlier. Sheldon, a devout Catholic, often wore his Ansett bomber jacket when he met Joyce. An Ansett union delegate had given the jacket to him in the wake of the airline's collapse in 2001, and he wanted to let the Qantas CEO know he was prepared for a fight.[19] With the full knowledge of Julia Gillard and the treasurer, Wayne Swan, Albanese had the two key protagonists in his electorate office holding what he believed were constructive talks away from the public grandstanding.

Sheldon and Joyce eventually walked out of the office, giving the minister hope from their feedback that a breakthrough could be reached. Sheldon had called off industrial action planned for the following Wednesday.[20] Later that afternoon, Joyce sat down for another chat with Albanese in his electorate office. The face-to-face meetings were on top of numerous text messages and phone conversations between the pair.

In the midst of the dispute, the government was preparing for one of the biggest events on its calendar that year. The Queen and world leaders such as the British prime minister, David Cameron, were due to arrive in the country in less than two weeks for the Commonwealth Heads of Government Meeting in Perth. Foremost in the ministers' minds was avoiding any travel disruptions caused by the industrial row during the three-day leaders' summit. The government bureaucracy had been planning with airlines for the extra flights needed to carry the heads of state and their entourages.[21]

Qantas believed the Transport Workers Union was fundamental from a political perspective. The union's members at the airline were blue-collar workers, which represented the power base of the Labor Party and in turn the Gillard Government. A settlement with the union would be a boost to Qantas gaining the support of the government in any efforts to end the dispute with the two other unions, which represented pilots, who were paid between \$150 000 and \$500 000 a year, and licensed aircraft engineers, whose salaries ranged from \$120 000 to \$150 000. It was hard to see an outpouring of public support for them gaining pay rises. In contrast, ramp handlers at Qantas were the poor people of the Qantas workforce, earning a base salary of about \$50 000. Importantly, a deal with the Transport Workers Union might force the other two unions to settle.

The talks with the Transport Workers Union hinged on a breakthrough over the ratio of Qantas ground staff to workers from labour-hire companies. Airlines were increasingly outsourcing their ground-handling jobs – known in the industry as 'below-the-wing' roles – to companies such as Menzies and Toll Dnata, a joint venture between Toll Holdings and Dubai's Dnata. The rationale was simple: the ground-handling companies employed staff on lower wages than their counterparts at Qantas. Slashing costs was all-important for airlines, and targeting ground-handling work was one way to do it.

A year earlier, Qantas managers had discussed in internal briefings the long-term option of ending the company's ground-handling operations by 2020. Confidential documents tagged '2020 Vision' revealed that the airline was looking at exiting what it called 'below-the-wing' ground-handling by the end of the decade. Roles such as baggage handling were a 'commodity service' and cheaper and more efficient to contract out to specialist providers. By the end the decade, the 'job for life' with 'good pay' and flexible working conditions would no longer exist for Qantas' ground handlers under the 2020 Vision. For Qantas managers, the outsourcing of ground-handling work would mean 'less staff and people matters to manage'. The leaked documents revealed that Qantas had also talked about increasing the automation of so-called 'above-the-wing' roles such as check-in, as well as using technology to help reduce the need for staff at entrances to airport lounges.[22] The vision was based on underlying assumptions that included 'more overlap' of the company's two-brand strategy of Qantas and Jetstar.

It was against this backdrop that the Transport Workers Union wanted a minimum of 55 per cent of ground-handlers employed by Qantas and was pushing for a wage rise of more than 3 per cent a year. Both were unpalatable to Qantas. It wanted a lower ratio of inhouse staff to workers employed by contractors, with annual wage rises capped at 3 per cent. A rise of more than 3 per cent would send a signal to the other unions that they, too, could push harder. The Transport Workers Union also wanted side letters to be included in the enterprise bargaining deal, which Qantas opposed because once in the agreement they would be open to arbitration.

The job-security clause the Transport Workers Union was fighting for in the public arena was broad. Joyce had made clear that he would not agree to any commitments over securing jobs. How could any CEO guarantee that the jobs would still be there in five years' time? More than anything, the union's claim was a rallying cry to its members to convince them that their jobs were under threat. In the longer term, this would be a likely outcome as Qantas followed other airlines in turning to outsourcing to lower its labour bill. Qantas believed it had no choice, as it competed against airlines that employed staff on salaries significantly lower than its own. Virgin had started life as an idea on the back of beer coasters, free of complex labour agreements that had been built up over decades and ran to hundreds of pages. Australia's second-largest airline did have a unionised workforce but agreements were originally negotiated on the basis of it operating as a low-cost carrier.

On October 25 Richard Woodward was driving to his Sydney home when he received a call. The contact told him that Qantas had booked thousands of hotel rooms via a broker in Los Angeles, Singapore and London. Woodward immediately phoned the pilots' union's president, Barry Jackson, to tell him about the tip from someone he regarded as a reliable source. The pair agreed that Qantas must have been making contingencies for a potential wildcat strike by members of the Transport Workers Union. A wildcat strike would affect only airports in Australia, but they reasoned that the union may have engaged support overseas from unions such as the Teamsters in the United States. Anything other than Qantas readying for strike action by other unions seemed too preposterous to imagine. Their thoughts quickly turned to the annual shareholder meeting in three days' time, and they decided to leave it to see what happened there.[23]

The next day, Joyce and Sheldon met again at Albanese's electorate office in Marrickville. This time – a Wednesday – they had been summoned by the minister after he had received a call to say that the negotiations had broken down. Albanese wanted to bring Joyce and Sheldon together in the desperate hope of rekindling talks that less than a week earlier had shown signs of a breakthrough. A few kilometres away at the Mercure hotel on the edge of Sydney Airport, the negotiating teams from Qantas and the Transport Workers Union were also meeting in a last-gasp effort to salvage an in-principle settlement. But like the meeting under way between Joyce and Sheldon, the chance of reaching a deal was further out of reach than ever. The union planned to push ahead with one-hour stoppages at airports around the country on the Friday, the day of the Qantas annual meeting. The Qantas managers later walked out of the Mercure hotel and drove back to the head office knowing that any hope of a breakthrough in the negotiations had been dashed. There was no deal, and no end in sight to the dispute.

The following day, Strambi and his direct reports who had been involved in planning for a lockout met again in Building A, the main offices for management. The buildings on Qantas' campus on Coward Street near the airport were dull office blocks built in the 1970s. They did not fit the perception of airlines as glamorous companies. The executives did not believe that the unions would think for a minute that they were considering playing the lockout card. As detailed planning of the lockout reached its conclusion, Strambi's executives charged with running the day-to-day operations of the airline also had to prepare for ground staff stopping work for an hour around the country the next day, which had been timed to coincide with Qantas' annual shareholder meeting.

With preparations gaining momentum at the highest levels, the circle of people in the know again widened. A verbal directive on the Thursday reached a select group of managers in Qantas' middle ranks. They were told to begin planning for one scenario – and only one. The verbal command was couched in implicit terms but was stark nonetheless. They were told Qantas' 144-strong fleet of planes could be grounded within the next few days if the stand-off with the three unions was not brought to an end. In some cases, managers were pulled out of meetings to be delivered the command to prepare for a 'what if' scenario. Once told, they had to decide quickly what their departments needed to do if planes ended up parked on airport aprons for an indefinite period. Some walked into quiet parts of their offices at the Qantas headquarters to chat with colleagues who had received the same command.

The gravity of the directive quickly dawned on managers who had long ago become accustomed to dealing with crises in an industry that seemed to be forever on the brink. 'There are a few times in my life when I have turned white – that was one of them,' one recalled later.[24] It wasn't fear of looming danger. Rather, it was a realisation of the far-reaching consequences of grounding the entire red-tailed fleet, and the enormous amount of work that lay ahead. They knew it would strand tens of thousands of passengers in an instant, the vast majority of whom would need to be put up in top-notch hotels as far afield as London, New York, Hong Kong, Tokyo and Johannesburg.

Under a shroud of secrecy, the Qantas managers began working in cells within their own company. 'It was very clandestine. There was no traceability in terms of emails to you to say, "Give an assessment",' a former Qantas manager recalled. 'It was all verbal discussion in fairly tight areas.'[25] Pairs in different parts of the operational areas of the airline began planning for the raft of potential flow-on effects from a grounding of the fleet. They did not know whether the grounding of the fleet – if it did eventuate – would last four hours, eight hours, a day or a month. They just knew that they had to plan – and fast. Some managers didn't believe the grounding would last very long. They thought the two sides would quickly be forced to the negotiating table – or that was what they pinned their hopes on. Their lives would be turned upside down if the unprecedented step was taken.

One of the first questions on their minds was the likely timing. This was imperative. They wanted to know how long they had to prepare for it. 'This weekend – it might be Saturday,' was one reply. Everything was implied; definitive answers were not given. Those in the know in middle management were not aware of the full picture; all they could do was read between the lines of the directives from above. But they had to understand the urgency of the situation or, as is often human nature, they would put off their planning for another day. What they did know was that they were working towards something occurring at the weekend, which coincided with one of the busiest couple of days on the Australian calendar. 'There wasn't much thought given to it the first time [it was mentioned in middle-management ranks in mid-October],' a Qantas manager recalled. 'The second time, you knew something was coming.'[26]

In Perth, the Queen was about to open the biennial Commonwealth Heads of Government Meeting. It was the first time CHOGM had been held in one of the world's most remote cities.

For the prime minister, it was a chance to rise above domestic politics and step onto the international stage. Gillard was hosting fifty-three Commonwealth leaders. Perth was in lockdown for the three-day event, one of the largest international gatherings the city had hosted. In Melbourne, staff at Flemington Racecourse put the final touches to marquees huddled beside each other in the Birdcage for Derby Day. The marquees would play host on the Saturday to Australia's rich and powerful as the worlds of business, politics, entertainment and sport intersected for a day of partying, networking and betting. It was the main drawcard for the country's political class during the Spring Racing Carnival, which kicked off on the Saturday and climaxed with the 'race that stops the nation' – the Melbourne Cup – the following Tuesday.

By the Friday, the Qantas managers who had been told to start planning for a grounding of the fleet were told that if it was to happen, it could occur on the Saturday afternoon. 'Well, what time?' a manager asked. 'Work on being told around five o'clock,' was the response. They did not know what was occurring further up the chain of command. They took orders, and did as best they could to prepare.

The planning under way in the mid-level ranks at Qantas' headquarters on the Friday was occurring less than 10 kilometres from where a showdown was about to take place. The sense of anticipation had seldom been greater for a Qantas shareholder meeting. Clifford, Joyce and the rest of the executive team and the airline's board were about to stare down their adversaries from the union movement.

Qantas had taken every precaution for the meeting, which was to be held in a 945-seat auditorium at the University of New South Wales, in the Sydney suburb of Kensington. It raised a sense that something big was about to happen. At the entrances to the auditorium, security guards stood beside metal detectors, screening everyone who entered. 'A condition of entry is that all personal items are subject to inspection,' a sign read. After the threats to Joyce months earlier, Qantas was taking no chances. To the unions, it was an overreaction.

'It is a continuation of Qantas trying to ramp up this dispute, whether it is in terms of alleged death threats or alleged chaos at airports,' a spokesman from the engineers' union, Peter Somerville, said.[27] About twenty police officers milled around outside the auditorium, making it clear that they were on hand in case anything turned nasty.

The size of the crowd outside grew in the lead-up to the start of the AGM at 11.00 a.m. Union members, some carrying banners, stuck close to their leaders from the Transport Workers Union, the Australian Licenced Aircraft Engineers Association – including Qantas' enemy number one, Steve Purvinas – and the Australian International Pilots Association. The pilots wore their non-uniform red ties, one of their few acts of protest during the industrial dispute. Their other act of rebellion had been to alert passengers to their cause when they made public announcements during flights. Journalists and cameramen darted among the union officials for their comments. Qantas' PR staff watched on from a short distance away. The gulf between the two sides was enormous.

The crowd was noisy but it wasn't antagonistic. Many people, including elderly shareholders who turned up, were surprised at the high level of security. If there was going to be a showdown, it would be in the Sir John Clancy Auditorium as Joyce and Clifford squared off with their union rivals. Those gathered outside speculated about what was going to come from the meeting. Some union members who were Qantas shareholders prepared their questions. It was their chance to put their demands to Clifford, Joyce and the rest of the Qantas board. Both sides were trying to anticipate what the other would say and do over the next few hours. About a dozen protesters from the Occupy Sydney movement, as well as university staff who brandished banners with 'UNSW staff support Qantas workers' walked around outside the meeting.

In a show of defiance, ground staff and baggage handlers who were covered by the industrial agreement in dispute had already begun rolling one-hour strikes across the country. The first members of the

Transport Workers Union walked off the job at Brisbane and Cairns airports in the early hours of Friday morning, followed by their colleagues at Sydney and Melbourne airport at 8.00 a.m. Other airports would be hit later in the day. Before the AGM began, Sheldon told reporters that ground staff had endorsed further industrial action at their hour-long stop-work meetings earlier in the morning. He also made it clear that the unions would be honing in on Joyce's pay and Qantas' expansion into Asia, which threatened their members' jobs. 'Qantas is quite clear about escalating the industrial dispute, and all forms of action, including one-hour stoppages, four-hour stoppages and the potential for 48-hour stoppages, are being contemplated as we speak,' Sheldon said.[28] With those words, the unions had given Qantas the further justification it believed it needed for the unprecedented events that were to follow.

By the time Clifford, Joyce and the rest of the board filed on stage in the auditorium at 11.00 a.m., Qantas had already cancelled 129 flights and delayed 387 over the previous three months due to the protracted industrial dispute. In the process, 70 000 passengers had been disrupted. The airline had also grounded seven planes because of a growing backlog of maintenance. All up, it put the cost of 'union action' at $68 million – or $15 million a week in lost revenue. Qantas' forward bookings had collapsed. The travelling public was deserting the airline, compounding its woes. Demand for corporate travel up and down the east coast of Australia had slumped 40 per cent in the week before the AGM, compared with previous years.

Back at Qantas headquarters, managers who had been told to plan for the possibility of a grounding walked to other departments to talk to those who had been similarly briefed. Departments could not plan in isolation. Qantas' call centres had to be ready to act because they would be inundated with calls from stranded passengers. But first those managing the call centres had to know what they were going to tell customers about hotel accommodation and alternative flights home. They could not do this without speaking to other departments.

The Saturday was the only firm date Strambi's direct reports or their underlings had received of a possible lockout. It was still only a possibility – a decision had yet to be made. But every effort was under way to ensure a smooth execution of the plan if the 'go' button was pushed. Some executives in Strambi's team began phoning their senior staff. They could not tell them what they were planning for. Instead, they warned them that they believed the unions might be up to something over the weekend following an expected firestorm at the AGM. 'We don't know what it is, we don't know when it will happen but you need to stay off the sauce if you can and try to hang around at home, and keep your phone handy,' one said. The executives were prepping their staff to ensure they had as many hands ready to assist as possible if the command was given. They could not tell their foot soldiers the real reason why they had to be available. 'I wanted them to be around so they could go in and help out, but I couldn't tell them why. So we made up a little story,' one recalled.[29] It left the middle managers thinking something was about to blow the next day – the Saturday – but nothing of the magnitude that it was to become. By the Friday, Qantas cabin crew managers were flying to Los Angeles and Singapore where they would wait to answer questions in hotels where flight attendants would be staying in the event of a grounding.

During the near four-hour annual meeting, Joyce traded verbal blows with the union heavyweights. He accused the unions of trying to 'stop management from making necessary changes'. After the meeting, journalists were bussed a short distance from the auditorium to a conference centre on the university's campus where Joyce and Clifford would speak. It was highly unusual. The venue for the media conference was just a short walk away but Qantas had gone to extraordinary lengths to ensure it had planned for every contingency. It feared that unions might storm the media conference, which seemed highly unlikely to those of us watching the events unfold from a distance. Rather than hold it next door to the auditorium, they decided to hold it further away on the university campus. It again highlighted the frayed nerves at the highest levels. Apart from trading verbal blows at the annual meeting, the union members were restrained. No one was arrested. The most noise outside the auditorium came from Occupy Sydney, a loose-knit group that had emerged from a global protest movement against inequality and had nothing to do with the industrial dispute.

After shuffling into the press briefing with a limp, Clifford emphasised that the AGM had been a 'watershed moment'. Voting by shareholders on the resolutions, which included adoption of the renumeration report for the executive team, had revealed overwhelming support for management. Joyce told reporters that Qantas jobs were on the line but declined to say how long the dispute could drag on before he would start axing them. 'It's a situation that for us is not sustainable and we need the unions to come to the negotiating table with sensible alternatives. If this was to continue it will cost jobs because the airline can't continue to take these type of hits.'[30] Journalists walked out of the room unaware of the frenetic activity behind the scenes at Qantas' main offices or what was to follow the next day. I chatted with Vanda Carson, a friend and colleague from a rival newspaper, about the unusual vibes we got from Qantas' top brass and their underlings. The lengths Qantas had gone to to prepare for any eventuality at the annual meeting – however unlikely – was strange, but we had no inkling of what was to come next.

Qantas staff who had endured hours at the AGM headed back to the airline's main offices in suburban Mascot. A number of those in the know were again bunkered down in a meeting room on the management floor on Level 9. Their planning over the weeks had resembled a covert, black-box operation. In the early evening, Joyce popped his head in and told them to go home and rest. It would be a big day tomorrow.

10

D-DAY

October 29, 2011, began early for those in the know. Some arrived at the Qantas headquarters near Sydney Airport as early as 7.00 a.m. on that Saturday morning. They knew they had an almighty day ahead of them given the planning they had endured over the previous weeks. But they still did not know how the day would turn out. All manner of scenarios were playing out in their minds, and some had a sick feeling in their stomach about what was about to happen.

It was not just those at the top of the airline's hierarchy who were walking into the offices, many dressed in jeans and T-shirt. Middle managers who had been told on the Thursday to begin planning for a possible grounding of the fleet turned up for work on their rostered day off. They wanted to be ready to spring into action in case it did happen. There was no point sitting at home waiting for the phone to ring. If the decision was made, they wanted to be at the Qantas offices ready to tell their staff, and begin the massive job they faced of dealing with 98 000 passengers who would not be catching their flights. The middle managers did not know what was unfolding at the top echelons of the company on that Saturday morning. They were holding out hope that Qantas' fleet of aircraft would not be grounded. For the rest of the Qantas staff, the Saturday started as just a normal shift. They had no idea of what was about to unfold.

But an inkling of what was about to transpire was circulating – it was just that it was not the unions that were about to ground the airline. The headline on a story in the Saturday edition of Melbourne's *Herald Sun* newspaper screamed: 'The Dying Kangaroo: Jobs warning as union threatens to ground Qantas for 48 hours'. Joyce had not mentioned the possibility of a grounding of the airline when he fronted the media conference after the annual meeting on the Friday. 'That is very hard for us to determine,' he said when asked how long the dispute would have to drag on before he started axing jobs.[1] But later that day he gave an interview to Simon Benson, a senior political reporter whose stories appeared across News Limited's tabloid newspapers, including the *Herald Sun* and *Daily Telegraph*. He told Benson that if the industrial dispute 'goes on for more than a year, we estimate we will have to shut down half of Qantas operations. That's 50 per cent of Qantas, gone. This would have very grave consequences for jobs.' And then the killer line: 'If these unions walk off the job for two days we would be left with no choice but to ground the airline until they returned to work.'[2] The blame game for what was yet to happen was already under way.

At 10.30 a.m., the Qantas board, which included former Commonwealth Bank chairman John Schubert and former Australian Defence chief Peter Cosgrove, dialled in for a teleconference. Over the next hour, Joyce gained their support for his decision to ground the airline later that day at 5.00 p.m. The planning that had been under way for months began to be put into action. Shortly after 11.00 p.m., Qantas told printers at Focus Press to start rolling their presses. The Sydney printing firm had been retained for some time to print lockout notices for thousands of Qantas workers in the event that Joyce decided to choose that option.[3] The Qantas chief executive also began phoning those of his executives who were not in the loop. He couldn't get hold of the Jetstar chief executive, Bruce Buchanan, until midday. Buchanan was in Melbourne talking to architects about work on his house. At noon, Joyce's executive committee met and set about executing the plans to ground the airline at 5.00 p.m., and lock out staff the following Monday at 8.00 p.m. They were still hoping the grounding and lockout would not happen, banking on the government stepping in to terminate the dispute as soon as its ministers were told what Qantas planned later that day. 'There was still a big thought that once the decision was made and the call was put in to the PM that she would step in and instantly call it off, and as a result, no aircraft would need to be grounded,' an insider said. 'That was the overarching strategy.'[4]

That afternoon, Anthony Albanese was playing tennis in a social competition at the Marrickville and District Hardcourt Tennis Club in Sydney's inner west. In the middle of a game, the federal transport minister got a call at 1.38 p.m. from one of his advisers to say that the Qantas chief executive wanted to speak to him urgently, and to expect a call. The call didn't come. Standing on the side of the tennis court, he rang Joyce's mobile at 1.51 p.m. but couldn't get through. 'What a time to ring!' Albanese, dressed in his coloured tennis gear, said sternly in a message he left on Joyce's phone.

Four minutes later, Albanese tried again without any luck, before repeating the exercise at 1.58 p.m.[5] Finally, Albanese's mobile rang with Joyce on the other end of the line shortly after 2.00 p.m. The Qantas chief executive told him that he would be grounding Australia's largest airline in less than three hours and locking out staff on the following Monday. Albanese told him unequivocally that he thought it was a bad decision. 'I reminded him that CHOGM was on in Perth and if he's going to pick any time to ground the airline, ever, that that would do maximum damage. I said, "Why would you do it tonight? People would be stranded. If you are going to do this, why wouldn't you at least give me some notice?"' Albanese recalled later. 'He was like, the decision has been made. We were being told, not asked.'[6]

Working to a prepared script, Joyce told Albanese he was doing it on the basis of safety. During their five-minute conversation, he informed the minister that if news leaked before 5.00 p.m. he would ground the fleet immediately. It was an extraordinary demand a company was making of a government. Qantas feared that chaos would have ensued at airports around the country if word had leaked out.

Once off the call, Albanese tried to phone the prime minister. Gillard was holding court with seventeen heads of state on the other side of the country. 'We were concerned about any disruption in the lead-up to CHOGM, and here we were being told it was being grounded in the middle of CHOGM,' Albanese said later.[7] The transport minister also rang his departmental secretary, Mike Mrdak, to ask him to find out whether the Civil Aviation Safety Authority believed there was a threat of Qantas staff sabotaging planes if they knew they were about to be locked out. The department later told him they had no advice that that would be the case.

A cascade of phone calls from Qantas began to be made to other ministers and state premiers. The workplace relations minister, Chris Evans, was at an under-seventeen cricket match in Perth when Joyce phoned to tell him of Qantas' intentions. Martin Ferguson, the tourism minister, who was regarded as the most sympathetic towards Qantas in Cabinet, was enjoying a day at the races. Weeks earlier, the Victorian frontbencher had lashed out at the engineers' union for encouraging passengers to fly with Qantas' rivals in the lead-up to Christmas because of the dispute.

From his office on the ninth floor at Qantas' headquarters, Joyce had spoken to the relevant ministers and did not expect to speak to Gillard because he knew she was busy with CHOGM in Perth.[8] Olivia Wirth phoned Gillard's chief of staff, Ben Hubbard, to tell him what Qantas planned. She told him Joyce would be available to speak to the prime minister if she wanted.[9]

At the inner-Sydney tennis club, Albanese left his fellow players standing on the court, telling them that they would understand later why he had to cut short their game. He raced home to change into a suit. With the prime minister showcasing the nation to world leaders in Perth, her ministers went into crisis mode on the other side of the country. Albanese phoned the treasurer, Wayne Swan, who organised a telephone hook-up of key Cabinet ministers including Evans, Ferguson, the finance minister, Penny Wong, and the assistant treasurer, Bill Shorten, to determine a course of action.[10] This was a crisis for the government, too. The country's largest airline was about to be grounded and tens of thousands of passengers stranded around the world on a weekend. World leaders would also be left wondering how they would get home while the fleet was grounded and a lockout of a large chunk of Qantas' workforce was planned for two days' time.

The government believed Qantas had dumped the problem in its lap to be fixed. Before the teleconference started, Albanese spoke briefly with Gillard about the government's course of action. As former industrial relations minister and the architect of the Fair Work Act, Gillard knew the legislation back to front. Shortly afterwards, the ministers who dialled into the teleconference from around the country quickly decided to send the dispute to an emergency hearing of the industrial umpire by using Section 424 of the Fair Work Act. To Qantas' dismay, the government had decided against invoking Section 431 of the industrial relations laws, which gave ministers the powers to terminate the dispute immediately. It would have allowed Qantas to keep flying. The senior ministers decided that Albanese would lead its counterattack later that afternoon. After being given an ultimatum by Qantas, the government believed it needed to get on the front foot or the airline, the Opposition and the unions would quickly fill the vacuum.

After changing into a suit, Albanese drove from his home in Sydney's inner west to the Commonwealth Parliament Offices, the home for Cabinet ministers when they were in the city. On the drive into the central city, he phoned staffers and thought about lines he would need for the media conference later. Joyce had told him the grounding would occur at 5.00 p.m. Albanese needed a counter line to Qantas'. The government did not want Joyce to be able to get away with telling the world that he had been forced to ground the fleet; it did not believe this was the case. But without a quick response from the government, Qantas' line would become the dominant view.

Before 5.00 p.m., the Department of Foreign Affairs and Trade notified overseas posts what was about to happen. Ambassadors, consul-generals and their staff needed to know because they were about to have to deal with stranded Qantas passengers overseas. To the department's astonishment, some had heard rumours that a grounding of the Qantas fleet was a possibility.

Journalists first got an inkling something big was about to happen when Qantas' PR team hit the send button on an email at 4.14 p.m. In the media release, marked 'urgent', journalists were told Joyce would turn up on Level 3 of Building A at the airline's headquarters for a media conference in three-quarters of an hour. It was highly unusual for a chief executive to call a media conference on a weekend. It had to be a big deal.

11

GROUNDED

Shortly before 5.00 p.m., Alan Joyce took a lift with one of his minders down six floors from Level 9 in Building A at Qantas' headquarters on Coward Street near Sydney Airport. Once out of the lift, they began the short stroll along the corridor to a room on the third floor where journalists and cameras had been corralled for a hastily arranged media conference to hear an announcement they had only been told was big. Before Joyce got to the waiting journalists, a text message bleeped on the screen of Lyell Strambi's mobile. 'We are go,' it read. With those words, the die had been cast on this last Saturday in October 2011. There would be no turning back.

About ten minutes earlier, in anticipation, Strambi had set up a conference call with his direct reports, including the head of cabin crew, Samantha Taranto, and the executive manager of ground operations, Matt Lee. Some of Strambi's executives had written short scripts beforehand to read out to their own managers when the nod was given. With Strambi on one line, his confidants were about to dial into their own conference calls to feed the message down the line.

'Alan is going in now. He's made the decision. You now need to go and put in place your plans,' one told his direct reports.[1] As the words ricocheted through the organisation, emails began appearing in the inboxes of senior staff outlining what was about to happen and what they would need to do. With the push of a 'send' button on a mobile phone, the middle managers had been drawn into the vortex. The CEO was holding a media conference and in ten minutes all hell was going to break loose.

Earlier, some staff not yet in the know had turned up at Qantas headquarters and at airport terminals in jeans and T-shirts. They had no idea why they had been dragged into the office on a Saturday. For all they knew, the Transport Workers Union was about to launch strike action.

Standing in front of TV cameras that fed his image live to network news bulletins, Joyce started reading a prepared speech. 'A crisis is unfolding in Qantas,' he began. With the unions 'trashing our strategy and our brand', Joyce insisted he had no option but to force the issue by locking out staff who were covered by three agreements under negotiation. 'Killing Qantas slowly would be a tragedy for Qantas and our employees,' he said. It would be fifty-five sentences into his carefully crafted speech before he uttered the crucial lines. 'The lockout makes it necessary for us to ground the fleet,' he declared. 'We have decided to ground the Qantas international and domestic fleets immediately. I repeat, we are grounding the Qantas fleet now. Obviously, those flights that are currently in the air will complete their scheduled sectors. However, as from now there will be no further Qantas domestic or international departures anywhere in the world.'

So far, Qantas had put the cost of the industrial dispute at $68 million and a loss of $15 million in revenue a week. While the grounding would begin immediately, the lockout of staff would not start until 8.00 p.m. on the following Monday. 'We are locking out until the unions withdraw their extreme claim and reach an agreement with us,' Joyce said.[2] The grounding of Qantas' red-tailed fleet would drag in parts of the airline's workforce that were not involved in the dispute, such as pilots who flew short-haul routes in Australia and domestic and international flight attendants. Joyce's words quickly began making headlines around the world on TV broadcasters such as the BBC and CNN.

Within eight minutes of the start of Joyce's speech, the command to ground the fleet had worked its way to every part of the Qantas operations, from London and Los Angeles to Darwin, Sydney and Perth.[3] Planes on taxiways were turned back to terminals and aircraft parked at gates began offloading shocked passengers who only minutes earlier had been easing themselves into their seats for their journeys. An air-traffic controller directed a Qantas aircraft taxiing to a runway at Sydney Airport for a flight to Melbourne to radio the company before going any further. 'That sounds interesting. We'll hold short and I'll let you know,' a pilot from Qantas Flight 453 replied. A moment later, he requested clearance to taxi back to the domestic terminal. 'I'll see you on the next one,' the air-traffic controller said. 'Your guess is as good as mine when I'll talk to you next, mate,' the pilot responded.[4] Joyce's decision to ground the fleet would disrupt 98 000 passengers already sitting on Qantas planes or who were due to hop on its services over the next few days. Like front-line staff, passengers did not receive text messages or emails to give them forewarning that their travel plans were about to be up-ended. Rebecca Morrison was stranded at Sydney Airport with her three-year-old daughter after their flight to Brisbane for her best friend's wedding was cancelled. 'I always fly Qantas because of their reliability and quality and reputation. That's completely gone now,' Morrison said. 'The CEO of Qantas probably has little-man syndrome. The way he acted, I have no sympathy for him.'[5]

With the command from their bosses, shocked staff went out into airports and did what they had been told. Few read the list of prepared notes detailing what they should do. Time was precious. Staff ensured that passengers disembarked from planes and were sent home or put up in hotels. In a worst-case scenario, Qantas had expected arguments and fights to start. Travel plans would be thrown into disarray. Some customers were sure to miss weddings or funerals. But mayhem did not break out. Instead, staff and passengers appeared so stunned and disbelieving of what was occurring that an air of order was maintained in airport terminals around the country and overseas.

People were simply dumbfounded. They were not given a chance to think through what was happening at lightning speed. Cabin crew who were shepherding people from planes were as much in the dark about what was happening as passengers. They were simply following orders. Four flights were to be stopped from leaving London on the Saturday, stranding about 1500 passengers at Heathrow Airport. In Los Angeles, a Qantas jet readying for take-off was called back to the airport gate, and its passengers offloaded. Several more passenger jets sat idle at Los Angeles International Airport. Qantas' decision had also put other airlines, such as Air New Zealand, in a bind. They relied on Qantas ground staff to load and unload their planes at Australia's five main airports. At Flemington Racecourse in Melbourne, word about the Qantas grounding spread like wildfire through the well-groomed crowd drinking in the marquees and left the racegoers who had flown to Melbourne for Derby Day from other states wondering how they were going to get home.

At 5.15 p.m., Qantas gave formal orders to couriers to deliver to staff lockout notices, which had rolled off presses at Focus Print in Sydney earlier in the day. Five minutes later, Qantas phoned a broker to book 2000 hotel rooms in Los Angeles and 800 in Singapore. Shortly afterwards, the airline booked accommodation in Australia for stranded passengers.

Qantas still had sixty-six planes in the air. The airline had decided not to tell pilots who were flying about the unprecedented events under way on the ground. It deemed it a risk to safety because it believed pilots could be distracted while in the air. But it knew there was a chance some pilots would hear about the grounding. Word had a habit of spreading quickly, even at 40 000 feet. Pilots on long-haul flights often tuned into ABC Radio Australia or spoke to pilots on other aircraft via air-to-air communications. The captain of a 747 flying from Dallas to Brisbane, one of the longest runs in the world, was listening to the news on Radio Australia in the middle of the night when he heard that his airline had been grounded. Steve Anderson, the captain of the 747 who was also a secretary of the pilots' union, checked in with Qantas' operations control centre in Sydney but was told they had no information to relay to him. This was despite the fact that Qantas had prepared a statement to be read to any pilots who phoned in. The statement confirmed Qantas had been grounded but emphasised that it did not pose a safety risk to their flight. They were told to fly onto their destination where they would be met on arrival and all would be explained.

The hardest job fell upon the shoulders of Qantas staff at airports. Flight attendants could offload passengers before catching a taxi home; pilots walked off planes parked at gates or on airport aprons and headed to a hotel or home; aircraft engineers dropped their tools and left for the day. But staff at airports had to deal with passengers and their long list of questions in emotional, trying circumstances. How would they get to their wedding now? When would they be able to catch another flight? When would Qantas be flying again? Where would they be staying tonight? The airport workers had only just heard the news themselves. They were just beginning to learn what steps they should take to deal with passengers such as Walter Matthews, a Perth resident who had been left stuck in Sydney on his way home from a rugby trip to New Zealand. 'Everyone is totally stranded. They said go away and find another flight,' he said. 'Everyone is getting really pissed off. I was fine until the lady said there was no solution.'[6] By the end of the day, Qantas would book 10 247 passengers into hotels, including 8485 in rooms in Asia, Europe, the United States and South America, and 1762 in Australia's state capitals.[7]

At 5.27 p.m. Samantha Taranto pushed the send button on an email to flight attendants around the network. The cabin crew were not involved in the industrial dispute, and Taranto wanted to assure them that they had not been locked out. She told flight attendants in London, Singapore and Los Angeles that Qantas had cabin-crew managers at hotels for them to speak to. At the Hilton in LA, Nick Bull and Helen Gray were waiting in the crew room; in Singapore, Josh Rogers and Denise Harriman were in a conference room in the Swiss Hotel; and in London, James Ellis was at the crew hotel.[8] 'We will have management and my direct reports working overnight so we can continue to provide you with the most up-to-date information,' she wrote. The email would later be used as evidence of the extent of planning Qantas had undertaken in the lead-up to the grounding. It showed this was not a spur-of-the-moment response to an industrial dispute. Why had the cabin-crew managers been sent to outposts in the Qantas international network before Joyce had made his decision? Staff at Qantas' office at Los Angeles International had become suspicious when managers from Sydney turned up unannounced in the days before the grounding. 'The people who turned up, we never saw those people. We might speak to them on the phone or by email but we would never see them,' a Qantas staffer at Los Angeles recalled. 'They were all management level. When the grounding was announced, it was like, oh, that's why you are here.'[9]

While Joyce had been speaking, Albanese's media minder, Jeff Singleton, alerted journalists to a media conference with the transport minister on the tenth floor of the Commonwealth Parliament Offices on Phillip Street in central Sydney, not far from Qantas' city offices. At 5.45 p.m., Albanese fronted the cameras and journalists. Clearly angry, he said he was 'very concerned about Qantas' actions of which we were notified only mid-afternoon'. In the 1989 pilots' strike, one of the most damaging industrial disputes in Australia's history, the government had been able to make contingency plans. It had called in the Royal Australian Air Force and allowed international airlines to fly on domestic routes. This time, the government complained there was no warning. Australia depended on aviation like almost no other country. Albanese told journalists the government would be making an urgent application to Fair Work to terminate all industrial action at Qantas.[10]

At its headquarters, the well-prepped Qantas machine was working like clockwork. Qantas' PR team went into overdrive as calls came in from global broadcasters such as CNN and BBC, and journalists from the major TV and newspaper outlets. It was not only the large media outlets that wanted to know what was happening. Small newspapers and radio stations wanted to find out what it meant for their readers and listeners. Joyce had made the biggest gamble of his career. The fact that word of the grounding had not leaked testified to the loyalty of his inner circle.

But neither he nor his inner sanctum knew whether the months of planning and strategising would pay off. With a single decision, the man with the thick Irish brogue from Dublin's outer suburbs had almost stopped a nation. After months of unions threatening stoppages, calling them off at the last minute, and in some cases seeing them through, it was Qantas that was taking action against a large part of its workforce. Throughout, Joyce had not shown signs of anxiety or nervousness to his staff. He was cool under pressure. The question now was whether his extraordinary act would bring the dispute to an abrupt end. More importantly, once the dust settled, what would be the final toll?

After the media conference, Joyce and his team took the lift to the ninth floor of Building A. They began working their way through a long list of key people to contact. Calls were made to the chief executives of Qantas' largest corporate clients and other influential business leaders. Media-company bosses such as Rupert Murdoch's son, Lachlan, were called. In the days leading up to the Saturday, senior Qantas staffers had ensured they had phone numbers for key people who would need to be called to brief them about the lockout. The airline needed to speak to corporate clients who spent millions of dollars a year on travel to gain their understanding and ensure they returned with their account intact when it was over.

There was one hiccup. Qantas realised at 8.00 p.m. on the Saturday night that people could still book tickets online. Half an hour later, the website was closed. The mistake of selling tickets to consumers when the fleet had been grounded would later put Qantas in the firing line of the Australian Competition and Consumer Commission. But it was a small glitch considering the complexities involved in shutting down an airline within minutes.

Attention quickly turned to a new battleground. Late on the Saturday night, a full bench of Fair Work Australia in Melbourne began hearing the Gillard Government's application to terminate the industrial action by both Qantas and the unions. In Sydney, Qantas managers and lawyers carrying large folders of evidence filed past TV camera crews, lights blazing from their equipment, into Fair Work's offices on William Street, just down the road from Kings Cross. Drunks, boy racers in their souped-up sports cars and other young partygoers passed by outside. Qantas was joined in the hearing room in Sydney by the Transport Workers Union's national secretary, Tony Sheldon, and lawyers for the three unions. In Canberra, silks for the government began presenting their case to Fair Work for the dispute to be terminated. The three rooms in different cities were connected by video conference, which made for an awkward hearing. Several times people had to be told to mute their microphones. After a long day, most people were running on adrenaline as the debate dragged on into the early hours. Everything would hinge on the outcome of this hearing.

Qantas wanted the industrial dispute terminated. The unions wanted it to be suspended for up to four months to allow for more negotiations over their enterprise bargaining agreements. In the early hours of Sunday morning the hearing was adjourned, before resuming again in the afternoon. At about 2.00 a.m. on the Monday morning, the commissioners ordered the dispute to be terminated, giving both sides twenty-one days to bargain to reach a settlement, or to let a tribunal force a compulsory settlement. The commissioners ruled that the decision by Qantas to ground its fleet and lock out staff 'threatens to cause significant damage to the tourism and air-transport industries'.[11] It was enough for them to order an end to the dispute. Qantas had cancelled almost 450 flights since Joyce had ordered the fleet to be grounded two days earlier. In contrast, the commissioners ruled that the unions' actions were unlikely to threaten the two industries. In effect, it was Qantas' action – not the unions' – that was of a sufficient magnitude for the industrial umpire to end the dispute.

Qantas set about returning to the skies the moment the decision was made. Shutting down an airline had been an extraordinary step. It was a highly complex machine comprising aircraft and workers spread around the world in different time zones. Switching it back on was equally challenging. It was like starting a new airline. Planes had been parked all over the world. Pilots could not simply start their engines and take off. Flight schedules had to be organised and passengers rebooked on services. Shortly before 4.00 p.m. on Monday, October 31, the Civil Aviation Safety Authority gave Qantas approval to resume flying and a short time later its first planes began to soar into the skies from airports around Australia.

At about 6.00 p.m., as the crisis centre at Qantas' headquarters was gradually wound down, staff heard that Joyce would be walking in to thank them for their efforts. The centre was full of screens and dominated by a long table for meetings, while next door in a support room desks were wired up. With managers and other support staff crammed into the crisis room, a spontaneous cheer erupted as Joyce walked into the crisis centre with Lyell Strambi. Standing at the front of the room, Joyce looked slightly overcome with emotion as he recognised his senior managers for their work. For those in the room, it was a mixture of relief and satisfaction that they had succeeded in bringing the dispute to an abrupt end. 'People were really supportive, in that room at least. We were successful in the sense that the action had stopped – not successful in other senses but successful in the sense that it had been brought to a conclusion,' one executive recalled. 'It was absolutely spontaneous when [Joyce] came in. There was no plan to say, let's give him a round of applause.'[12] But it highlighted the gulf between Joyce's loyal lieutenants and large swathes of the Qantas workforce and customers who would not easily forget or forgive.

Joyce had cast the die, and in the process had become a household name. He would forever be known as the man who grounded Australia's national carrier. The unprecedented action was to make the waterfront dispute more than a decade earlier pale in comparison in shock value. The dispute between Chris Corrigan's Patrick Corporation and wharfies lasted much longer but did not instantly affect almost 100 000 people who had no part to play in the stand-off. For almost an entire nation – apart from a tiny, select group of individuals – this had come entirely out of the blue. The grounding was to polarise Australia. The big end of town applauded Joyce for taking on the unions, but many individual Australians and customers believed the action was over the top.

The blame game began in earnest on the Monday. Unions, politicians and the media sought answers to who had known what and when – and who was to blame. The grounding had gone almost without a hitch, apart from Qantas continuing to sell tickets via its website until it was closed at 8.30 p.m. on the Saturday. The Coalition attempted to blame the culmination of the dispute on the Gillard Government. It claimed the government should have used its powers to stop the grounding going ahead as soon as Qantas forewarned it on the Saturday afternoon.[13]

Joyce also told journalists he had suggested on 'multiple occasions' that the grounding was a possibility, which was denied by the government. Albanese rang Joyce on the Monday to tell him that he would be holding a media conference later that day to point out that 'at no stage did you give warning that you would be grounding the airline'.[14] Gillard also phoned Joyce to give him an earful. In parliament, the prime minister accused Qantas of extreme action. 'Qantas had alternatives. I have made it very clear to the CEO of Qantas that I do not believe this extreme action should have been taken,' she said. 'The advice from Qantas was crystal clear that they had made the determination to do so. They were not consulting with the government; they were not asking the government to do anything. They were grounding the planes at five o'clock – no ifs, no buts, no maybes; they were grounding the planes.'[15]

The event did play to Labor's strengths. Labor was attacking Qantas management for a lockout of staff who were members of trade unions – the backbone of the party. The government accused the Coalition of knowing about the planned grounding and acting in unison with Qantas. Their claims gained credibility when the shadow treasurer, Joe Hockey, told the ABC's *7.30 Report* that Qantas had been saying 'weeks ago' that it was considering a grounding or lockout as an option. 'They had been saying it publicly and privately around Parliament House for weeks,' he said. Hockey confirmed that he had heard it personally from a Qantas representative, whom he did not name.[16] A day later, Hockey changed his position to say that he had not known about the grounding and lockout until 4.45 p.m. on the Saturday. The opposition leader, Tony Abbott, also refused to answer questions when journalists first asked him about when he had known about the lockout and grounding. He later told parliament that he had had no prior knowledge and had been alerted to the action only fifteen minutes before Joyce began his media conference at 5.00 p.m. on the Saturday.[17]

On the day of the Qantas' annual meeting, Abbott had demanded that the prime minister 'get active' to end the dispute. In contrast, Peter Reith, a former industrial-relations minister in the Howard Government, had told Sky News such federal intervention was 'old thinking' and 'an idea that we have effectively abandoned for very good reason'.[18] He also wrote a column published in the *Weekend Australian* on the day of the grounding headlined: 'Government intervention a backward step'.

Six days after his decision to ground the Qantas fleet, Joyce walked into the lion's den in Canberra when he appeared before a Senate committee hearing. Senators wanted answers – and a smoking gun. The Qantas chief executive had insisted he had not made the decision to ground the fleet until the morning of October 29. But a long line-up of Labor and Greens senators claimed it had been orchestrated and the decision made before Saturday. They believed they had proof: cabin-crew managers flown to Singapore and Los Angeles, and hotel rooms booked before Joyce announced the grounding. In front of the senators, Joyce described as 'conspiracy theories' claims made about the grounding. He told the senators that he had not thought there was a prospect of grounding the fleet when he walked into the Qantas annual meeting in Sydney. But as talk of 48-hour strikes and the dispute lasting for another year began to ramp up, he said he had decided the next day to call a board meeting where he made the decision to ground the airline. 'The only alternative that was left to me was to bring this to a head,' he said. While he insisted a decision had not been made until the Saturday, Joyce admitted that Qantas had been planning for the possibility of a lockout for weeks. 'We had looked at a lockout as an alternative for a long time and we had planning documents looking at how we would do a lockout, what it would entail. That is why we came to the decision that once we made the lockout we had to ground the airline immediately,' he told the Senate hearing, a year to the day after the Qantas A380 superjumbo had narrowly avoided disaster over an Indonesian island. The planning showed that, if he decided to lock out the staff, he would have to make an immediate decision to ground the airline due to safety concerns. The air-safety regulator had told Qantas it was keeping an eye on the impact of the industrial dispute. The three-hour grilling descended into a slanging match when Labor senator Doug Cameron told Joyce he was a 'bit like Richard Nixon' for trying to talk his way out of things. Joyce shot back: 'This is a bit like a McCarthy trial.'

Taking questions from senators on notice, Qantas later insisted that it had sent the managers to Los Angeles and Singapore earlier in the week because the unions had indicated that they were planning to ramp up industrial action around the time of the AGM.[19] However, the pilots' actions had been limited to wearing non-uniform red ties and making on-board announcements; the engineers had done nothing more extreme than what they had been doing for weeks; and the TWU had given notice seventy-two hours in advance of one-hour work stoppages around the country on the Friday. Why this required cabin crew to be sent to overseas airports on the Friday in readiness was highly questionable.

In the end, Qantas had pulled off an elaborate and high-stakes act without being sprung. The airline had shocked its own workforce with the scale and complexity of the operation, as well as the government, the 100 000 customers due to fly over the two days and the nation. Peter Cosgrove, a Qantas director and a former Australian Defence chief, later told the *Sunday Telegraph*: 'It was more impressive than anything I've seen in the military.'[20] His comments gave an insight into the extent of the planning that had been under way for months at Qantas in the lead-up to the grounding. The element of surprise had been everything.

Qantas had stopped a potentially drawn-out industrial dispute in its tracks. But it came with a high financial toll. In the end, Qantas put the cost of the dispute at about $200 million, a sizeable part of which was due to its own decision to ground its planes to end the stand-off. While not easily quantifiable, the cost to its relations with its workforce, the federal government and ultimately its customers was far greater and longer lasting. The grounding had given Virgin Australia a free kick. Well-heeled consumers who had so far baulked at flying on what they tagged a budget airline had had no choice but to try Virgin for the first time. And some liked what they experienced.

Qantas had put its fight with unions ahead of its passengers. After the grounding, it quickly stepped up its attempt to win consumers back with free tickets on flights anywhere in Australasia. But for some, the major disruption forced upon them without any notice would not be something they would easily forget. How quickly would someone who had missed a funeral or wedding forgive an airline that had made the decision to ground its fleet to halt an industrial dispute? Many veteran aviation executives believe travellers should have come first, and the rest would have followed for shareholders, management and the workforce. In a time of crisis, you play to your number-one audience: the consumer. Qantas didn't. Almost 100 000 passengers around the world were inconvenienced by a text message. It crossed almost every part of Australian society. 'I told Joyce at the time that I didn't believe the decision had been made that morning to ground the airline at 5.00 p.m.,' Albanese said later. 'There are logistics that have to be put in place. He insists the decision was made that morning – it's for others to judge. I remain to this day of the view that it was a big strategic mistake for Qantas. What Qantas forgot was that yes, they were locking out their employees, but they were also locking out their customers. And that hurt the Qantas brand.'[21]

Many within the senior echelons at Qantas believed the grounding was the right decision to make at the time. The question was whether it was worth the pain in the long run. The unions may not have won their demands for job-security clauses to be inserted into new employment agreements, but their members still achieved annual pay increases of about 3 per cent. Given the amount of pain inflicted, many within the top rungs at Qantas felt that the grounding should have resulted in a more significant shake-up of the company. 'The grounding is a very good example of making a tough decision but not capitalising on it,' a former Qantas executive said. 'It didn't result in any concessions.'[22] They wanted Qantas to be rid of the generous labour agreements. Three years' later, the airline would have to begin negotiations again with the same three unions.

12

REMAKING VIRGIN

With a single decision, Alan Joyce had given John Borghetti a gift. For the first time, passengers loyal to Qantas had no choice but to fly on its rival over several days in late 2011. Borghetti had acted swiftly in the wake of Joyce's decision to ground the Qantas fleet. Speculation had been circulating within the airline industry early on the Saturday afternoon that a shutdown was imminent. Journalists were alerted to the press conference at 4.14 p.m. at Qantas' head office. At his home in the inner Sydney suburb of Glebe, Borghetti switched on his television late in the afternoon to watch Joyce shock the world with his order for Qantas planes to be parked immediately at airports around the world. As Joyce delivered his speech, Borghetti dialled into a teleconference with his senior executives to prepare for a deluge of stranded passengers. The Virgin executives were not about to let a rare opportunity to gain a march on their rivals slip through their fingers. Trying to predict how long the grounding would last, his executives phoned their counterparts at Air New Zealand, Singapore Airlines and Etihad to see whether they had spare planes. In the end, they were not needed because Qantas resumed flying three days after its passenger jets were parked at airports around the world. But just a short spell gave Qantas' loyal passengers the first reason to try its competitor. 'The grounding was definitely pivotal because it opened the door for Virgin to say to our customers, "Come and try us",' a Qantas executive said later. 'Up until then, we had the market locked up and it was very difficult for people to change their habits.'[1] While the vast majority of customers returned to Qantas, Virgin needed just a small proportion to take a liking to its service to help eat into its rival's grip on the most lucrative part of the travel market.

Borghetti had walked out of Qantas for the last time on May 4, 2009, exactly thirty-six years to the day since he began in its mailroom in Melbourne aged seventeen. Unemployed and aged fifty-three, he did not know what he would do next. After spending his entire working life at Qantas, he had simply had enough of the volatile world of airlines. As part of the conditions of his contract at Qantas, he could not work for a rival company for six months anyway. He pondered working in other industries and later took several minor board positions to keep himself busy. Head-hunters searching for new chief executives at Ireland's flag carrier, Aer Lingus, and Gulf Air in Bahrain approached him to see whether he was interested. But he did not want to leave Australia. The country had been his home since he had migrated at the age of seven from Italy with his parents, Mario and Anna, younger brother, Mauro, and sister, Rita. Neither he nor the rest of his family spoke any English when they arrived in Melbourne in 1963. They were from Marta, a village north of Rome, and began carving out their new lives in Melbourne's northern suburbs. His father ran a coffee shop on Bourke Street in the central city, and later turned it into a restaurant. John Massimo Borghetti developed an almost obsessive-like focus on finer details. The trait matched the way he later carried himself in public. His designer Italian suits, well-pressed shirts, fine ties and cufflinks marked the man. He modelled himself as his very own brand.

Within months of his departure from Qantas, he started fielding calls from David Baxby and Rob Thomas, two directors at Virgin Blue. They sounded him out about putting his hand up for the chief executive's position at the airline. Virgin had also hired Heidrick & Struggles, the executive recruitment firm Qantas had used two years earlier, to help find a successor to Brett Godfrey. In September 2009, Baxby invited Borghetti to the grand prix in Singapore. The Virgin director was one of Richard Branson's closest lieutenants and had done his homework on the former Qantas executive. Borghetti, a self-confessed car nut, had a small fleet of Porsches, BMWs and Alfa Romeos housed in a Sydney warehouse. Among his prestige cars was a Porsche 911 that he liked to take for a spin on weekends. The real reason for Baxby's invitation was to line up a meeting with Branson, who was in Singapore to watch his Formula 1 racing team. Two months earlier, Virgin Blue's largest shareholder had bumped into Flight Centre's founder, Graham Turner, in Barcelona. Over lunch in the Spanish city Turner, or 'Skroo', as he was known, had urged Branson to make Borghetti the next Virgin chief executive.[2] Now in Singapore, Branson sat down for lunch with Borghetti. It was a chance for Branson to size up Borghetti as a potential successor to Godfrey. Borghetti had not met Branson before but he walked away from their causal meeting thinking that he was sharp despite his clown-like public persona.

On a bitterly cold day in London in January 2010, Borghetti walked into a meeting with Baxby and Virgin Group's partner, Patrick McCall. Often seen wearing a velvet jacket and jeans, Baxby was a thirty-something former Goldman Sachs banker who also oversaw Branson's aviation assets, including Virgin Atlantic and its large stake in Virgin Blue. He was based at Virgin Group's headquarters in Geneva but his job often meant he was on the road. The non-compete clause in Borghetti's contract with Qantas had ended, and he was free to decide whether he was willing to return to the industry he knew best. He understood better than most the challenges in leading an airline that counted Qantas as its main rival. Qantas was a formidable competitor with a vice-like grip on two-thirds of Australia's domestic market. Borghetti had built a solid reputation from his decades at Qantas. It would be in jeopardy if he could not improve Virgin's fortunes. In April 2010, he returned to London to meet Virgin Group's chairman, Peter Norris. After sharing similar views on an overarching strategy, Borghetti decided to put his hand up for the chief executive's job at Virgin Blue. He later met the rest of the airline's board and believed he could work with them. 'I knew it would be hard but, frankly, I needed a job – not because I needed the money but mentally I needed a job,' he said later. 'It was the only one that was stimulating enough.'[3]

In early May 2010, Virgin staff and executives from the aviation and tourism industries crammed into the Ivy, a large nightclub in central Sydney, for 'Brett Unbuckled'. The party dropped the curtain on Godfrey's decade-long tenure at Virgin. More than 200 guests, including Alan Joyce, Geoff Dixon and Rob Fyfe, the Air New Zealand chief executive, who stood out in his pink jacket and jeans, arrived to farewell the quick-talking former accountant. A prerecorded farewell message from Branson, who had just run the London Marathon, was beamed onto a screen. Max Moore-Wilton, the outspoken Sydney Airport chairman and former secretary of the Department of the Prime Minister and Cabinet under John Howard, had the crowd in stitches as he regaled them with anecdotes. Later that night, Dixon, Joyce and Godfrey posed for the cameras, linking their arms in an act that would seem unthinkable for two of them years later.

The following Monday, Borghetti walked into his new office at Virgin's headquarters in Brisbane, almost a year to the day after he had departed Qantas. He inherited a senior-management team loyal to his predecessor and cool about what he planned for the airline they had built from scratch. Virgin paid a premium for its new CEO. Under the terms of his contract, Borghetti was able to earn as much as $4.5 million in his first year in the job, $1.8 million more than Godfrey had been able to make. The airline he was charged with leading was at the crossroads, sandwiched in no-man's-land between Qantas and budget airlines Jetstar and Tiger Airways. Godfrey's final eighteen months at the helm had been tough. After years of profits, Virgin had slumped to a $160 million loss in 2008–09 and been forced to resort to a heavily discounted capital-raising to shore up its balance sheet. It more than doubled Virgin's shares on issue and forced Branson, the airline's largest shareholder, to do what six months earlier he had said was not on the cards: inject up to $80 million to get the deal away. Both Branson and Godfrey, who had a 2 per cent stake in Virgin, had watched their own net worth fall in tandem with the airline's share price. Godfrey had described it as probably the 'toughest time in commercial aviation history in its 100-year existence.'[4] Virgin's long-haul international airline, V Australia, had been launched in early 2009, in the aftermath of the global financial crisis. What seemed like a good idea a few years earlier had become a financial noose due partly to bad timing. V Australia burnt through cash as it competed against Qantas, United Airlines and Delta Air Lines on the Australia–US route. Almost a decade after its launch with just two planes, Virgin's dream run had come to an abrupt end.

Within three weeks of his arrival, Borghetti was forced to warn that profits would plunge after a rapid fall in demand from leisure travellers. Under pressure from large investors and analysts following the profit warning, he sought to allay their concerns by unveiling his longer-term plans for Virgin earlier than he wanted to. From the outset, he had been loath to reveal his cards for Qantas to see for fear of it stopping him in his tracks. Within three months, he had divulged part of his plan to grab a bigger slice of the business market from Qantas rather than scrap over lower-yielding leisure travellers. In one fell swoop, he began axing unprofitable routes, rescheduling flights, overhauling the airline's four brands and forming alliances with other international airlines, such as Etihad. His aim was to give business travellers what they wanted: greater flight frequency and better products and services both in the air and on the ground. Virgin would begin flying bigger aircraft such as twin-aisle A330s between Australia's east and west coasts. 'I wasn't wanting to do that until eight months later because I wanted to get some things in place so we would catch people by surprise,' Borghetti recalled later. I thought, the moment I bring it forward, that's it, because I know what Qantas management would have done when I was there.'[5] He had spent his last five years at Qantas fine-tuning its services and in-flight products. Now, he was attempting to do the same at its rival.

As he did, more roadblocks began to appear. On the eve of Virgin's tenth-anniversary celebrations in a hangar at Melbourne Airport, competition regulators in Australia and the United States dealt two telling blows to his ambitious plans to remodel Virgin. In the space of two days, they flagged that they would thwart Virgin's plans to form alliances with Air New Zealand and Delta Air Lines.[6] It was a major setback to Borghetti's ambitions to use airline alliances to stop Virgin's international business from burning a hole in its bottom line. A week later, Borghetti found out first hand how hard it would be to convince rusted-on Qantas flyers to switch to Virgin. 'Do you fly Virgin Blue?' he asked a gathering of more than 300 business people in a Sydney hotel. He was taken aback when just a small number of people raised their hands. 'There's a bit of work to do, isn't there?' he said sheepishly. To large investors, it was an understatement. 'It's a bit like Kmart trying to take on DJs [David Jones],' said Paul Fiani, one of the fund managers who had baulked at the $11 billion takeover bid for Qantas in 2007.[7] A month later, Borghetti's fears about the challenges of reinventing Virgin were realised. A computer meltdown played havoc with the airline's booking system for eleven days, causing severe disruptions to flights. It was hardly the way for Virgin to win over discerning business travellers from its arch rival.

Weeks later, in early October 2010, Borghetti flew to Washington, DC on a rescue mission.[8] Virgin's proposed alliance with Delta, which Godfrey had unveiled a year earlier, lay in the hands of the powerful US Department of Transportation. It had signalled its opposition to the deal, and had a track record of sticking to its guns. Accompanied by his government relations chief, Jane McKeon, and another executive, Merren McArthur, Borghetti checked into the Four Seasons Hotel in the US capital. His executives visited the Australian embassy to drop off briefing papers and to meet Kim Beazley, the former Labor leader now ensconced in Washington as the Australian ambassador. Judging by his mood, Beazley had had a hard day at the office. The next day Beazley, Borghetti and his executives walked into the Department of Transportation's new head offices a short distance from Capitol Hill. They were there to convince the department's secretary, Ray LaHood, and his deputy, John Porcari, to drop their opposition to the alliance with Delta on the Australia–US route. The meeting was scheduled for just half an hour, but Borghetti was willing to take any small chance to change their minds – even if it meant flying to the other side of the world for a short meeting. With the flick of a switch, Beazley turned on the charm to win over the chief transport bureaucrats. A few weeks later, Australia's physically imposing ambassador to Washington got a chance to whisper in the ear of the US secretary of state, Hillary Clinton, when he accompanied her on a flight to Australia.

In May 2011, the US Department of Transportation overturned its decision – one of the first times it had changed its mind on an airline alliance.[9] It meant Borghetti was able to pull out the Cartier pen he had been gifted at Qantas and used only for special occasions to sign a deal that had almost been lost. Borghetti, or 'JB', as he was known, had cultivated long-term relationships among Australia's political and business establishments over decades. Now, they were paying off in spades.

While he emphasised that Virgin would remain steadfast in pursuing his 'game-change' strategy, in reality his long-term plans had to adapt to a quickly changing environment. Across the Tasman, Air New Zealand had been evaluating internally whether to invest in Australia. Under the leadership of Ralph Norris and his successor, Rob Fyfe, New Zealand's flag carrier had been reshaped into a more nimble airline. The silver-haired Fyfe and his executives were conscious of the need to secure a foothold in its most important overseas market, and the valuable passenger traffic that flowed from Australia onto its network. However, the memories of its disastrous foray into Australia a decade earlier remained raw in the minds of many. The collapse of Ansett had forced the New Zealand government to mount a NZ$885 million rescue of its flag carrier in 2001, resulting in it taking a controlling stake. Air New Zealand executives later referred internally to the 'Ansett shuffle' whenever they found themselves in need of a way out of a tricky situation. Aside from opposition from within the airline, politicians needed to be convinced that Air New Zealand was not about to repeat the sins of its past. In January 2011, the airline cast the memories aside to snap up a 15 per cent stake in Virgin, making it the second-largest shareholder after Branson. The day of the purchase, Air New Zealand managers made presentations to their staff. Among the slides was one titled: 'Why this investment is *not* Ansett Mark II'.

Within months, Air New Zealand raised its shareholding to almost 20 per cent. The acquisition cemented the trans-Tasman alliance it had formed with Australia's second-largest airline a year earlier. In business, there is nothing like skin in the game to focus minds. More importantly, Air New Zealand's move put it at the front of the queue in the likely event other investors began eyeing a slice of Virgin.

With his plans out in plain view for Qantas to see, time was of the essence for Borghetti as he set about remodelling Virgin. He began building new lounges at airports that business travellers had come to expect of premium airlines. He tarted up Virgin's loyalty scheme and set about refreshing the cabin interiors of its planes with leather seats and business-class cabins. He devoted twin-aisle A330s to the transcontinental route between Australia's east coast and Perth. Business passengers might happily travel on single-aisle Boeing 737s on short hops from Sydney to Melbourne, but they had higher expectations when flying five hours into the jet stream to Perth. Branding was a top priority for Borghetti. He hired Dutch-born designer Hans Hulsbosch, who had played a major role in branding and design at Qantas for more than two decades. The airline removed the brash edges that had been synonymous with Branson in favour of a more refined style.

In early May 2011, Borghetti united the airline's domestic and international operations under the one brand as Virgin Australia. As part of the rebranding, it dropped the red livery from its planes in favour of white licks of paint. Qantas stressed that it had been investing in in-flight products and lounges to counter its rival, but Borghetti believed his rival had underestimated his plans for Virgin. 'They belittled us and they said we weren't going to be able to do it. That gave us twelve months until May 4, 2011, when we launched the new airline,' Borghetti recalled. 'The old Qantas management wouldn't even allow me to finish my sentence at the presentation before they'd absolutely hammer us. But [Joyce] didn't, and that was a big free kick for us – a twelve-month gap was heaven sent.'[10] However, the danger for Borghetti in his mad dash to turn Virgin into a credible competitor at the premium end of the market was an increase in its cost base. A narrowing of the gap in operating costs with Qantas risked removing one of its major advantages too soon.

At the same time, Virgin was working away on plans to nullify one of Qantas' secret weapons: the prestigious Chairman's Lounge. Qantas had long been adept at using flight upgrades and access to invitation-only lounges as a way of courting rich and powerful individuals. Before he left Qantas in 2009, Borghetti's role as third-in-charge of the airline included oversight of the Chairman's Lounges. At Virgin, his answer was 'The Club'. Hidden behind doors marked 'private', they featured à la carte menus, personalised levels of services, luxury facilities and escorts to accompany members to terminal gates. Membership to The Club was invitation-only. It represented a secret war between Qantas and Virgin in their attempts to entice chief executives, chairmen and politicians. Neither Virgin nor Qantas donated money to political parties, but they lavished the country's decision-makers with free access to their exclusive lounges, flight upgrades, iPads and other devices. Politicians of all stripes were beneficiaries of the airlines' largesse.

While the airlines went out of their way to publicise other offerings, both Qantas and Virgin ensured that their staff did not divulge details about their extravagant lounges for their powerful passengers. 'No comment' was the regular reply to questions. The secrecy was a clever way of adding to the allure of the lounges tucked away in discreet locations at airports in Australia's major cities. For the airlines, big bucks were on the line. They kept watch over who walked into their lounges. The airlines used a variety of criteria to choose their members. A rule of thumb was that the airlines needed to be able to generate about $1 million a year in revenue from corporate clients before they received a personalised invitation to use the exclusive lounges from either airline's chairman or chief executive. At its heart, the airlines' munificence created a sense of obligation among recipients.[11]

For Borghetti and Joyce, the battle was forever changing. Neither could afford to stand still. By the second half of 2011, Joyce was trying to outfox the three unions as much as Borghetti. Qantas also had plans under way to set up an ultra-premium airline in Singapore, and new Jetstar offshoots in Japan and Hong Kong. Joyce had so many balls in the air that he risked not paying the level of attention to Virgin that it deserved. The Qantas Group was a complex business. The focus at executive meetings was increasingly on Qantas' troubled international operations, which meant managers of other parts of the business felt they were not receiving enough attention. 'If you are part of the executive team of Qantas, then you go to every one of those meetings and you are called up to long day strategy sessions, investor roadshows, media sessions and annual results and board meetings,' a former executive recalled. 'You were constantly getting people called in to solve the core Qantas problem.'[12]

Like Joyce, Borghetti lived and breathed work. Saturday mornings were his one moment of freedom from the demands of running an airline. This meant he had high expectations of the executives around him. After taking the reins in 2010, he set about removing the vestiges of Godfrey's leadership team and installing trusted lieutenants from Qantas. The long list of Qantas refugees at Virgin included Jane McKeon, Roger Lindeman, Hope Antzoulatos, Judith Crompton, Will Owens, Neil Thompson, Roz Wheatley and Mark Hassell. On the flip side, some of the executives who had served under Godfrey left Virgin for Qantas after seeing the writing on the wall. They believed Borghetti was entering a war of attrition with Qantas that Virgin didn't need to.

From the outset, Borghetti's mantra was that his sights were on the long-term horizon. If it stuck to its plans, Virgin would eventually reap the rewards. But he and the rest of his executive team opened themselves up for criticism. Borghetti was paid a Qantas salary at Virgin before he had delivered tangible benefits to shareholders. His salary and those of his executives were based on what they were doing to reinvent the airline. They were reshaping it at breakneck speed but the success of the new model had yet to be reflected in Virgin's bottom line. Advisers to large investors Institutional Shareholder Services and CGI Glass Lewis took exception to the quantum of short-term bonuses for Borghetti in 2011. However, a large protest vote from minority shareholders against the salaries and bonuses for Virgin executives was symbolic, because key stakeholders such as Branson and Air New Zealand supported the pay deals. For the next three years, CGI urged investors to vote against Virgin's executive-pay card because of a 'lack of justification' for what it deemed high levels of pay for Borghetti.[13] In 2012, his pay package totalled $4.07 million, while a year later it was $3.7 million.

Apart from the risk of a rising cost base, Virgin's potential Achilles heel was the arrival of three major shareholders: Air New Zealand, Singapore Airlines and Etihad. While they would ensure that Virgin would last the distance in its fight with Qantas, they risked posing a challenge for management if they became restless with the airline's direction and results. Their interests conflicted to varying degrees. The New Zealanders had a habit of poking their noses into Virgin's affairs more than Singapore Airlines or Etihad. Because of their proximity to Australia and their larger shareholding, the Kiwis seemed to think they had a greater right to meddle in Virgin's affairs. As long as the three shareholders were content with the strategy it was fine, but any major disagreements in the longer term risked making life unbearable for management.

As he remoulded Virgin, Borghetti constantly cautioned his executives not to underestimate Qantas. They regularly heard him talking about Qantas holding 'lots of hollow logs' – a reminder that an airline twice Virgin's size could pull rabbits out of its hat. On the other side, Qantas was forever evaluating Virgin. Qantas analysed whether it was gaining the most from its own two airline brands in the international and domestic markets. In evaluating the domestic arena, game theory exercised the minds of Qantas' strategy team and senior executives. At its simplest, it was a process of evaluating the likely reactions of Virgin or Tiger Airways to a decision. It meant that if Qantas believed Virgin or Tiger was about to enter a route that it did not fly, it might consider starting its own services or Jetstar's to put it ahead of a competitor. This might result in stopping its competitor from pushing ahead with plans that would pose a threat. Like pieces on a chess board, Qantas and Virgin continually tried to predict what the other was about to do in the domestic market. 'You map it out and say, "If they pull out of there, can they do this?"' a former Qantas executive said. 'The problem with game theory is that you never know whether you're leading or following.'[14]

In public, Borghetti painted the battle with Joyce purely as business. But it was very personal. The events in his final days at Qantas had supercharged his ambitions. 'I tell my executives this: you don't judge a company by the way they treat you on the way in. You judge them by the way they treat you on the way out,' he said later.[15] His attempt to reshape Virgin as a viable competitor to Qantas put him on another collision course with Joyce. Their war in the domestic market threatened to become a nuclear winter for both airlines, and a case of who could last the distance.

13

DEAL WITH THE DEVIL

In early July 1999, a negotiating team from Australia's transport department flew to Dubai for talks with their counterparts from the United Arab Emirates (UAE). The team was led by Tony Wheelens, a senior bureaucrat for the federal government department. Qantas' government lobbyist, John Kerr, and his counterparts from Ansett, Jane McKeon and Anne Buttsworth, were among the group that travelled to the fast-growing city of skyscrapers on the shores of the Persian Gulf. Dubai stood in contrast to Abu Dhabi, the capital of the UAE, which near the turn of the century was still a backwater. In Dubai, the two sides had a lot at stake as they negotiated a deal to give airlines from both countries greater access to air routes between Australia and the UAE. On the other side of the negotiating table from the Australians was a delegation led by the chairman of Emirates, Sheik Ahmed bin Saeed Al Maktoum, the son of the former ruler of Dubai. Two years earlier, Wheelens had led a mission to the Gulf state to negotiate air-traffic rights. This time, Emirates was again eager to boost flights to Australia.

Despite protestations from Qantas, the pressure was on to reach an agreement. The meetings in the UAE in mid-1999 came just a month after the federal transport minister, John Anderson, and the treasurer, Peter Costello, had announced a loosening of the tight restrictions on foreign airlines flying to Australia. Under sweeping changes to aviation policy, the limits on airline capacity and flight frequency on routes from Australia to other countries agreed to under bilateral air-rights agreements were to be relaxed significantly. The caveat was that Australian airlines had to be offered the same rights by the foreign airlines' home countries.[1]

On July 13, 1999, Anderson unveiled the outcome of the negotiations in Dubai. The new air-services agreement with the UAE unleashed forces on Qantas that were not as apparent to onlookers at the time as they would be fifteen years later. The deal was the first the federal government signed under its more liberal policy towards international air services. In response, Qantas' chief executive, James Strong, attacked the government for signing a deal that would allow Emirates to increase flights from seven a week to twenty-five within two years.[2] Qantas' well-founded concern was that it would be exposed to a new wave of competition on the kangaroo route to Europe. The agreement gave Qantas the right to fly to the UAE but it had no plans to take up the opportunity – its flights to Europe were routed through Singapore. The deal opened the way for Emirates to step up its efforts to boost traffic from Australia onto its fast-growing international network, which radiated from its hub in Dubai to destinations around the world. Behind the scenes, Qantas staffers would spend hours writing dirt sheets on Middle Eastern airlines in the years ahead. The lobbyists' task in Canberra was to do their best to slow the advance.

But the gate to Australia had been rammed open, and the agreement was followed by similar deals with other countries, including Malaysia, Thailand and Hong Kong, in the following years. Qantas' grip on protected routes in and out of the country had been prised away, forcing it to compete against a growing list of airlines whose operational costs were much lower. Three years after the treaty with the UAE was signed, another airline was born that would gain access to the rights to fly to Australia. Its name was Etihad. For the public, the greater competition meant lower fares. Anderson would later be nicknamed the minister for Qantas. Following the march towards privatisation and deregulation of the aviation industry begun by Paul Keating in the early 1990s, the Howard Government had unleashed a new force on Australia's once heavily protected airlines.

By 2012 Alan Joyce found himself boxed into a corner. After Singapore blocked his attempt to set up a new airline and talks with Malaysia Airlines foundered, the Qantas chief executive needed an alliance with another airline to stem the growing flow of red ink from the airline's international operations. He also needed a win. Joyce had been outstepped by Borghetti, who had delivered a masterstroke in securing Singapore Airlines as a strategic partner for Virgin in June 2011. Borghetti had teamed up with one of the most prestigious airlines and, together with code-share deals with Air New Zealand, Delta Air Lines and Etihad, had built a sizeable international network. Code-share deals are common in the aviation industry, and involve airlines marketing their partner's flights and placing their flight code on their services. They allow airlines to widen their distribution without having to fly their own expensive planes on routes. With the emergence of new competitors, Qantas was becoming isolated and losing its grip on a seat at the top table of global aviation.

The viable candidates for an alliance partner had been reduced to Emirates. Under the leadership of Tim Clark, Emirates had shunned airline alliances. With a rapidly growing aircraft fleet, Clark preferred Emirates to fly its own planes to destinations around the world that it could gain the rights to fly to. But it needed more passengers to fill its fleet of planes. Emirates was eager to boost revenues from Australia, its second-most important market after the UAE. Barry Brown, a Sydneysider with decades of experience in the airline industry, had taken the job of overseeing Emirates' operations in Australia and

New Zealand in mid-2010. A lover of golf, he was the consummate networker. Working closely with Clark, he set about formulating a strategy to increase Emirates' grip on the Australasian market. 'We both decided that Qantas was plum for us. We needed domestic feed and access to the corporate market,' Brown said later.[3]

About a year after he took the senior role in Australia, Brown met Qantas' commercial chief, Rob Gurney, for a drink. The pair's paths had crossed frequently during their decades in the industry. Aviation is a small, almost incestuous, business. Airline executives know each other well. They travel to large industry conferences and engage in hallway conversations. Many have worked with each other previously. Brown and Gurney talked about the possibility of Qantas and Emirates establishing an interline agreement, one of the most basic forms of airline cooperation. Emirates' interline agreement with Virgin Blue was about to end after the Australian airline had decided to team up with Emirates' fast-growing rival, Etihad. Brown and Gurney took the idea back to their respective head offices and the airlines' strategy teams began running the numbers on a basic agreement. The talks had begun as both airlines reached a crossroads in Australia: Qantas needed an alliance partner to help stem losses from its international network, while Emirates needed to secure more passengers to fill its superjumbos flying to Australia and New Zealand.

The door had been edged open. In late March 2012, Project Lawrence was born. Under the leadership of Jayne Hrdlicka, Qantas' strategy team began working on the possibility of an alliance with Emirates. The team was given a blank canvas because it was merely an idea that had been lobbed into their court. Their job was to see what it could be turned into. The team later made presentations to Gurney and Qantas' other senior executives. But by May 2012, Gurney was no longer the point man for the talks. He had become a casualty of one of the biggest reshuffles of Qantas' executive ranks since shortly after Joyce had taken the reins in late 2008. Under the banner of greater accountability, Joyce had decided to split Qantas Airways in two, creating separate business units for its domestic and international flying operations. Both would have their own chief executives in Lyell Strambi and Simon Hickey, the former boss of Qantas' frequent-flyer division. It meant there was no longer a role at Qantas for Gurney, and he departed the airline. He later emerged as the chief executive of Jetset Travelworld, a poorly performing travel company part-owned by Qantas.

The burden for creating a model for a deal between the two airlines fell on the shoulders of Qantas. Its strategy team needed to come up with options to take to Emirates for negotiations. Emirates was geared towards growing its flying business on its own rather than expanding its reach through alliances. Apart from a failed investment in Sri Lanka, it had not jumped into bed with another airline to form a deep relationship. In contrast, partnerships were in Qantas' DNA through years of forming them – or attempting to. In simple terms, Emirates had an extensive network to Europe that Qantas needed if it didn't have its own. Qantas' long-term alliance with British Airways gave it two-stop links to continental Europe but it was a poor substitute for Emirates' one-stop flights from Australia to continental Europe via Dubai. The kangaroo route to Europe had become what strategists termed a 'commodity route' because dozens of airlines competed on it.

Qantas had long identified flying to Europe as its problem child. In 2012, it still had a large amount of capital – six A380 aircraft and three Boeing 747 jumbos – dedicated to flying to London and Germany. A daily flight to Frankfurt – its only service to continental Europe – was on borrowed time as losses mounted. Qantas was on a hiding to nothing on routes to Europe as it competed against a growing number of airlines, especially those from the Middle East and Asia. Except for British Airways, all of its rivals had lower cost bases. Qantas' competitors were growing their international networks while it was shrinking as the economics of flying multiple routes declined due to their unprofitability.

Both Qantas and Emirates had been casting a close eye over each other, trying to determine what they could get out of an alliance. Clark, an Englishman who had been part of the team that started Emirates nearly three decades earlier, liked to visit his airline's Wolgan Valley Resort every couple of years. The luxury resort at the western foot of the Blue Mountains near the New South Wales town of Lithgow had been his pet project. Brown and his fellow Emirates executives saw it as an opportunity to bring the two airlines' senior management teams together when Clark was due to visit in May that year. A meeting at Wolgan Valley was a chance to dip the litmus paper into the pot to see whether there was chemistry between Joyce and Clark. If the pair did not gel, a strategic alliance between the two airlines would not work. A business relationship was based on trust. If it turned sour and ended up in court, it was as good as dead. Winning a legal argument would not bring two sides back together.

On a weekend in early May, Wolgan Valley became the setting for what Brown later referred to as the airline industry's equivalent of Camp David. The two executive teams sat down for lunch on the Saturday to break the ice, followed by the beginning of broad discussions in the afternoon at the resort's old homestead. The five top executives from each airline stayed that night at the resort's villas, and regrouped again on the Sunday. The fear of being sprung was never far away in an industry notorious for leaks. Even among people who showed no interest in big business, Joyce had become a highly identifiable figure in Australia in the wake of the grounding of the Qantas fleet six months earlier. It would take only one guest at Wolgan Valley to tweet that they had spotted Joyce to blow the airline's cover. 'We were a bit concerned that it would leak out – Alan was a bit recognisable at the time,' Brown recalled.[4] As it turned out, the Qantas and Emirates executives managed to sneak in and out of the luxurious hideaway without having to read about their rendezvous in newspapers the next day. Joyce and Clark did not settle on a model for an alliance but agreed to enter negotiations over the following months.

A small team from Qantas spearheaded the talks. Decisions had to be made in super-fast time. Hrdlicka and Markus Svensson led the team, which ran a dual process of writing the internal business case and negotiating with Emirates to bring it to fruition. The shuttle diplomacy fell upon the shoulders of Svensson. He had to make multiple trips to Dubai to negotiate the finer details of a deal. The pressure to nut out an agreement that would usually take as long as two years to complete was immense. Svensson and his team found themselves arriving in Dubai after a fourteen-hour flight from Sydney, and heading straight into meetings with their counterparts from Emirates. Early on, Joyce and Clark had targeted September 6 as the day they would announce the deal. The setting of a date focused the two teams, ensuring the talks over an alliance did not drag on. But the fact that Qantas had highlighted the woes its international business was suffering did not help it in the negotiations. Emirates' hand was strengthened because it was aware of the world of pain Qantas' international business was in, though Qantas later believed it had received a better ten-year deal than Emirates realised. Joyce and Clark remained in regular contact as their teams delved into the details. Clark was often his media minders' worst nightmare because he would not stick to their scripts. Unlike many other chief executives, he was willing to answer questions from journalists that revealed more about the airline than others would. He was also not afraid to walk into a verbal stoush with rivals. With decades of experience, he was a man who knew the industry inside out.

Clark and Joyce had agreed to meet in Beijing, where the annual meeting of the airline industry's peak global body was to be held for the first time in June 2012. Not wanting to be discovered, they sat down to talk about the potential for an alliance at the Park Hyatt, a short distance from the prying eyes of hundreds of other airline executives and journalists at the China World Hotel.[5] The talks had to be conducted in a covert manner to avoid the world finding out about what the two airlines were up to. While Qantas remained silent publicly,

Clark told Australian journalists in Beijing that he had 'put the feelers out' for a code-share deal with Qantas. But he sought to keep under wraps the real extent of what was going on behind the scenes. 'We are looking at all sorts of things and possibly we will engage with Qantas at some point to talk about a code share,' Clark said in the foyer of the hotel near Tiananmen Square.[6] He was equivocal on one point: Emirates would not be tipping in any money to buy a stake in Qantas. He also made a subtle dig at previous management, pointing out that Emirates had attempted a code-share deal with Qantas in 1996 only for the Australian airline to 'abandon it'. There had been no love lost between Clark and Geoff Dixon. The Australian had railed against Middle Eastern airlines such as Emirates boosting flights to Australia throughout his seven-year tenure as Qantas chief executive. Dixon was well known for his ability to lobby federal politicians in Canberra to ensure Qantas' interests came first.

Qantas' fears about the growing threat from Virgin were realised in June when Etihad became the second foreign airline to emerge on its share register, with a 5 per cent stake. Qantas immediately went on the offensive. Joyce and his government-relations team, spearheaded by Olivia Wirth, flew to Canberra to lobby against Etihad building a cornerstone stake in Virgin. The team circulated a dirt sheet among politicians decrying a foreign airline investing in its domestic rival. 'Etihad will cross-subsidise Virgin's domestic business with the specific aim of weakening Qantas. Virgin/Etihad will be able to flood the market with capacity until its competition is forced to significantly reduce its own operations, or worse,' Qantas warned in the briefing paper. 'The first impact of such a strategy would be to reduce marginal regional routes such as those to the Northern Territory and North Queensland.'[7] Qantas had fair grounds to argue the point: the foreign-ownership restrictions imposed on it were far more onerous than those imposed on Virgin. Months earlier, Virgin had opened the way for more foreign airlines to invest in its domestic business, which was its money-spinner and most attractive to investors. Despite the ghosts from its disastrous investment in Ansett, Air New Zealand had swooped on Virgin to buy a cornerstone stake in early 2011. The Kiwis' purchase pushed Virgin close to its 49 per cent foreign-ownership cap.

At its de facto head office overlooking Sydney's Circular Quay, Virgin had established Project Rutherford to search for ways to open its share register to more overseas investors. In a slick legal manoeuvre, Borghetti's team had hatched a plan to split Virgin's international and domestic operations into two separate entities. They identified a loophole that allowed more foreign investors, such as Etihad, to buy into Virgin's domestic business while ensuring the airline retained its lucrative rights to fly on international routes as an Australian carrier. Qantas had a valid claim that it was disadvantaged. But it failed to mention that behind the scenes it was trying to stitch together its own deal with another Middle Eastern airline with deep pockets.

Qantas and Emirates stuck to the deadline for their alliance. To fanfare, Joyce and Clark fronted the media for a deal-signing ceremony at the Westin in Sydney's Martin Place on September 6. 'This agreement represents a step-change for the aviation industry,' Joyce trumpeted at the media conference. 'This is the biggest arrangement Qantas has ever entered into with another airline.'[8] The ten-year deal would give Qantas passengers access to more than seventy destinations in Europe, the Middle East and North Africa on Emirates jets. But it would result in Qantas ditching its 747 jumbo services between Singapore and Frankfurt – its last remaining destination in continental Europe – leaving it with two A380 services a day to London's Heathrow Airport. Its long-standing alliance with British Airways would be scrapped, as well as code-share deals with Cathay Pacific and Air France on routes to Rome and Paris. Under the main agreement were multiple smaller deals to complete the alliance, which resulted in the airlines earning commissions for selling each other's flights. The deal was a way for Qantas to stem losses from a part of its business it believed was in structural decline. It would be able to avoid having to inject substantial amounts of new capital into its European network. Analysts from Macquarie Bank estimated the value to Qantas of a code-share alliance with Emirates at up to $90 million a year in pre-tax earnings. To them, it was the 'missing piece in the earnings bridge for Qantas' in turning around its international operations, which a month earlier had chalked up a $450 million annual loss – more than double the figure of the previous year.

To critics, it signalled a further retreat and the possibility of Qantas ending up as a mere regional airline. Qantas had raised the white flag in the face of an aggressive onslaught from Middle Eastern and Chinese airlines. 'It's a code share on steroids but not real steroids,' an aviation veteran exclaimed.[9] It appeared an act of desperation. The risk lay in exposing Qantas' moneyed customers to a rival. Qantas had gifted Emirates access to almost ten million frequent-flyer members, the cream of the Australian travel market it had guarded closely for years. In their eyes, the alliance also weakened Qantas' position in Canberra when it needed to lobby against further increases in flights on routes to Australia by Asian and other Middle Eastern airlines.

Weeks after Joyce had forged the alliance with Emirates, Borghetti delivered another surprise. In one fell swoop, Virgin bought a 60 per cent stake in Tiger Airways' Australian operations, made a takeover bid for West Australian airline Skywest and tightened its ties with Singapore Airlines. To fund the deal, Virgin issued $105 million worth of shares to Singapore Airlines, giving it a 10 per cent stake. Having spent the previous eighteen months reshaping Virgin more as a full-service airline, Borghetti had created a Qantas 'Mini-Me' with the addition of a budget airline and a regional carrier. The company's cost base was lower than that of Qantas and Jetstar, and it now had the backing of four cornerstone shareholders in Etihad, Air New Zealand, Singapore Airlines and Richard Branson's Virgin Group. Less than two decades earlier, Qantas had been in a pitched battle in the domestic market with Ansett. 'History suggests that domestic aviation is ultimately a two-horse race,' said Rod Eddington, the former chief executive of British Airways and Ansett. 'What we are seeing . . . is a return to a two-horse race. But the horses are more multifaceted than they were before.'[10] Now, Qantas, Jetstar and its regional subsidiary were slugging it out against Virgin, Tiger and Skywest.

It signalled another chapter in the deeply personal contest between Borghetti and the man who had beaten him to the top job at Qantas. It also ensured Singapore Airlines would remain hitched to Virgin. Airlines constantly changed dance partners. A strategic alliance did not guarantee that an airline would remain faithful, whereas skin in the game kept eyes from wandering. Borghetti was conscious of the potential for a gatecrasher before Singapore Airlines bought its stake. The *Financial Review* revealed that Qantas had attempted to scuttle Virgin's new alliance.[11] Shortly after Virgin had announced its deal, Qantas had approached senior executives at Temasek, the Singapore government's investment arm, which had a majority stake in the country's flag carrier. The talks had ended not long after they began. While Temasek was willing to talk, Singapore Airlines was not. Qantas had broken what some believed to be a cardinal rule in Singapore: it had gone over the head of a potential dance partner to ask its parent for its hand.

Borghetti's dealmaking, too, carried risks. Tiger had notched up losses of more than $200 million since it had launched services in Australia in 2007. As a result, the top post at the budget airline had been a revolving door: it had had four chief executives in four years. But it suffered its biggest setback in 2011 when the Civil Aviation Safety Authority grounded it for six weeks due to safety concerns. Tiger had been a disruptive force in the market for both Virgin and Qantas–Jetstar but its grounding severely tarnished the budget airline's brand. In his push to create a Qantas Mini-Me, Borghetti risked overstretching his management team and the company as the battle with his rival intensified.

However, it also increased the pressure on Qantas to complete its own deal with Emirates. The amount of work required behind the scenes with Emirates was mind-blowing. Qantas had to shift its major international hub from Singapore to Dubai, requiring a retiming of flights and change of aircraft. The $50 million cost to Qantas of the switch underscored the complexities of the move. At the same time, the two airlines still needed to demonstrate to competition regulators that their deal would not disadvantage the flying public. A rejig of its network resulted in Qantas ditching routes between Adelaide and Singapore, and Perth and Hong Kong, sparking complaints it was abandoning Western Australia and South Australia. Qantas countered that people in Perth and Adelaide would have more ways of travelling to Asia and Europe via its new partner Emirates.

The shift of hub to Dubai ended a well-worn path to Europe for Australians. Qantas had launched the so-called kangaroo route on a drizzly night in Sydney on December 1, 1947. At Kingsford-Smith Airport at Mascot, around a thousand people had turned out to farewell twenty-nine passengers and eleven crew aboard a Lockheed Constellation, affectionately known as a Connie. The four-engine plane was one of four Connies that Qantas had taken the keys to two months earlier. Qantas' founder and chairman, Hudson Fysh, was on hand for the ribbon-cutting ceremony where he delivered an airmail bag to the plane's captain, Ken Jackson. It would be another four days and stopovers to refuel in Darwin, Singapore, Calcutta, Karachi, Cairo and Tripoli before the passengers and crew reached their final destination in London.[12] Qantas had begun flying to Singapore twelve years earlier, allowing passengers to connect to an Imperial Airways flight to London. But the triple-tailed Connie's departure from Sydney on this wet night two years after the end of World War II was the first time a Qantas plane had flown all the way to London. The cost of a return fare to London then was £585, a small fortune when the average weekly wage in Australia was little more than £7. Over the next sixty-six years, tens of millions of Australians would fly on other Qantas planes, such as the Boeing 707 passenger jet and the 747 jumbo, to London's Heathrow Airport. In doing so, the kangaroo route helped to build a sentimental attachment to the national carrier.

Qantas' new alliance with Emirates would end the long hop to London via Singapore. Instead, Qantas would fly two A380 superjumbos from Melbourne and Sydney each day to London via Dubai. In contrast, Emirates would fly twelve times a day to its home city of Dubai from five Australian airports – Brisbane, Sydney, Melbourne, Adelaide and Perth. For many Qantas long-haul pilots, the alliance and re-routing signalled the end of an era. It brought down the curtain on eateries and bars that had become their homes away from home when they were passing through Singapore on their way to Europe or southbound to Australia. For more than four decades, generations of Qantas pilots had met at Fatty's, a restaurant in one of the city's bustling shopping districts. Fatty's was a tradition among Qantas pilots. Every night, they were guaranteed to be found eating at the Chinese restaurant in Bugis Junction run by two brothers. One was known as Skinny. 'You build up myths and traditions when you go to that kind of place – it is the absolute passing of an era for most of us,' Qantas A380 captain Richard Woodward said. 'There are quite a few guys with nostalgia in their eyes.'[13]

In Joyce's mind, the predicament facing Qantas' international operations left little room for nostalgia. Within six months of announcing the 'partnership of equals', Qantas and Emirates had gained regulatory approval and their alliance was ready to fly. Under huge pressures, the airlines had been able to pull off a complex deal in super-fast time. Early on the morning of March 31, 2013, a Qantas A380 superjumbo and another from Emirates soared low over Sydney Harbour in parallel to mark the start of the airlines' alliance. Later that day, a Qantas A380 captained by Richard Tobiano climbed into the skies from Sydney's Kingsford-Smith Airport bound for Dubai. On board were Alan Joyce; Tim Clark; the federal transport minister, Anthony Albanese; Olivia Wirth and her partner Paul Howes, the then 32-year-old secretary of the Australian Workers Union; and a large contingent of Australian television celebrities and journalists.

The so-called 'party flight' kicked off several days of lavish proceedings. In a giant marquee beside the Atlantis resort on Dubai's artificial island known as the Palm, hundreds of guests gathered for a gala dinner for the launch of the alliance. They included a rollcall of Qantas executives such as Lyell Strambi and Simon Hickey, and Australian television personalities including Hugh Sheridan, Chris Brown and Carrie Bickmore. With the Melbourne television presenter Eddie McGuire as MC, the night became an Australian affair as singer Jessica Mauboy and TV host Kerri-Anne Kennerley delivered numbers on stage. But it was the American singer Gloria Gaynor who later brought the crowd to its feet when she delivered her disco anthem 'I Will Survive'. The choice of song was not lost on those present, which included senior government bureaucrat Mike Mrdack and former federal MP Bruce Baird.

Late the next day, a large contingent travelled in a convoy of four-wheel-drive vehicles into the desert. Atop a sand dune, Joyce mingled with the crowd as they waited for the main spectacle – a sunset in the desert. It was a sight to behold as the sky turned shades of orange and red before the sun dipped below the horizon. As darkness began to descend, the crowd was shepherded back into the vehicles for a short trip over the dune to their final destination. Awaiting them was a site that resembled a Bedouin camp, erected at the foot of a sand dune. The night was to finish with camel rides, Wirth and Howes flirting with each other like young lovers and Clark puffing away on a cigar as camp fires roared.

Weeks later in Sydney, Qantas threw a lavish gala dinner to showcase its Emirates alliance and a new uniform for its flight attendants. The guests who strode the red carpet to the hangar included actor John Travolta, supermodel Miranda Kerr and Irish singer Ronan Keating, and a long list of kingpins from Australia's business community, such as the Nine Network's boss, David Gyngell, News Limited chief executive Kim Williams, and Fairfax Media's chief executive, Greg Hywood. At one end of the giant hangar sat a Qantas A380 superjumbo, glistening under the lights. Almost a thousand guests sat down to the black-tie dinner in Hangar 96, which included a performance by Australian singer Tina Arena. Qantas spared no expense as it put on a night to rival any other.

Over the next year, the hype gave way to a more conservative tone about the deal. Qantas would not put a figure on the benefits of the alliance to its bottom line, and it was no longer something to be highlighted when Joyce fronted investors and journalists. In less than two decades Emirates had gone from flying just twice a week to Australia to almost hitting its cap of eighty-four flights allowed under the bilateral air-rights agreement between Australia and the UAE, giving it the largest market share of any foreign airline flying to Australia. By late 2013, it had surpassed Singapore Airlines as the largest foreign airline to fly to the country. Almost 10 per cent of the passengers who walked on or off planes at Australia's international airports flew Emirates. In contrast, Qantas' international market share had shrunk from 33 per cent to 17 per cent. The decline looked slightly less dramatic when Jetstar was included, with the airline group's share down by almost seven percentage points to about a quarter of the market.[14] But it was evidence of the large shift in market power with the emergence of the fast-growing Middle Eastern airlines and the looming threat from state-backed Chinese carriers. Emirates had become a powerhouse of world aviation, and the cigar-smoking Clark its key architect. Like slowly peeling away the layers of an onion, the opening-up of air routes to Australia was a further removal of the shackles of protectionism. Other parts of the Australian economy had long been exposed to the harsh world of globalisation. By 2013, workers in the car industry – one of the country's most protected industries – would feel the direct impact on their lives of the removal of trade barriers and subsidies. Like the car manufacturers, the ability of Australian airlines to compete against foreign carriers had been severely diminished.

For Qantas, the question was whether the alliance was the 'partnership of equals' that Joyce had trumpeted when he signed the deal in September 2012. 'In the short term it was a positive for them but we will see what happens in the long term,' Flight Centre's managing director, Graham Turner, said. 'Are [Emirates] just going to swamp Qantas [on routes] to places like Europe? You get into bed with a big player – the Goliath or the gorilla of international airlines – and that is one of the risks you might take.'[15] To its supporters, Qantas had done a deal it needed to do to stem a flow of red ink. To its sceptics, the airline had made a strategic blunder by getting into bed with a new giant of global aviation.

14

COLD WAR

Geoff Dixon and Alan Joyce regularly drank together at high-end bars in Sydney's central city. Among their favourites were Rockpool, a plush restaurant and bar run by Dixon's close friend and celebrity chef Neil Perry, the Sofitel Wentworth and the Park Hyatt in The Rocks. For Dixon, Rockpool was a place to be seen, while the other hotels were places to meet for confidential conversations. On the water's edge, the five-star Park Hyatt offered views of the Opera House and the 'Toaster', a luxury apartment building. Apart from featuring a quieter bar, the four-storey hotel was a convenient meeting place for the former Qantas chief executive and his successor. Dixon's two-storey penthouse in the heritage-listed Metcalfe Bond building, which he had bought in 2010 for $7.75 million, was just a 100-metre stroll from the hotel. A short distance away, an old brick chimney stood beside the Harbour Bridge as a monument to the area's hard-living past.

Joyce lived about 600 metres from Dixon and his wife, Dawn, in the luxury Cove apartments, near the Four Seasons Hotel in The Rocks. He had bought his three-bedroom, three-bathroom apartment for almost $4.6 million in late 2008 when he shifted from Melbourne to begin his new role as Qantas chief executive.[1] From the forty-second floor of the building designed by renowned Austrian-born architect Harry Seidler, he gazed north out over the Sydney Harbour Bridge, Circular Quay where ferries docked, and the Opera House, Sydney's crown jewel. But for the Quay West apartment building towering in front, Dixon's penthouse would almost have been visible from Joyce's wave-shaped balcony.

Like Joyce, Dixon lived and breathed work. When he had handed the baton to his successor in November 2008, Dixon was about to turn sixty-nine, an age when most people are long into retirement. After he left Qantas, he remained a director of the James Packer-controlled casino operator Crown and sat on a number of other boards. Dixon and Packer knew each other well from their time as Qantas directors. In mid-2009, Dixon joined the Tourism Australia board and within a year had become its chairman. His personal interest in Qantas remained well after he severed his official ties in March 2009, when his consultancy contract ended. For Joyce, his predecessor was a mentor who had guided him into one of the most prestigious jobs in corporate Australia. Joyce was young for a chief executive, and lapped up the advice as he navigated a highly complex business through the economic turmoil wrought by the global financial crisis. Their tight bond was well known even after Dixon left Qantas. In his role as Tourism Australia chairman, Dixon often turned up with Joyce to high-powered dinners. To onlookers, the Qantas chief executive and his predecessor seemed inseparable. With a 27-year age gap, their friendship appeared to have a tinge of a father–son relationship.

Dixon's connections ran deep in Australia's business and political establishments. Apart from his close relationship with Packer, his network extended to advertising mogul John Singleton, retail billionaire Gerry Harvey, investment banker Mark Carnegie, trucking magnate Lindsay Fox, and a long list of executives who had passed through Qantas and other airlines over decades. Many of his friends and associates epitomised a larrikin side of Australia. It was a persona they liked to promote. They were from a generation that placed a high value on the Australian ideal of mateship, indulging in long lunches and drinking. Their interests in life outside business in pursuits such as horseracing, Australian football and rugby league was the gel that helped keep many of them connected. They had cultivated extensive networks and built a certain amount of goodwill and trust into their relationships. The businessmen met regularly for lunch and dinner at restaurants such as Rockpool and Machiavelli, the aptly named eatery for business and political types in central Sydney – places where business leaders, like bulls pouting in a ring, showed where they stood in the pecking order. To some extent, they all needed each other. The big end of town was a little fishbowl that became smaller the longer you swam in it.

They had different degrees of friendships and levels of trust. Peter Gregg, the former Qantas chief financial officer, was friends with Singleton but not nearly as close to the radio-station owner and ad man as Dixon. During his tenure as the marketing boss at Ansett in the early 1990s, Dixon had infuriated Singleton when he dumped the airline's contract with his agency. But in early 1994, Dixon had shifted to Qantas to become its head of marketing and corporate affairs and within a year had hired Singleton's firm to run a multimillion -dollar marketing campaign to help revitalise the airline's image.[2] It was to become a long-term relationship. Following on from advertising agency Mojo, the larrikin ad man's firm was later the creator behind Dixon's idea to fly children's choirs to locations around the world to sing Peter Allen's song 'I Still Call Australia Home'. The campaign ran for more than a decade, tugging at the heartstrings of Australians and connecting them to the airline's brand. Over the years, a number of choirs, including the Australian Girls' Choir and Boys' Choir and the Gondwana National Indigenous Children's Choir, sang at locations as diverse as Uluru in Central Australia, a Maasai village in Tanzania, atop the Brooklyn Bridge in New York and the Great Wall of China.

But behind these colourful personas lay serious businessmen who dealt in serious dollars. Dixon and Singleton had investments in pubs that went back decades. In his home town of Wagga Wagga, Dixon had invested money in the Turvey Tavern to help out his mate, Col Lyons, who ran it. The pub was 100 metres from Harris Park, where Dixon had played rugby league for the Wagga Wagga Magpies as a youngster. A short distance away was the Wagga Leagues Club, one of the town's institutions, which Dixon's father, Arthur, and rugby-league legend Arthur Summons spent decades overseeing. Over the years, Dixon, Singleton and, later, Carnegie built a small pub empire that included institutions such as the Bellevue Hotel, once a drinking den for Labor faithful, in the upmarket Sydney suburb of Paddington. In the aftermath of the global financial crisis in 2008, the trio took advantage of a buyer's market. Indebted owners of pubs had found themselves forced to sell for a lot less than what they had paid. In 2010, they bought Kinselas in the inner-Sydney suburb of Darlinghurst for $12 million and the Steyne in Manly for $28 million.

For these businessmen, another deal was never far away. By 2010, Dixon, Gregg, Carnegie, Singleton and former Allco executive chairman David Coe had bought into an aeroplane leasing company, Global Aviation Asset Management. One of Australia's richest families, the Liebermans in Melbourne, had controlled the company for several years, and gave the job of overseeing it to former Macquarie banker and Allco director Greg Woolley. Their worlds were deeply enmeshed. All five businessmen except Singleton had had a part in the $11 billion bid for Qantas in 2006. At Macquarie Bank, Woolley had been the head of the investment committee for the takeover offer for Qantas. As evidence of the close world of Australian business, Woolley had dealt with Dixon and Gregg when they were kingpins at Qantas. The airline leased a large number of passenger jets from Global Aviation Asset Management.[3] A year later, in August 2011, the group pocketed a tidy profit on its investment when it sold Global Aviation Asset Management to an American leasing company for

US$1.4 billion, a point the high-profile businessmen were only too happy to tell the financial press about.

Shortly afterwards, rumours began circulating of a takeover tilt for Qantas as its share price languished near record lows. To many investors, the speculation seemed more hot air than believable. Qantas' share price sank despite reports of a $3 billion bid by a mysterious private-equity firm. In most circumstances, the prospect of a genuine takeover bid would breathe life into a company's share price. For Joyce, the conjecture was the last thing he needed as he dealt with the full-blown industrial dispute and the question marks over plans for an ultra-premium airline in Asia. 'Unless there is something more firm out there . . . we are not going to set horses racing,' he told journalists.[4] Behind the scenes, Dixon, Gregg and their inner circle of business associates and friends had bought into Qantas. With Qantas' shares depressed, they saw a buying opportunity and bought a small stake. Gregg and Dixon knew the airline inside out, and believed investors were seriously undervaluing it.

In late November 2011, Dixon told *The Australian* that he was among a wealthy group of investors, including Singleton and Carnegie, who had considered buying a strategic stake in Qantas but eventually shelved their plans. 'All we did was have a look at it. And we looked in a serious way. We had some very top people looking at it and had a lot of people interested,' he said. Dixon insisted the group was interested in Qantas only as a buying opportunity, and he supported the way Joyce and his executives were running the airline.[5] While they sold out of Qantas for a healthy profit, his comments kept alive speculation about the group's intentions for months to come.

With Qantas trying to second-guess the group's intentions, the catch-ups between Joyce and Dixon for glasses of pinot became far less frequent. One night at the Park Hyatt in Sydney in March 2012, the pair was engaged in a deep conversation, Joyce pressing a point to Dixon, who sipped on a glass of his favourite red. It would be one of their last meetings.

In the background, the loose group of business associates, including Carnegie, Gregg, Dixon, Singleton, and Gerry Harvey and wife, Katie Page, were buying back into Qantas. 'We disagreed with the direction of the business. We disagreed that a great brand and a great business and a great icon of our country was getting damaged in a way that wasn't right,' Gregg recalled later. 'There were others that agreed with us and put some money where their mouth was and we tried to do something about it. It wasn't just the old brigade with their sweaters on, sitting around a camp fire.'[6]

This time, they were trying to convince Qantas' major institutional shareholders that a change in direction at the airline was needed. In early June 2012, Joyce spooked the market when he warned Qantas would sink into the red for the first time since it had been floated in 1995. The share price plunged almost 19 per cent in a single day and continued to fall over the following week, wiping more than $1 billion from the airline's market value. It prompted Qantas to go on the counterattack. The chairman, Leigh Clifford, rushed to Joyce's defence, insisting he had the full support of the airline's board. His comments echoed those of a year earlier, when Clifford had denied suggestions of a rift between him and the man he had hired. It was a catch-22 for the chairman. A company chairman rushing to publicly support his chief executive often fuelled further speculation and raised the very questions such comments sought to quash. With its share price hovering near a record low, Qantas readied its defences for a prolonged destabilisation campaign by the consortium of high-profile private investors. Many in the loose group were well versed in the dark art of plays on companies.

In response, Qantas reactivated an internal defence team put in place less than a year earlier amid the media speculation that Dixon and Gregg were part of a consortium running a ruler over the business. The airline hired bankers from Macquarie to give advice on a defence strategy, and Citigroup to keep an eagle eye on its share register for signs of unusual levels of trading.[7] The manoeuvring highlighted the role reversals from five years earlier, when Macquarie had orchestrated the $11 billion takeover bid for Qantas that gained the backing of the airline's directors, who included Dixon and Gregg. Now, the Australian investment bank was helping Joyce and Clifford repel a group whose key players included Qantas' former chief executive and its key numbers man. Carnegie, the financier who spearheaded the renegade group, had also advised the Qantas board during the takeover bid in 2006.[8] Rushing between meetings at an airline conference in the centre of Beijing, Joyce was battling a hidden enemy back in Australia at the same time as he was holding secret talks with the Emirates president, Tim Clark, about forming an alliance on the kangaroo route to Europe.

Qantas began drawing new battle lines. Management believed the actions by a consortium that included two of its former executives bordered on an act of treason. A year earlier, the syndicate had snapped up shares in Qantas because it reasoned the market was undervaluing the stock. This time, it was undermining Joyce and the rest of the Qantas management. The ginger group was intent on agitating to put Qantas on a different course, and campaigned behind the scenes against it forming the alliance with Emirates. Carnegie and his team analysed various options, including a sale of Qantas' frequent-flyer division and a partial float of Jetstar on the stock exchange. Carnegie's focus was on making money, while Dixon and Gregg still dreamed about charting Qantas' course. They were a bunch of men whose connections in some cases stretched back decades.

The syndicate invested a lot of time and money into their plans. Singleton helped create a new brand campaign for Qantas that was ready to go should they win support. Drawing on help from his old mates from the legendary advertising agency Mojo, Singleton oversaw a new theme song for Qantas that included a bit of the new and a bit of the old from the previous Spirit of Australia campaign. Like the old, it tugged at the heartstrings. 'It was ready to rock and roll. It was an upbeat part of the old one with some new stuff interwoven into it,' an insider said.

In early September, Barry Jackson and Richard Woodward, the leaders of the long-haul pilots' union, strolled down the long entranceway into what was billed an 'urban oasis'. In the inner-Sydney suburb of Paddington, the modern building with a Balinese theme served as the offices for Carnegie, the money man masterminding the consortium's strategy. Jackson and Woodward were in the lion's den and felt way out of their depth talking about high finance with Carnegie over the next forty-five minutes. The renegade group needed support from as many parties as possible, and the pilots were a key group within the Qantas diaspora. 'As we walked out, we were saying to ourselves, "We are only bloody pilots, and we need some serious advice here",' Woodward recalled. The pilots were open to talking to the group of investors because at the very least it would give them an insight into the power plays going on behind the scenes and what these meant for their members. Later, the Transport Workers Union's national secretary, Tony Sheldon, organised a meeting between a manager of a large industry super fund and the pilots' union to give them a better insight into the high-stakes game.

Sheldon also paid a visit to Carnegie's office to hear his battle plan. At its simplest, the ginger group planned to build a cornerstone stake in Qantas of up to 20 per cent, gain three board seats and agitate for management change. The latter was music to the ears of union leaders such as Sheldon, who wanted nothing more than to see the back of Clifford and Joyce after their public dust-ups during the industrial dispute a year earlier. The syndicate's overarching strategy in the talks was to create an accord with the union movement. For the unions, it meant giving ground on workplace agreements. For the syndicate, its proposed pact with the unions meant growing Qantas and, in turn, jobs. The pilots were told that if they wanted another meeting they would need to speak to Gregg, the consortium's choice of chief executive for Qantas. 'This has all the hallmarks of them trying to keep themselves in the game,' Woodward said.[9]

By now, Qantas and the syndicate were watching each other like hawks. The renegade group had acquired a 2 per cent stake in Qantas. But their grand plans had little chance of success without the support of Qantas' large institutional investors. Qantas was desperate to learn about the extent of the secret briefings by the consortium. It also wanted to seek assurances from its key shareholders that they remained supportive of Joyce's strategy. The nerves of Qantas executives were tested when one of its staffers spotted Gregg chatting over dinner with a prominent Sydney fund manager in mid-September in Hong Kong after an investor conference. Gregg also spoke with Andrew Sisson, the fund manager from Balanced Equity, which had one of the largest stakes in Qantas. Five years earlier, Sisson had gained national prominence after he refused to accept the $11 billion private-equity bid for Qantas. Carnegie and his team presented their plans to Sisson, too. But Sisson would not budge this time, either. He was sticking like glue to Joyce and his strategy, and was not about to change his mind after Gregg's and Carnegie's approaches.

The rebel group's strategy was straight out of the US playbook of shareholder activism. It was a necessity: the days of cheap credit were over, making it more difficult to raise the capital to launch a full-scale assault. The foreign-ownership limits on Qantas also made their job harder. The two sides were left to engage in a guerilla campaign, backgrounding shareholders and the media in an effort to undermine and flush out their enemy. The history of the individuals involved on both sides added an extra touch of bitterness. Qantas became desperate for a resolution to a campaign against its strategy. Joyce and his executives did not want the agitators to gain momentum and create a beachhead in a battle that threatened their place at the controls of the national airline.

But the renegade group's plans were foundering as Qantas' largest shareholders showed little desire to side with it. The group needed an investor with deep pockets. In a last gasp, transport mogul Lindsay Fox helped arrange meetings with China Southern, arguably the best-run of the big three Chinese airlines, in late 2012.[10] His private transport company, Linfox, had connections in Asia through its businesses there, as well as offices in Hong Kong and Shanghai. The Fox patriarch had been on the periphery of aviation for most of his life. He had entrusted his son, David, to look after the family's aviation assets. More than a decade earlier, Fox and another billionaire, Solomon Lew, had formed a consortium named Tesna to rescue Ansett from administration. The businessmen had ditched their plans to resurrect Ansett but their attempt had highlighted the Foxes' interest in aviation. Apart from their large trucking interests, the Fox empire included an airport at Avalon, near Geelong in Victoria. The airport relied heavily on Qantas for its income. One of Qantas' three heavy-maintenance bases was at Avalon where its Boeing 747 fleet was maintained. Jetstar was the only airline to still fly to the airport after Tiger Airways pulled out following its forced grounding by aviation-safety authorities in 2011. Qantas had long signalled the end of maintenance at Avalon, while the gradual reduction in Jetstar services threatened the airport's viability. It left the Foxes worried about Avalon while the syndicate, which had a small stake in Qantas, had gone from trying to convince the airline's largest shareholders to back its plans to searching for a new investor.

One night in late 2012, Carnegie, Dixon, Gregg and a number of others from the syndicate walked through the doors of Boomerang, Fox's Spanish-mission-style mansion in Sydney's swanky suburb of Elizabeth Bay. Fox had bought the heritage-listed waterfront home for $21 million in 2005, and later spent millions of dollars on renovations. On this night, the guests sipped glasses of wine as they chatted on Boomerang's patio, which boasted spectacular views northwards over Sydney Harbour. The reason for the gathering was to meet executives from China Southern's strategy and network planning teams, who were in Sydney on other business. The meeting at Boomerang was a chance for both sides to size each other up. The Chinese were eager to hear a presentation from Carnegie and his team about the potential opportunities in Qantas. Based in China's third-largest city, Guangzhou, China Southern needed to increase passenger traffic from Australia, one of its most important international markets. The presence of two former Qantas bigwigs at the meeting at Boomerang helped to boost the group's credentials in the eyes of the Chinese. In his role as Tourism Australia chairman, Dixon had been a frequent visitor to China, which had become the second-biggest source of foreign visitors for Australia in a matter of a few years. His time in China meant he had formed strong relationships with those in the senior ranks at the large Chinese airlines.

Both the Chinese and the Australians walked out of Fox's trophy home encouraged by their meeting but acutely aware of the major hurdles. If China Southern was to jump on board as a partner, it would not be able to do so quickly. The Chinese needed approval from their political masters in Beijing, which made quick decision-making near impossible. Under one potential scenario, China Southern would build on the 2 per cent stake in Qantas that the syndicate had acquired. But the problem was that the moment the market caught a whiff of a large investor such as a Chinese airline building a stake in Qantas, its share price would take off, removing any opportunity to buy at a low-ball price. The bigger question for the Australians was whether China Southern was the right investor to bring in. Doubt began to fill the minds of the key proponents as questions kept piling up. The prospect of a state-backed Chinese airline bankrolling the purchase of a cornerstone stake in Australia's flag carrier would be politically sensitive. As the grounding of Qantas' fleet in 2011 had demonstrated, the airline was deemed central to the nation's interests. The Qantas Sale Act prevented foreign airlines from buying more than 35 per cent of Qantas' shares. Apart from having to satisfy the foreign-ownership restrictions, the Foreign Investment Review Board was guaranteed to more closely scrutinise a deal in which a Chinese airline was financing the purchase of a major stake. Under the Foreign Acquisitions and Takeovers Act, aviation is one of seven sensitive sectors.

The Chinese later hired lawyers to act as legal advisers on a purchase of a 10–15 per cent stake in Qantas.[11] But the China Southern executives could not tell the syndicate whether they had the support of the central politburo in Beijing. As the weeks passed, the financial investors in the syndicate became concerned that the talks with China Southern were not going anywhere, and soon wanted to sell their holdings in Qantas. With doubts about the Chinese, and Qantas' major shareholders sticking with Joyce and Clifford, the group of agitators stood little chance of seeing their plans bear fruit. The talks with China Southern were their last gasp at reviving their plans for Qantas. But they, too, were dead in the water. 'We had a wonderful management team with Gregg and others, but it fell over,' Singleton said later.[12]

The key protagonists from both sides could not avoid each other in the small world of Australian business. On a Saturday night in mid-November, Bruce Buchanan was celebrating his fortieth birthday at the Bronte Surf Life Saving Club.[13] Buchanan had handed in his resignation as Jetstar chief executive six months earlier after Joyce suggested he take the reins as boss of Qantas International. The job to turn around the international division's fortunes was immense, and Buchanan had chosen to exit the airline group. On this early summer's night, a raft of airline executives and other high-profile business identities Buchanan had come to know well during his nine years at Jetstar mingled at the party. Among them were Dixon, who had developed a close relationship with Buchanan, and David Fox. As they chatted over a drink, Alan Joyce walked into the surf club and quickly spotted the pair. They were left in no doubt that they were personae non gratae.

The following Monday, the *Financial Review* reported that Gregg and Carnegie had been talking to senior union officials and some of Qantas' largest shareholders about an alternative strategy for Qantas.[14] Their agitation strategy was finally playing out under the full glare of the media. That day, Joyce sent an email to Qantas' senior managers urging them not to be distracted and insisting that his five-year strategy had the full support of the board. 'Rumours about this type of agitation have been doing the rounds for many months,' Joyce said in the email. 'We have not received any formal or informal approaches regarding a takeover. And I have no intentions of supporting any private-equity bid.' The agitators kept their heads down, apart from Singleton, who let fly that Qantas 'is being sacrificed – it is being given to Emirates'.[15] On one side were Clifford and Joyce, and on the other a group of businessmen who had some of the largest contact books in corporate Australia. It quickly cast a spotlight on the relationship between Dixon and his protégé. Their days of chats over glasses of fine wine were well and truly over. But their parting attracted more interest than most because the pair had been so close and had such high public profiles.

Just over a week later, it turned into all-out war in public between the top echelons of Australia's business establishment. Joyce had been scheduled months in advance to speak at a gathering of the National Aviation Press Club in central Sydney. Here was his opportunity to end his enemy's slow-burn strategy. With a room full of journalists and airline-industry stalwarts, Joyce rounded on Dixon and others in the consortium he branded APA Mark II, a reference to the failed private-equity bid five years earlier. 'The consortium is determined to stymie the Qantas–Emirates partnership,' he said, pointing his finger firmly at Dixon, who had been 'very much out there briefing against the company'. 'Qantas is of the view that as chairman of Tourism Australia, Mr Dixon is in a position of significant and untenable potential conflict.'[16] A day earlier, Joyce had written to the federal tourism minister, Martin Ferguson, to inform him that Qantas would cut funding to the country's peak tourism body unless Dixon resigned as Tourism Australia chairman or split from the rebel group. Qantas poured tens of millions into the industry body's coffers for marketing campaigns each year.

That night, Tourism Australia's board held an emergency meeting at its offices overlooking Darling Harbour in Sydney. The directors, including former Virgin Blue chief executive Brett Godfrey, emerged to give Dixon their full support and declared that his investment in

Qantas was not an unmanageable conflict of interest. Ferguson, who was close to Dixon, left the matter in the hands of the board to resolve, a signal he would be backing the former Qantas chief executive.

Neither side would back down. But the consortium's strategy appeared half-baked. Some onlookers were disparaging, pointing out that if the rebels were serious they would have got all their ducks in a row first before making a quick overnight play for Qantas. 'It's just some harebrained scheme from yesterday's heroes,' an influential adviser to large institutional investors said. 'It is seriously embarrassing for them – talk is cheap. It's like the Keystone Cops' takeover plan.'[17] The syndicate had been unable to gain the support of Qantas' largest shareholders, nor raise the money needed. The loose group of high-profile businessmen were unwilling to throw more of their own money into a high-stakes gamble. By January 2013, the consortium had sold its 2 per cent stake for a tidy profit. 'The market didn't agree with us and we decided that there was no point going further and divested. The large institutions obviously had greater faith in the management strategy than ours. Whether you are right or wrong doesn't really matter – they didn't do it,' Gregg recalled. 'The institutional investors own the company. If they don't buy into a strategy of change, then you have got no hope.'[18]

But the battle between Joyce and Dixon showed no sign of ending. Joyce would not bow from his refusal to inject money from Qantas into Tourism Australia campaigns until Dixon was removed from his post. Dixon stayed silent in public, and remained chairman of the peak tourism body. Dixon felt that he had handed over an airline whose coffers bulged with $3 billion in cash only for his successor to make strategic missteps such as the Emirates alliance. To Joyce and his executives, Dixon had steered Qantas during boom times and benefited from a vacuum left in the market by the collapse of Ansett. They had been left to deal with what they believed was a lack of structural change to the business during the halcyon days. 'This business, it didn't just get bloated all of a sudden. It got bloated because we didn't make the changes in terms of labour for the last ten years, and I'm sure Geoff finds that very uncomfortable to live with,' a Qantas executive said. 'But that is the reality of it. He didn't want to take the unions on. He wants to be remembered as the hero. He didn't make the tough calls in transforming the business.'[19]

The falling-out between Dixon and Joyce was of Shakespearean proportions. The once-close allies had turned on each other, and neither would back down. Emotions ran high because of the cocktail of personalities. It was a far cry from the days when the pair would heap praise on each other. Dixon had described to journalists how his successor was 'very, very bright but so at ease with that intelligence that he's also very engaging'. Joyce had labelled Dixon his mentor. Not only had Dixon hired Joyce to Qantas, promoted him to Jetstar chief executive and rebuffed accusations from his executives that he was protecting his protégé, but he had played a big part in Joyce's ascension to Qantas chief executive.

Now, they were sworn enemies. The impact of their row rippled through Australia's aviation and tourism industries, placing many, such as Tourism Australia's chief executive, Andrew McEvoy, in an awkward position as they tiptoed around the stand-off. Tourism Australia was forced to find alternative revenue sources to fill the hole left by Qantas, which diverted millions of dollars of spending on marketing into state tourism coffers. For Qantas, the dispute had distracted Joyce and his executives from resolving other challenges facing the airline.

In the tight-knit world of Australian business, Joyce and Dixon could not avoid each other. Four months later they were brought together in a very public way following the death of a former Qantas chief executive James Strong. The lives of Strong and Dixon had been intertwined since they had first met in the early 1980s at Northern Territory mining company Nabalco. After working in Gove for the bauxite miner, Dixon had set his sights on becoming a diplomat. Following a brief spell working in Canberra, he had scored a gig in the Australian consulate in New York in 1976. But within a short time, he had returned to Australia and Strong hired him to work for the Australian Mining Industry Council. Strong later left the council for Australian Airlines (formerly known as Trans-Australia Airlines) with Dixon in tow.[20] With Strong as chief executive, the airline's management team included Dixon as boss of its commercial operations and Gary Toomey as its chief financial officer. Strong left Australian Airlines in 1989 and Dixon later went to Ansett. But they would work together again four years later when Strong was given the task of folding Australian Airlines into Qantas and, as chief executive, overseeing the merged airline's public float in 1995. Dixon served in various roles under Strong before replacing him as Qantas chief executive in March 2001. The pair knew each other inside out.

On a blue-sky day in Sydney in early March 2013, a Qantas A380 superjumbo roared low over the city centre in salute to Strong's contribution to the country's aviation industry. Strong, who was born in the northern New South Wales town of Lismore in 1944, towards the end of World War II, had died eight days earlier of lung complications from surgery in Sydney at the age of sixty-eight. At the Recital Hall, some of Australia's best-known identities from the business, sporting and arts worlds filed in to pay their respects to the Qantas director who had become known as 'Mr Bow-Tie'. Among those who walked to their seats near the front of the hall were Dixon and his wife, Dawn, and Joyce and his partner, Shane Lloyd. The other mourners included Gregg, five-time motorcycle champion Mick Doohan, former world motorcycle champion Casey Stoner, federal government ministers Simon Crean and Peter Garrett, former NSW premier Nick Greiner, Reserve Bank board member and Fairfax Media chairman Roger Corbett, and one of the country's best-connected business leaders, David Gonski.

Standing on the stage, Joyce told the audience that the man known for his signature bow ties was a 'true gentleman but also a fighter; an opera buff and a revhead, a mountain climber and a bookworm;

a businessman and a dreamer'. For Dixon and Joyce, it was the first time they had been seen together in public since their falling-out had become very public five months earlier. After the service, they spoke briefly in the foyer of the Recital Hall where the high-profile attendees gathered before departing. A day later, Qantas said its position on Dixon had not changed.

Gregg, Dixon and their co-investors had not expected the ferocity of the response from Qantas. It was important to remember that they were businessmen who had had their fair share of ugly disputes in their long careers. They were people who lived for the rush of dealmaking, and were well accustomed to the rollercoaster ride that entails. Perhaps it should not have been a shock. Joyce and Clifford defended their positions. After all, they believed they were under attack from a group of high-profile investors, including former Qantas executives who had had their day in the sun steering the airline. At stake were not only their positions but the future direction of Qantas, an airline all sides claimed they had foremost in their minds. It was a case of former executives who could not let go of the airline they had spent years working at. They had been unable to resist the temptation to attempt to return to the stage. The battle lines had been drawn. There would be little forgiveness from any of them, and years later the two sides were still refusing to back down. They were tearing themselves up over personalities and ego.

15

PROJECT LANTERN

Pansy Ho was a renowned socialite in Hong Kong, regularly appearing in the gossip pages of the city's newspapers and magazines. The tabloids christened her 'Party-Girl Pansy' for her exploits in bars such as Sevva. From its deck on the twenty-fifth floor of the Prince's Building in central Hong Kong, revellers looked out at skyscrapers and old Star ferries bobbing in Victoria Harbour on their way to nearby Kowloon. At night, the city switched on its magic as lights lit up the crowded skyline in the Chinese territory. A short walk from Sevva was another of Ho's favourite eating places. Isola, an Italian restaurant at the foot of the second-tallest tower in Hong Kong, the IFC, offered panoramic views of the harbour and Kowloon on a good day. On a bad day, the smog from China's manufacturing heartland in the Pearl River Delta was a reminder of the cost of progress. Her frequent visits to the city's top bars and restaurants made her a regular feature in *Hong Kong Tatler*, the high-end magazine that chronicled the personal lives of the city's rich and famous.

By mid-2013, Pansy Ho had become crucial to Alan Joyce's aspirations in Asia. More than a year earlier, the Qantas chief executive had flown to Hong Kong to unveil plans to launch Jetstar Hong Kong as part of a joint venture with one of China's big-three airlines, China Eastern. Trumpeting its 'first-mover advantage', Joyce spoke of the 'huge potential' for the new budget airline to tap into mainland China, where airline passengers were forecast to surge by 50 per cent to 450 million by 2015. 'We think this will be a long-term partnership with China Eastern and we don't see the need for any other partners to be involved in it,' he said.[1] Under his ambitious plan, Jetstar Hong Kong would launch flights from Chek Lap Kok Airport by the middle of 2013. It would start with three Airbus A320 aircraft before quickly growing to an eighteen-strong fleet by 2015. Qantas and China Eastern would each invest up to US$99 million in the new budget airline over three years. Joyce and his executives had spent a lot of time trying to build relationships with their counterparts at China Eastern. It was a frustrating experience as connections were built only to be rendered pointless when Chinese executives shifted to top jobs in other parts of China Inc. After plans for RedQ, the ultra-premium airline, had been consigned to the bottom drawer two weeks earlier in 2012, the Australian airline group's hopes for expansion in Asia rested firmly on Jetstar.

Before it settled on China Eastern, Qantas had been sniffing around for other partners for a budget airline in Hong Kong. Cathay Pacific was among the parties Qantas approached about becoming an investor. But its advances were rebuffed. 'They were offered Jetstar Hong Kong first and they said no,' a former Qantas executive said. 'Cathay is really hard to understand because there is Cathay management, then there is Swire as a shareholder and then there is Air China and the Chinese government. You never know who is blocking it.'[2] Despite being founding members of the oneworld airline marketing alliance, the relationship between Qantas and Cathay Pacific had been tetchy for decades. Their trust of each other went only so far. Like many affairs between companies, it often fluctuated based on the personalities in the CEO chairs. The relationship between the two airlines had been stretched in the 1990s but Geoff Dixon and his counterpart at Cathay, David Turnbull, had got on well personally. Turnbull later played a role in the Macquarie Bank-orchestrated $11 billion bid for Qantas in 2006 as a director of Allco Finance Group. Dixon and Qantas' chief financial officer at the time, Peter Gregg, relished the chance to chat over drinks, which appealed to Cathay's senior executives. Their rendezvous when Turnbull was chief executive of Cathay Pacific included time sipping fine wine on the launch *EQV* – owned by the airline's parent, Swire – as it cruised around islands in Victoria Harbour. Most of Cathay's executives heralded from the English establishment, and rotated in and out of the airline from Swire. Many had worked at Swire for life – or, at least a good part of it. Plucked from the top British universities and inducted into a company that traced its roots to Liverpool in the early nineteenth century, they earned their stripes by working at Swire's businesses as far afield as Papua New Guinea and Geelong, in country Victoria.

Under Joyce, the relationship with Cathay was about to be tested. Within months of him unveiling his plans for Jetstar Hong Kong, Cathay had shown that it would be a thorn in the side of Joyce's ambitions in the Asian financial hub. Cathay had bitten its tongue until August 2012, when it highlighted to Australian regulators in an unrelated matter the hurdles Jetstar Hong Kong would face in establishing itself in the Chinese territory. The shot across the bow was the first signal Hong Kong's flag carrier would aggressively defend its home turf from any new upstart. Jetstar was unperturbed, emphasising several weeks later that it had lodged its operational blueprint for the airline with Hong Kong regulators and announcing it would soon begin hiring up to a hundred pilots and flight attendants. Jetstar had a project team in Hong Kong led by Nick Rohrlach, an executive in strategy at the budget airline in Australia and a former consultant at Boston Consulting Group. But Joyce's intention to launch flights by the middle of 2013 quickly began to look overly ambitious. Hong Kong regulators were in no rush to grant Jetstar Hong Kong approval.

As the months dragged on without any response from them, it became evident Jetstar would need a local investor to help it gain approval.

Qantas and China Eastern needed to put a local face on their new airline. They hired an investment bank to search for another strategic shareholder. Pansy Ho's Shun Tak was at the top of the list of interested investors. In early June 2013, Shun Tak emerged on Jetstar Hong Kong's register with a 33 per cent stake, diluting Qantas and China Eastern's interests to a third each. Under the deal, each party would inject up to US$66 million in the new airline. For Qantas, the dilution of its stake was a small price to pay. The new airline would stand little chance of ever flying without the support of Shun Tak, which had begun in the 1970s as a ferry operator and later expanded to include a helicopter shuttle service between Hong Kong and Macau. Under the revised plans for Jetstar Hong Kong, Ho would become chairwoman and steer the effort to seek regulatory approval. 'Pansy is of the belief we have a strong case and Pansy is leading the charge on that,' Joyce said later.[3]

Away from the social circuit, Ho was one of the most feared women in Hong Kong and Macau, the former Portuguese colony. The fashionista was the right-hand woman and daughter of Macau gaming billionaire Stanley Ho. One of the Asian godfather's seventeen children to four wives, Pansy had emerged as the heir apparent to the Ho business empire. In Macau, the Hos controlled everything from casinos and shopping centres to transport, tourism and property assets. Through their connections and business interests, the family had a strong influence on the territory's government. Stanley had built his empire in Macau from scratch after escaping from Hong Kong when the Japanese invaded during World War II. Establishing kerosene and construction companies, he expanded into gambling in 1970 when he opened the Lisboa casino. Several years later, the Lisboa's gaming halls were the backdrop for a scene in the James Bond film, *The Man with the Golden Gun*. Over the next forty years, rivers of gold flowed from the Hos' monopoly licence on gambling in the Portuguese outpost.

Stanley Ho was also connected to the dark underbelly of the gambling industry. In 1988, a report by the Department of Justice in the United States highlighted his associations with Asian organised crime. Four years later, a US senate committee investigation concluded that, while not a member of Asian organised crime, he was linked with individuals and business associates who were. In the early stages of negotiations with a company owned by Pansy Ho to operate a casino in Macau, American gaming powerhouse MGM conducted background checks on both her and her father in 2003. Private investigators hired by MGM noted in several confidential reports that Stanley was 'linked closely' to the two major triads in Macau – the 14K and Sun Yee On – and had 'strong ties' to North Korea. According to a US report, Australian gaming authorities found he was 'unsuitable to hold a gaming licence'.[4]

The Hos' tentacles stretched to Hong Kong, where Pansy had held court at the listed transport conglomerate Shun Tak as its managing director since 1999. However, she could not escape her father's shadow. Investigators for US casino regulators found that she had gained the vast majority of her wealth through multimillion-dollar gifts from, and business relationships with, her father. Following a four-year investigation, the gaming regulator in the US state of New Jersey directed MGM in May 2009 to sever ties with Pansy Ho after it deemed her 'unsuitable' due to her 'dependence on her father and her associations with individuals connected to organised crime'.[5] In Macau, one of her brothers, Lawrence, had been a business partner with Sydney billionaire James Packer in a casino operation since 2004. The joint venture later became known as Melco Crown Entertainment and proved a savvy bet for Packer as Macau's status as a mecca for Chinese gamblers grew in tandem with the wealth on the mainland.

Pansy Ho was the antithesis of budget travel, often flying in her Bombardier corporate jet. 'She is a very shrewd businesswoman and a very tough lady. I would go as far as to call her ruthless in the way she operates, but I have a grudging respect for her,' said Andrew Pyne, a former government lobbyist for Cathay Pacific and an ex-adviser on aviation matters to Hong Kong's last governor, Chris Patten. 'Within the whole empire there is a quite a lot of internecine squabbling, to put it kindly, and she has come out at the top of it.'[6] Qantas' hopes for a budget airline that, like its rivals, would cram passengers onto planes, rested on Pansy Ho acting as the key to the door to Hong Kong and mainland China. She was an aviation enthusiast with a penchant for shiny new toys. She was also a believer in the low-cost airline model. But her political clout was greater in Macau than Hong Kong. She could not shake her family's reputation in Macau. Most locals in Hong Kong perceived her as heralding from Macau despite her substantial investments in the former British colony and her immersion in some of its elite social circles.

It was not the first time Australian airlines had courted Hong Kong's richest woman and Shun Tak. In 2004, the Hos' transport conglomerate was one of the companies Virgin Blue had talked to about setting up a budget airline in Macau to operate flights to mainland China. David Huttner, the strategy boss at Virgin, had been dispatched to Macau for weeks in an attempt to prise the door open. Virgin was trying its luck at gaining a licence to run commercial flights out of Macau, which was a much cheaper place to base planes than neighbouring Hong Kong. Huttner also talked to Viva Macau about the airlines cooperating, but it quickly became clear to his counterparts in Macau that Virgin did not have a lot to offer them. The talks fizzled out and Huttner flew home empty-handed. Before long Qantas, ever vigilant to what its Australian rival was up to, got an inkling of what Virgin was attempting to do and wanted to join the search for dance partners.

In January 2007, the then chief executive of low-cost carrier Viva Macau, Andrew Pyne, met Dixon and Gregg at the Pan Pacific hotel in Singapore. The senior Qantas executives were in the city-state for other meetings, and an evening encounter with Pyne, a former

Cathay executive, was a chance to explore opportunities. Dixon and Gregg put on the table their desire to grow the Jetstar brand throughout Asia and their belief that Macau was a good entry point to China for Jetstar. Their brief introduction ended with plans to meet again in Australia; they later exchanged emails. But the fleeting interactions quickly ran aground. Viva Macau was unable to demonstrate to Dixon and Gregg that it could be transformed into a Jetstar offshoot. The airline was flying twin-aisle Boeing 767 aircraft and, in order to operate as a proper low-cost carrier, needed smaller Airbus A320 or Boeing 737 planes to fit the short-haul budget model.

At the same time as the talks with Viva Macau were under way, the Qantas executives were knocking on other doors in Macau. The Australian airline had serious discussions with Air Macau, of which Pansy Ho was an executive director, in the months before Dixon stepped down as chief executive in November 2008. But like those with Viva Macau, the negotiations with Air Macau amounted to nought. It was just as well. Viva Macau collapsed in early 2010, and Air Macau remained a bit player in the region years later despite hundreds of thousands of Chinese flocking to the city's gaming dens annually. While short-lived, Qantas' dalliance with the two airlines highlighted its ambitions to set up an airline as part of a joint venture on the doorstep of mainland China, and expand elsewhere in Asia. It could not do so on its own because of the high level of regulation that constrained aviation in the region. The talks with Air Macau in 2008 helped to build bridges with the Ho family that would later become useful in Qantas' attempts to set up Jetstar Hong Kong.

Years earlier, Qantas had pushed the button on expanding Jetstar into Asia. The airline had won goodwill from the Singapore government for continuing to fly via the city-state when an outbreak of severe acute respiratory syndrome (SARS) in 2003 caused panic in Asia. The epidemic had a devastating effect on air travel, including that in and out of Australia. Changi Airport's terminals almost resembled a ghost town at the height of the pandemic, its departure halls deserted as large numbers of people decided against travelling. The goodwill from the Singaporeans provided an opening for Qantas, which favoured setting up a low-cost airline in the South-East Asian country. Over the next year, Peter Gregg and other executives flew repeatedly to Singapore for meetings about setting up a new budget airline. The objective of Jetstar Asia was to feed passengers from South-East Asia to its hub in Singapore.

Out of Jetstar Asia developed a concept of a broader Jetstar business whose operations would extend from Australia to other parts of Asia besides Singapore. Gregg later pushed for the launch of Jetstar International, which was to fly long-haul routes from Australia directly to destinations in Asia. In 2005, Qantas also began negotiations with AirAsia, a low-cost airline based in Malaysia. In the Grand Hyatt in Singapore, Gregg held negotiations with AirAsia's founder, Tony Fernandes, about how the two airlines could bring their networks together so that Jetstar Asia and AirAsia would not cannibalise each other on routes in South-East Asia. Conor McCarthy, a former colleague and mate of Alan Joyce's at Aer Lingus in Ireland, had a 5 per cent stake in AirAsia. McCarthy had helped draw up the blueprint for Jetstar several years earlier in Australia, and had been a link between the two airlines. It was difficult to do anything in Singapore without being sprung. On this occasion in 2005, Qantas had booked a room for the secret talks with Fernandes, and the hotel staff in the Hyatt, unaware of the sensitivities, posted a sign on the door declaring it a Qantas-AirAsia meeting. Walking into the meeting with his AirAsia cap on, Fernandes proved a difficult man to deal with because he pushed hard for the upper hand. 'Tony is easy to get on with but he knows what he wants and he will do everything around it to get where he wants to,' Gregg recalled. 'It came to nothing as a lot of these things do. It is very hard to consolidate in this industry, forgetting about the government regulations and the personalities involved.'[7]

At the same time as the talks with Fernandes were under way, Gregg, Dixon and Borghetti were holding tentative negotiations with Singapore Airlines about a merger. It again highlighted the fact that airlines constantly danced with multiple partners and were always on the lookout for prospective companions. A year earlier, Jetstar Asia had been unveiled in Singapore with the usual fanfare such events entailed. 'This is going to be a very, very substantial airline,' Dixon crowed at the time.[8] Qantas had a 49 per cent stake in the new low-cost airline, while the rest was split between two Singaporean industrialists and Temasek, the investment arm of that country's government. Singapore was to prove tougher than first envisaged, and it would be four years before Jetstar Asia stemmed losses to post a tiny profit. It would yoyo for years between losses and minuscule profits.

After Bruce Buchanan took the reins from Joyce at Jetstar in late 2008, he set about rearranging the ownership of Jetstar Asia in Singapore. Both Jetstar Asia and the Jetstar-branded joint venture in Vietnam were repair jobs for the lanky, thirty-something executive who grew up on the New South Wales central coast, north of Sydney. Qantas had a tense relationship with the other shareholders in Jetstar Asia. A few years earlier, Jetstar Asia had bought Valuair mainly because of its traffic rights to fly to the four largest Indonesian cities of Jakarta, Surabaya, Medan and Denpasar. But the small, loss-making airline was not properly folded into Jetstar Asia, leaving the Singapore business to operate two airline brands from the city-state to destinations in South-East Asia with a small fleet of aircraft. With a large number of minority shareholders, it was proving difficult to make decisions. In 2009, Qantas ended up buying out the minority shareholders in Jetstar Asia for $S25 million while Dennis Choo, a Singaporean businessman and long-time Qantas associate, took 51 per cent of the voting stock in the new holding company. This ensured that Jetstar Asia adhered to the Air Navigation Act in Singapore, and could gain access to air routes as a Singaporean-designated airline. But its journey was only to become harder as competition with other budget airlines intensified.

After the reshuffle in Singapore, Buchanan's focus turned northwards to China and Japan. Jetstar had to figure out how to gain access to domestic markets that had been out of bounds to foreign interests. Under Project Lantern, Hong Kong was targeted as the place for Jetstar to get a foothold into China. In order to fly to the mainland from Hong Kong, Jetstar had to gain access to bilateral air-rights agreements between China and the territory. The only way to do this was to have a budget airline operating as a Hong Kong carrier. Buchanan wrote the plan for Jetstar Hong Kong and presented it to Qantas' board twice in 2009 and 2010 as part of a blueprint for Asia. His job was to search and evaluate investment partners for the new airline, build a relationship with his counterparts at Chek Lap Kok Airport and put the initial project team together.

As time passed, the pressure to launch Jetstar Hong Kong grew. Access to slots at Hong Kong's sole commercial airport became harder. Cathay Pacific knew that if Jetstar Hong Kong was delayed, the budget airline would be severely restricted when it did eventually win approval to fly because it would have difficulty gaining airport slots. The new airline would have to wait years until a third runway was built at Chek Lap Kok Airport in order to grow its operations. The approval to fly from the city would mean nothing if it did not have designated times during the day when it could pull planes up to terminal gates at Hong Kong's airport to load and unload passengers.

For Qantas' unions, the Jetstar offshoots in Asia had long been a target. The long-haul pilots' union went to great lengths to prove its thesis that Jetstar's expansion in Asia was a black hole and that Qantas was heavily subsidising Jetstar. In 2011 at the height of their industrial dispute, the union hired auditors from PPB Advisory to crunch the numbers on whether the big losses Qantas was attributing to its international operations were inflated because it was subsidising Jetstar. Without Qantas giving them unfettered access to its books, it was impossible for the pilots and their auditors to substantiate their argument beyond broad assertions and flimsy raw numbers. Jetstar's

Asian offshoots were even harder to assess because the likes of Jetstar Pacific in Vietnam did not release annual accounts. Joyce dismissed the claims of cost-shifting between Qantas and Jetstar as 'in line with the moon-landing conspiracy theory that we didn't land on the moon'. He added, 'It is in line with "Elvis is alive and well and serving in a McDonald's somewhere in Manly." Qantas subsidising Jetstar is another one of these great conspiracy theories.'[9] Independent South Australian senator Nick Xenophon would pursue Qantas for years in an attempt to untangle the web of interrelated companies, and in the process became the airline's number-one public enemy.

As it worked away to set up an airline in Hong Kong, Jetstar was nearing the end of six years of negotiations for a licence to fly domestic routes in Japan. Months after Jetstar Hong Kong was unveiled in March 2012, Buchanan left the company and handed the baton to Jayne Hrdlicka, the head of strategy at Qantas and an American who had long been close to Joyce. Buchanan did not get the chance to watch the first flight of Jetstar Japan in July 2012, the culmination of years of talks with the Japanese regulators and its new business partners in the joint venture, Japan Airlines and two other shareholders. Japan was to be a tough market to break into because of the onerous conditions set on new arrivals by the country's regulators, but it offered a more promising future than Hong Kong.

After deflecting questions for months in 2013, Cathay Pacific ripped off the gloves in September that year when it filed its formal opposition to Jetstar Hong Kong with regulators. 'The setting-up of Jetstar Hong Kong is an attempt by a foreign carrier to gain access to Hong Kong's pool of traffic rights without a fair exchange of value to Hong Kong,' it thundered. 'Doing so would also open the door to similar attempts to grab Hong Kong's air-traffic rights by other foreign airlines based in rival aviation hubs to Hong Kong.'[10] Cathay had guarded the keys to Hong Kong for decades and was showing that it was not going to give them up without an almighty fight. It had everything to lose. Its fear was not a small budget airline that planned to begin flying with just three planes. Instead, its worry was that the arrival of Jetstar would open the floodgates to a raft of airlines, including the large state-backed Chinese carriers, wanting to set up shop on its home turf.

Rod Eddington, the former chief executive of Cathay and British Airways, summed up the challenge for Jetstar in setting up in Hong Kong, which was both a competitive aviation market and an expensive city in which to run a business. 'The two most competitive markets in Asia are Hong Kong and Singapore because everybody flies there and everyone wants traffic rights to these places,' he said. 'It's one thing to set up in Malaysia and Indonesia. But in Hong Kong and Singapore you are taking on two extremely successful, very combative major Asian players.'[11] The motto for Cathay's parent, Swire, was *Esse Quam Videri*, which meant 'to be, rather than seem to be'. In its campaign against Jetstar, it had shown it was living up to its maxim. The former British trading colony's location at the crossroads of Asia had been treasured for centuries. For airlines, Hong Kong was within five hours' flying time of all the major Asian financial centres, making it one of the world's most prized aviation hubs. Cathay was not about to cede ground to a small budget upstart from Australia.

Even with Hong Kong's richest woman on board, Joyce and his trusted boss at Jetstar, Hrdlicka, faced a protracted battle in gaining approval for Jetstar Hong Kong to fly. While Pansy Ho was well connected, she was up against the lobbying power of Cathay and its biggest shareholder, Swire, synonymous with the 'Pearl of the Orient'. Cathay also had a weapon on the mainland in its second-biggest shareholder, Air China, which was based in Beijing and close to decision-makers.

As it turned out, Jetstar Hong Kong had broken a cardinal rule by ordering planes before gaining the right to fly them. By November 2013, Jetstar Hong Kong's senior executives were searching for homes for its growing fleet of planes. The cost of the brand-new aircraft with fresh licks of paint parked on the ground indefinitely was mounting.

Early in November, Qantas proposed taking three A320 planes from Jetstar Hong Kong and storing at least two in Australia. In a leaked email to its chief executive, Edward Lau, and other executives on November 15, Jetstar Hong Kong's chief financial officer, Howard Cheung, called a management meeting in its offices in a bland four-storey building on the outskirts of Chek Lap Kok Airport to discuss a range of scenarios. They included weighing up the 'cost of storage in Toulouse vs Australia'.[12] The southern French city of Toulouse was a base for the planes' maker, Airbus. Hong Kong was not an option because of the high cost of parking planes. In the end, Jetstar Hong Kong's executives decided to store its first three aircraft in Toulouse indefinitely.

With losses mounting due to growth from competitors such as AirAsia, Joyce slammed the breaks on Jetstar's aggressive expansion in Asia in February 2014. Stiff competition in South-East Asia had stripped $29 million from Jetstar's earnings in six months. 'This is a significant reprioritisation of our growth to focus on the areas that we must continue to invest in,' Joyce said. But he was quick to emphasise that the losses in Asia were 'tiny in the scheme of things; it is a small investment and they are in the start-up phase. The big problem is domestic . . . it is certainly not Asia.'[13]

By early 2014, the number of Jetstar Hong Kong planes sitting idle in Toulouse had grown to nine. Joyce emphasised that it was not unusual for airlines to park planes during their start-up phases because of the difficulty of lining up aircraft deliveries with regulatory approval. Airlines typically placed orders for planes two years in advance of receiving the keys to them. He cited Virgin America parking more than fifteen aircraft while it waited a year before gaining traffic rights to fly in the US.[14] While this was true, Jetstar Hong Kong's long wait to get off the ground revealed that Joyce had been far too ambitious in his aim of having the new airline flying by the middle of 2013. Within months of his comments, Jetstar Hong Kong had sold six of its nine planes.

Jetstar's venture in Japan was also facing hurdles. In April 2014, Jetstar Japan had as many as six A320s parked at Tokyo's Narita Airport with their engines covered due to delays in regulators allowing it to set up a second base in the country. Six months earlier, Qantas had pumped another $60 million into the airline. Analysts at Macquarie Group had estimated Jetstar Japan was losing $50 million a year as it competed against other newcomers in the Japanese domestic market.

Jetstar was hamstrung in Asia by regulators, particularly in Hong Kong – with or without Pansy Ho. The financial centre was an opportunity worth trying but it was far from a golden goose. Joyce had overstated the ease with which Qantas would waltz into the lion's den to set up a fledging budget offshoot. 'Jetstar's approach to this market has been flawed at every stage – the way they handled Cathay, the initial overconfident view of the regulatory situation and even the people they lined up to support them politically,' said Andrew Pyne, the former Cathay Pacific executive.[15] Jetstar had morphed way beyond its original plan to service the domestic market, and was competing in a region littered with low-cost airlines.

16

MAYDAY

By early 2013, the war between Qantas and Virgin had become one of attrition. Both companies were forever running the numbers on the other's cash burn. It was a case of who could last the distance. At the outset, Qantas' internal analysis suggested Virgin was living on borrowed time, and would have to pull back from the costly attempt to snare a larger part of the lucrative business-travel market. 'The analysis we did looking at their cash burn against their investments, to the extent where we could, was always saying that they were going to run out of cash,' a Qantas executive at the time said.[1]

One of Qantas' trump cards was the special status that credit-rating agencies bestowed upon it. The airline's investment-grade credit rating had been hard won, and something it had gone out of its way to protect for years. It was one of only two or three airlines worldwide at any time to hold the rating, which allowed it to borrow money more cheaply than its rivals. But by 2013, Standard & Poor's and Moody's were becoming uneasy about their rating on Qantas. The jitters from two of the world's big-three ratings agencies piled pressure on Qantas to search for ways to protect its status.

Behind closed doors in early 2013, Joyce and his executives began appealing to the federal transport minister, Anthony Albanese, for government assistance. While Albanese was the key man to petition, Qantas had to detail much of its demands to bureaucrats at the federal Treasury and Finance Department in Canberra. It resulted in the Gillard Government considering two forms of assistance: a debt guarantee, or a so-called 'letter of comfort'. By midyear, the lobbying to gain support had reached a climax without the knowledge of anyone outside the top echelons of the government or Qantas. However, the airline soon hit a roadblock in trying to convince the government to act as a guarantor. The response from the two departments was that they opposed the government guaranteeing Qantas' debt but were relaxed about it offering a letter of comfort, which amounted to tacit support. 'The advice I got back from Finance and Treasury at the time was that if you did [give a debt guarantee], we want a stake in the airline,' Albanese said later.[2]

The government believed a letter of comfort was the best option because it resolved Qantas' main concern: credit-ratings agencies downgrading the airline to 'junk' status. '[Qantas] made the case, and I accept the case, that the aviation industry is an essential industry,' Albanese recalled. 'It was examined by Finance and Treasury, and by my department, and they felt in the end the letter of comfort was enough. And it was. I was in support of it, and had to think it all through obviously, and got approval, and it went back to discussions [with] Julia as PM, then Kevin [Rudd after he succeeded Gillard as prime minister in June 2013].' The government's willingness to allow the taxpayer to give implicit support to the airline in order to shore up its financial standing in the eyes of all-powerful credit-ratings agencies highlighted the special place afforded Qantas.

As Qantas secretly pressured the government, Virgin was pressing ahead with plans to widen its reach in Australia. In early May, Richard Branson flew to Perth from Europe for a rebranding of Skywest, the regional airline it had bought a year earlier, in Virgin livery. Two weeks earlier, Branson had halved his stake in Virgin. He sold almost 10 per cent to Singapore Airlines for about $122 million in a deal that further cemented the grip of Virgin's three airline shareholders. At Qantas, it reinforced fears within senior ranks that it was fighting a transnational battle in the domestic market against Singapore Airlines, Etihad and Air New Zealand. Between them, the three airlines had a combined stake of 47 per cent in Virgin and had signalled their intention to increase it further. No longer was Qantas' domestic business simply competing against Virgin, whose only major shareholder was a flamboyant English entrepreneur reluctant to dig deep into his pockets. Qantas was left to decide whether it could afford a fight on multiple fronts, including on international routes where it was under attack from Asian and Middle Eastern airlines.

After arriving in Perth at 2.00 a.m., Branson turned up later in the morning donning an Akubra hat as the headline act for the launch of Virgin's regional airline. His antics, waving flags and poking his head out of a plane's cockpit, came almost three years to the day after Borghetti had taken the reins at the airline. 'Qantas made the biggest mistake by not making him their chief executive,' Branson gushed to journalists in a marquee on the tarmac at Perth Airport. 'He came with a mission to prove Qantas wrong. He wouldn't say that himself, but I'm sure that's the case. We've been delighted that he has gone all out to show they made a dreadful mistake.'[3] Branson was right. Borghetti would not utter in public what Branson was keen to mention. But it was clear he had been given every incentive five years earlier to prove a point.

As they countered each other's moves in the domestic market, the battle between Borghetti and Joyce was costing both Qantas and Virgin dearly. Virgin posted profits in only one of its first three years under Borghetti, while Qantas slumped to its first loss since privatisation in 1995 under Joyce. 'They are both bleeding money unnecessarily,' a former airline executive said. 'It is egos, and it always has been in the airline industry. But in this case, there is a bit too much pride as well. There are only two airline groups [in the domestic] market and the fact that neither is making money is criminally insane. They can both be making money tomorrow.'[4] The increase in flights had escalated into all-out war between the pair a year earlier. Qantas had increased frequencies on domestic routes as it sought to repel Virgin's attempt to entice its lucrative corporate customers. It boosted services during peak hours on key business routes between Sydney, Melbourne and Brisbane, while reinstating Boeing 747-400 jumbos on the Sydney–Perth route and putting more A330 planes on the Melbourne–Perth run. For travellers, it was a godsend. Qantas' vow to aggressively defend its 65 per cent share of the domestic market resulted in the airlines heavily discounting fares. As a result, the earnings of both airlines went into freefall. 'It is game-on in the domestic market,' Matt Crowe, a Commonwealth Bank transport analyst, said. 'They are about to get a price war with Virgin and this is certainly pretty tough for earnings.'[5]

More than a decade earlier, Geoff Dixon had coined the 'line-in-the-sand' strategy as he sought to fend off Virgin Blue's advances. 'I get a stick every morning and go out on the beach and I change the line on the sand,' Dixon quipped in early 2002. 'It's a very fluid line in the sand.'[6] Under Joyce, the defence of its market share became one he would not budge an inch on. His line in the sand stood at a 65 per cent share of the domestic market for Qantas and Jetstar. Joyce's right-hand man, Lyell Strambi, later raised the challenge to Borghetti when he warned that Qantas and Jetstar would put on two planes for each one Virgin added in the domestic market. To critics, Qantas was forewarning its competitor. 'You never put an inviolate line in the sand – no army ever did that. Rommel was a genius in strategic withdrawals and Montgomery was not stupid enough to say we need to hold our line in the sand,' said Peter Stainlay, a former Qantas deputy chief executive, in reference to the desert campaign in North Africa during World War II. 'Qantas is like being in a battle without air support. D-day without air support could have turned out very ugly.'[7] Unbeknown to the Qantas executives in 2013, their line was to later become like France's Maginot Line in the early days of World War II.

With Qantas under assault, Albanese signed off on a letter of comfort for the airline on August 2, just days before the Rudd Government went into caretaker mode in the lead-up to the 2013 federal election. 'I was surprised by your advice that the ratings agencies have, to date, not considered the company as meeting the threshold tests,' he wrote in his confidential letter of comfort to Joyce. 'Whilst recognising that the ratings agency's determinations are not a matter for government consideration, I would expect the government's long-term and ongoing recognition of the critical importance of the company to the economic and social fabric of the country to be an important element of the ratings agencies' deliberations.'[8] Ironically, Albanese also highlighted to Joyce how the government had 'explicitly recognised' the importance of Qantas to the economy when he grounded the fleet in 2011. While Joyce was the recipient of the letter, the intended targets were the ratings agencies, which were now furnished with the knowledge that the government tacitly stood behind the national carrier. The Australian taxpayers' discreet backing did not go nearly as far as Qantas wanted but it was nonetheless a helping hand, and something not available to its rival.

Three weeks later, at its annual earnings results, the need for a letter of comfort stood in marked contrast to what Qantas was telling investors. The airline's shares rallied 14 per cent after it cut debt and costs, lifted its bottom line back into the black and resumed a buyback of up to $100 million of its stock. Qantas had been privately pleading for help while in public it was relatively upbeat about its performance. A day later, Virgin slumped to a $98 million annual loss. But concerns mounted within Qantas' senior ranks when they learned that Air New Zealand, Etihad and Singapore Airlines had set aside a $90 million loan for Virgin to draw down if it was needed in the war of attrition.

As Qantas resumed buying back shares in a sign its fortunes were sound, it was quietly stepping up its lobbying of the new Abbott Government for help. Joyce had installed a new man in Canberra in July to lay the groundwork for a renewed campaign. Andrew Parker, a one-time adviser to former Liberal leader John Hewson, was hired from Emirates where he had been a right-hand man to its veteran boss, Tim Clark. Parker replaced as Qantas chief government lobbyist Olivia Wirth, who became its marketing boss while retaining oversight of corporate affairs. Although Qantas insisted it was a promotion for Wirth, it was interpreted as a way of allaying concerns within Coalition ranks about her relationship with Paul Howes, the national secretary of the Australian Workers' Union. Howes, who at twenty-six had become the youngest leader of one of the country's largest and oldest unions, rose to national prominence in 2010 when he helped remove Kevin Rudd as prime minister and installed Julia Gillard. He represented the enemy for the Coalition.

Wirth had been central to Qantas' handling of politicians for several years. In the aftermath of the Qantas grounding in 2011, she and her team had sought to rebuild damaged relations with the Gillard Government. They had identified the most receptive politicians to lobby before working their way through to the least. All the while, she had kept Clifford away from Qantas' efforts in Canberra and minimised Joyce's dealings with the politicians before she thought it was time to wheel them out.

In early October 2013, Joyce, the Qantas chief financial officer Gareth Evans, Jetstar boss Jayne Hrdlicka and other executives walked into a hotel on Waikiki Beach in Honolulu. It was a one-night stopover on the way from Seattle to Melbourne to showcase Jetstar's first state-of-the-art Boeing 787 Dreamliner. A delegation of equities analysts and journalists were also on the trip. As they lined up to check in, news spread like wildfire among the executives that Virgin had announced a complex deal in the US to refinance twenty-four planes. They quickly pulled their smart phones out of their pockets to get a handle on what Virgin was up to and what the implications might be for both its rival and their own company. It highlighted the level of hysteria that constantly gripped Qantas' senior echelons about Virgin. At first glance, it appeared as though Virgin was resorting to desperate means to refinance. Smiles quickly returned to the Qantas people's faces as they checked in for a night in Honolulu. A month later, their hopes were dashed. Borghetti announced that Virgin would raise $350 million from investors in a deal underwritten by Air New Zealand, Singapore Airlines and Etihad. The financial footwork allowed the three major shareholders to further boost their grip on Virgin to as much as 70 per cent of the share register. In return for them digging deeper into their pockets, Virgin would offer each a seat on its board.[9] Importantly, it sent a clear message that they stood firmly behind it in the fight with Qantas. Virgin's tanks had been refuelled. Air New Zealand executives joked to themselves that they were now part of the 'coalition of the willing'.

The injection of new money was a pivotal moment in the fight between Joyce and Borghetti. Qantas faced a much longer battle than Joyce had anticipated. Now, he could not expect Borghetti to eventually retreat from the price war by scaling back Virgin's growth plans. Backed into a corner, Joyce pulled off his gloves in a very public fashion days later. In a well-orchestrated campaign that had had its genesis two years earlier, a letter was leaked to journalists in which Joyce demanded the Abbott Government block Virgin's $300 million capital raising because it amounted to a 'foreign takeover' by three state-backed airlines. Joyce claimed that the pumping of more money into Virgin by Air New Zealand, Etihad and Singapore Airlines threatened Qantas' very survival. However, he did not reveal that Qantas had gained tacit support months earlier from the Rudd Government in the form of a letter of comfort. As much as Virgin's three shareholders had some form of state backing, Qantas had quietly gained its own helping hand from the federal government.

The leak to the *Financial Review* of the letter from Joyce to the prime minister, federal transport minister and state governments had the desired effect, setting off a wave of media coverage about Qantas' plight in the days that followed. Qantas wanted a review of the motives of what it described as a 'virtual takeover of Virgin Australia by foreign airlines'. So large was the threat that Joyce emailed Qantas' 33 000-strong workforce urging a call to action, launched a public petition and dashed to Canberra to again press the urgency of the matter with politicians, including the treasurer, Joe Hockey, and the transport minister, Warren Truss. 'The agenda of these foreign airlines is to terminally weaken Qantas and Jetstar, force us to shrink our international business and sacrifice jobs,' he wrote in the email to staff.[10] Borghetti immediately went on the counterattack, lambasting the claims and hiring high-profile corporate lawyer Leon Zwier to decide whether Joyce could be sued. The descent into a verbal stoush revealed much about the battle between the two men.

The public jousting was just the tip of what was going on behind the scenes. With a new government in power, Qantas had a chance to press its case again for financial support. 'The government was new and I suppose we were all starting to feel one another out a bit about what our attitudes were to these sorts of issues,' Truss recalled. 'Joe [Hockey] was always of the view that when it came to Qantas, it was a fundamental part of the Australian economy.'[11] The helping hand Qantas was seeking was similar to the assistance the federal government had provided to Australia's banks during the global financial crisis. With the stakes rising, politicians were under pressure from both sides while journalists were backgrounded and selective drops were made. In Canberra, Qantas and Virgin targeted politicians who were sympathetic to their cause. The treasurer was top of the list within Cabinet. Although she had relinquished the reins as Qantas' chief lobbyist, Wirth's links to Hockey stretched back years to when she advised him as tourism minister in the Howard Government. An email trail revealed Hockey's office had kept an unusually close eye on the two airlines for a federal treasurer. The same day that Virgin sought to raise funds to give it the firepower to take on Qantas, a spate of emails were fired off between the treasurer's chief of staff, Grant Lovett, and a senior bureaucrat in Treasury.[12] The emails revealed high-level discussions up to November 27, less than two weeks after Joyce's letter to the Abbott Government.

On that day in late November, Hockey strode onto a stage at the InterContinental hotel in central Sydney. Calling for a national debate on Qantas' future, the treasurer flagged changes to the foreign-ownership restrictions on the airline or the possibility of government support. 'We still need to properly deal with the aviation transformation that has occurred in Australia, and deal with the legacy of Qantas continuing to have shareholding restrictions when their competition does not have exactly the same,' he told the Australia–New Zealand leadership forum.[13] While his comments were portrayed as off the cuff, they appeared to be anything but to an audience that included Qantas' government lobbyists and one of its public-relations staff. Their presence to hear Hockey raised eyebrows among others in the audience. Hockey had set the ball rolling as Qantas piled the pressure on the government to act before Christmas. That same day in late November, Albanese's letter of comfort to Qantas was leaked to journalists, giving credence to Hockey's calls for a national debate about the airline. While Hockey was a big supporter of Qantas, the transport minister, Warren Truss, was less enamoured of the cries for help. 'We don't want to be bankers for airlines,' Truss declared.[14] His office privately moaned about Qantas' backroom dealings. At its core, Qantas' strategy was about painting a doomsday scenario to engender government support.

Paranoia gripped the senior echelons of both airlines. Virgin became increasingly nervous about the inroads Qantas was making in Canberra. Some of the more agitated conversations Truss had during the period were with Borghetti. To counter his rival's claims, Borghetti publicly went on the attack by sending an open letter to ministers in which he criticised the prospect of government support for Qantas. Days later, the prime minister dampened expectations the government would offer a helping hand. The debate about financial assistance was quickly becoming entangled with calls for a loosening of the foreign-ownership limits on Qantas. They were different arguments. The Qantas Sale Act was a legacy of the airline's shift from government to private hands two decades earlier. Qantas' chief gripe was that different rules applied to its business than Virgin's. Under the 1992 act, foreign investment in Qantas was capped at 49 per cent, total ownership by overseas airlines at 35 per cent and a single foreign investor at 25 per cent. Qantas had a fair claim to make for the ownership restrictions to be lifted to allow it to be better able to attract foreign investment. But that was a different argument from gaining special assistance from the Australian taxpayer. Qantas moaned about the need for a level playing field yet it was asking for help its rival would not gain. 'Qantas was concerned about its future liabilities, its aircraft orders, debts coming forward, its rundown in cash reserves so that they were uncertain whether they could survive another shock,' Truss recalled. 'At some stages it reached almost hysterical proportions.'[15]

Joyce was playing to an era that placed a high value on a national flag carrier. However, top of mind for many travellers in the twenty-first century were cheap fares or, if they were going to pay top dollar for travel, superior comfort in the skies. For years the airline had been riding on the coat-tails of its legacy as a national carrier, be it flying rescue missions to Bali, Cairo or Darwin or injecting itself into the national psyche through slick marketing. Travellers' loyalty to one of the most recognised brands in Australia had become tenuous with the advent of intense competition. It could no longer command a premium over rivals who flew newer planes and boasted high-class in-flight products.

In early December, Qantas dropped a bombshell. Joyce warned that the airline would be forced to axe at least 1000 staff and consider major asset sales due to a slump in earnings. In sending a mayday call, he revealed a scenario in which Qantas was under attack from competitors in both its domestic and international markets. 'The challenges we now face are immense,' he warned.[16] He laid the blame squarely on Virgin, which in his view had been allowed to get away with creating an 'unprecedented distortion' of the domestic market. However, Joyce was not revealing in public what he was urging behind the scenes: financial assistance from Canberra in the form of a stand-by debt facility. In highlighting the urgency of its predicament, Qantas upped the pressure on the Abbott Government to put its concerns to Cabinet before Christmas.

A day after Qantas' profit warning, one of the big two ratings agencies cut Qantas to junk status.[17] Despite Joyce's cries, neither Truss nor Abbott showed signs of budging. 'Qantas is still a very strong business. It's got lots of assets. It's got a lot of goodwill. It's got lots of advantages in the domestic market,' Truss said at the time. Hockey also pulled back from his earlier position by indicating that the government would not be rushing to assist a private company.[18] Earlier in the week, former federal treasurer Peter Costello had urged the ministers not to buckle to Qantas' pleas. He reminded them that Qantas had mounted the strongest opposition to a government bailout when Ansett was on death's door. Politicians on both sides of the divide had become weary of what many perceived as crocodile tears from Qantas over the previous decade. 'There was a well-established history of the airlines being close to governments and talking about their problems,' Truss said later. 'I suppose there was a *Boy Who Cried Wolf* view about the frequency of those visits, so the airlines over time would have to put a stronger and stronger case that this really was Armageddon.'[19] With its cries for help failing to win over Abbott and Truss, Qantas decided to go to greater lengths to ensure its message was heard at the highest levels of government. On December 9, Abbott walked into the airline's first-class lounge at Sydney Airport to wait for a flight to South Africa to join other world leaders for the funeral of Nelson Mandela in Johannesburg. There to meet him was Joyce, who pleaded the airline's case directly to the prime minister.[20]

Months earlier, Hockey had declared an end to the age of entitlement. The government had resisted calls for assistance from fruit canner SPC Ardmona. Early December also marked the end of the road for another Australian icon. American automotive behemoth General Motors announced that it would walk away from manufacturing Holden cars in Australia by 2017. Its departure would lead to the axing of 2900 jobs at Holden's plants and threaten thousands more who were involved indirectly in the manufacture of cars. The confirmation from its masters in Detroit brought to an end years of uncertainty about the future of Holden's assembly line in Adelaide and engine plant in Melbourne's Fishermans Bend. Holden had started car-making in 1948, and its demise followed Ford's decision to retreat from Australia. Their exit cast doubt over Qantas' ability to cry for government help. Having built the first 'Australian car', Holden was as much Brand Australia as the Flying Kangaroo. A big helping hand for Qantas would be a hard call for a government to make when it had let the car-maker call time. Since it had taken office in September 2013, the Abbott Government had been signalling that it wanted to stand for minimal interference in the running of businesses and a freeing-up of markets. It was survival of the fittest. Assistance for Qantas would blow a gaping hole in its argument for an end to the age of entitlement, however it was spun.

Early in the new year, Joyce turned up with Evans and several other executives to Alan Davidson Oval in the inner-Sydney suburb of Alexandria. He had been searching for ways to involve the Qantas pilots in the bigger picture. The social cricket matches between three sides made up of Qantas pilots and management were seen as a chance to rebuild relations. Joyce, who preferred Gaelic football and soccer, watched on from the sidelines as Evans, an Englishman with a Welsh name, showed his talents as a bowler. As much as they tried, the chasm between Qantas management and the pilots appeared vast. 'There is still very little trust there,' one of the senior pilots said after the cricket games. 'It is not easy to rebuild a bridge between the two groups.'

It summed up relations between management and much of its front-line staff, and was not helped by the fact that Joyce had left the prospect of deep cost-cutting hanging over Qantas' 33 000-strong workforce for weeks. He would not reveal his hand until he delivered the airline's half-year earnings results in late February.

Qantas was also sending mixed messages. Joyce had painted a picture for politicians and the wider public of an airline fighting for its survival as state-backed carriers poured more cash into Virgin. In the wake of Moody's joining Standard & Poor's in cutting Qantas to junk status, the airline's chief financial officer had sought to reassure investors that the airline was a 'strong business with a track record for disciplined financial management'. Compared with the rhetoric about an airline in peril, it left politicians and the public wondering who they should believe.

As the countdown to Joyce revealing his hand neared, Qantas renewed its lobbying campaign in early February. In a closed-door briefing in Canberra to a group of Coalition MPs and senators, Joyce foreshadowed the magnitude of the extra costs he planned to strip out of Qantas. He emphasised that they would be proportionately greater than those of American Airlines when it had been placed in bankruptcy protection in 2011. But he was at pains to distance Qantas from Holden and fruit canner SPC Ardmona, which had failed to gain aid from the Abbott Government. 'Quite obviously, Qantas is not Holden,' Joyce told the audience, making special mention of Hockey, who had led the debate about the 'uneven playing field in Australian aviation'.[21] A day later, Hockey signalled that the government would throw Qantas a lifeline in the form of a debt guarantee. His reasoning for making an exception for Qantas was fourfold: the foreign-ownership limits imposed on the airline under the Qantas Sale Act; its role as an essential public service; its attempt to get its house in order; and the fact it was competing against a rival whose large shareholders were backed by governments. Hockey's stance gave Qantas hope. At Virgin, it stoked fears that its rival was about to gain a leg up from the government and triggered a fresh wave of lobbying of ministers. 'Any form of government assistance to Qantas is a means to enabling them to reinstate their monopoly,' Virgin countered.[22] Regional Express, a small airline that serviced regional destinations in several states, also warned a debt guarantee for Qantas would give it an unfair advantage.

On February 27, Joyce revealed the extent of his plans to trim costs over three years. At the Westin in central Sydney, he announced Qantas would axe 5000 jobs – or 15 per cent of its workforce – sell or defer fifty planes and freeze wages. His decision for Qantas to ditch the Perth–Singapore route due to large losses highlighted the shrinking of its international network. In six years, it had axed twenty-two international routes, including Sydney–Beijing and Melbourne–Auckland–Los Angeles, and introduced just four new runs. In contrast, Jetstar had launched eighteen new international routes over a similar timeframe. Joyce also revealed the cost of the battle with Virgin after Qantas posted a $235 million bottom-line loss, the largest since Paul Keating had cut the airline free from government ownership almost two decades earlier. 'We have already made tough decisions and no one should doubt that there are more ahead,' Joyce declared.[23]

Later that day, Tony Abbott effectively dashed Qantas' hopes of financial assistance. 'Governments do not save businesses,' the prime minister told parliament. 'What we do for one business, in fairness, we have to make available for all businesses.'[24] Hockey had been rolled, and in the process Qantas' hopes were dashed. With help from accounting firm PricewaterhouseCoopers, the federal Treasury and the Department of Infrastructure sifted through a mountain of paperwork to uncover Qantas' real position. 'The government had done some due diligence on what we thought Qantas' position really was – how imminent a collapse was,' Truss recalled. 'It certainly indicated that there were stresses within their balance sheet but we didn't feel a collapse was imminent. We weren't going to bankroll a capacity war for one of the airlines – even if one of them was Qantas.'[25] The only consolation for Joyce was that the government was willing to relax the restriction on foreign ownership of the airline. But it would be too little, too late. Joyce was adamant that Qantas' plight was not of its own making. 'There is nothing anybody in Qantas has done that has caused this issue,' he declared. Instead, he pinned the blame on three factors: a 46 per cent rise in capacity on routes in and out of Australia since 2009, fuel prices at record levels, and a competitor in the domestic market backed by state-owned airlines. 'It is just the fact that the environment has had a perfect storm against Qantas in every aspect,' he said.[26] Leigh Clifford, too, was not shy of sheeting some of the blame at previous management. 'In the benign economic conditions of the mid-2000s, when competition was limited, there was little appetite for serious reform at Qantas,' the chairman wrote in a newspaper column.[27]

Capping off a bad week, a Qantas A380 and one of its Boeing 747 jumbos scraped their wingtips as they were towed out of a hangar at Los Angeles International Airport. This forced the cancellation of two flights to Australia while repairs were made to the damaged aircraft. The scrap was a minor bingle but it was the last thing the airline needed. It highlighted the unpredictable nature of the industry, which never knew when it would be buffeted by another challenge. The following Monday, Cabinet considered the request from Qantas for a stand-by debt facility, or a $3 billion unsecured loan. Qantas got the same answer. 'They asked for it; we thought about it; and we rejected it,' Abbott declared later.[28] Qantas' hopes were finally dead. For all of the lobbying over months, Joyce, Clifford and the rest of the inner circle had little to show for their tactics. Once again, a high-stakes campaign had strained relations with some of the airline's key stakeholders. The failure to win support resulted in Joyce changing his rhetoric. Four months after painting a dire scenario for Qantas, he stressed that the airline 'continues to be an extremely healthy company' and emphasised the importance of the company holding its 65 per cent share of the domestic market.[29] The campaigning had again alienated many Australians, including those in powerful positions. 'Leigh Clifford needs to toughen up. Dixon and co. had to live through the Iraq War, September 11, SARS and a huge spike in fuel costs. Nothing too level about those playing fields,' wrote veteran media buyer Harold Mitchell in a newspaper column. 'I'm a great supporter of Qantas. But I won't travel Qantas again while the current chairman and CEO are there.'[30]

Project Harbour – the codename for Qantas' plan to gain government assistance – served as a reminder of how big business conducts campaigns. Apart from intense lobbying of political powerbrokers, spinning the message in the public domain was a major part of the tactics employed to further Qantas' interests. The game is usually played by identifying a media outlet that will give the company's version of events maximum coverage. Documents are leaked to a journalist whom the company believes will treat it favourably or give its cause prominent treatment. It becomes a win for both sides. In Qantas' case, it gains public attention, often with screaming headlines on the front page of a newspaper, while the journalist claims an 'exclusive' story. The strategy is played to varying degrees by large corporations as they serve their interests. The loser in this high-stakes game is usually the general public.

The botched attempt to gain assistance also raised questions about Joyce's tenure as Qantas chief executive. However, the immediate calls for a change of leadership came from those on the periphery, such as union officials and politicians. The people who mattered in deciding his future – Qantas' large institutional shareholders – remained silent, suggesting that they supported him seeing through his plans to strip out billions of dollars of costs. 'It is an industry issue – shareholders understand that,' a Qantas director said. 'Some of the shareholders have a good understanding of this business.'[31] The lack of public utterances from large shareholders indicated they were content that their messages to the Qantas board had been heard. Fund managers with large holdings in a company tend to speak out in public only when they feel that the company is not listening to them in private. Few fund managers held long positions in Qantas. For most large institutional investors, it had become a stock they dipped in and out of. It meant that Qantas management was less likely to be held to account by the people who could influence the airline's course.

To some airline veterans, Qantas was caught in a spider web. For years it had searched for ways to break free from its predicament but at every move it remained entangled. The strategic pressures on Qantas are immense, and the CEO's role is one of the toughest gigs in corporate Australia. Qantas has many stakeholders, each wanting something different for its own ends. In reality, the airline had beaten the odds to last as long as it had. Most so-called 'legacy airlines' in the United States have gone through bankruptcy protection, while other countries' flag carriers, such as Air New Zealand, have been bailed out by their governments. 'The threats are that large. The Australian government policy could be characterised as holding Qantas' nose just 1 millimetre above the waterline, and taking your benefit of cheap airfares,' a former Qantas executive said. 'The price of that is Qantas has to adjust to the many realities – that adjustment is relentless and painful every step of the way.'[32]

In the weeks following Joyce's radical overhaul, the first of the staff whose jobs were axed walked out of the door at Qantas for the last time. The departures included twenty-six senior managers, including the chief operating officer of Qantas' domestic operations, Matt Lee, Qantas International security chief Steve Tregarthen, senior engineering manager Gavin Harris, Jetstar executive strategy manager Max Kownatzki, and government lobbyist Euan Robertson.[33] As part of the shake-up, Qantas' domestic business cut regional general manager roles, resulting in the exit of long-time executives Ian Gay, Allan Williams and Ken Ryan. But the bloodletting throughout the airline did not extend to the top echelon of Qantas management, despite its ill-fated campaign to convince the government to furnish the airline with financial assistance and a muted response from investors to the $2 billion cost-cutting program. It left a sour taste in the mouths of many Qantas staff from the second tier of management all the way down to front-line staff. As they walked out the door for the final time, many began to question what the strategy was beyond stripping out billions of dollars in costs. 'They created the narrative without having any substance behind the narrative. It was corporate spin rather than how to get from here to there,' said a Qantas senior manager who joined the exodus. 'I am not disparaging of the company – I recognise the industry and the market it operates in are completely fucked. It has delivered some good initiatives but it hasn't delivered results and it has gone backwards. Alan does a good job of blaming external factors for not delivering your strategy. You can't blame them for not delivering the solutions.'[34]

While the axing of mid-ranking management and back-office jobs happened quickly, the culling of thousands of jobs from Qantas' large unionised workforce required significant negotiations. The airline's top echelons tried to enlist help from Greg Combet, a minister in the Gillard Government, to act as a link between the unions and management over the large cost-cutting initiatives and retrenchments. Combet was well versed in the politics of aviation from his high-profile role as secretary of the Australian Council of Trade Unions at the time of the Ansett collapse more than a decade earlier. He had first become a household name during the waterfront dispute in 1998 as the face of the unions in their battle with Chris Corrigan's Patrick Corporation. But in the end, the approach from Qantas to Combet amounted to nothing.

Qantas was also to undergo its first redundancy program for pilots in more than forty years. The retirement of its ageing Boeing 747 and 767 aircraft meant it would have more pilots on its books than it needed, which reflected the shrinking of its network. For a number of pilots close to retirement, this was a godsend as they walked away with a year's pay. One left with a redundancy cheque weeks before his sixty-fifth birthday. For a small number of younger pilots, an uncertain future beckoned as they walked out of a company they had become attached to over decades. 'You miss the people. You miss the flying. All pilots become a bit like adrenaline junkies. Like all drugs, you have to give them up eventually,' said Ian Woods, a Qantas 747 pilot and former president of the pilots' union, shortly after leaving the airline he had worked at for thirty-four years. 'The last chapter for the airline is whether the contraction of Qantas International continues. It is not dead yet but it is harder to breathe life into it the longer it goes on without a change. I don't want Qantas to fail. You have to change the strategy, the legislation and the manpower cost base. To get them changed, you need new leadership.'[35] To many younger pilots, those departing had enjoyed the airline's best years and were now walking away clutching large cheques and amazing memories of a bygone era.

In May 2014 Qantas finally blinked. Staring at a loss expected to top $1 billion, the airline froze capacity in the domestic market for the first three months of the new financial year. It was a bitter pill to chew for Joyce and his executives. Five months earlier, Gareth Evans had warned in a newspaper column that abandoning its line in the sand at a 65 per cent share would 'effectively be waving the white flag'.[36] 'Anyone who advocates this kind of approach does not understand the way business works. We plan to keep strengthening our competitive advantages, not walking away from them,' he wrote. But the Qantas executives had little choice. Large investors became increasingly anxious about the strategy leading to bigger losses. A minor consolation came two months later when a compromise deal was agreed between the Coalition and Labor to relax the ownership restrictions on Qantas. However, this removed the limits only on a single overseas investor owning more than 25 per cent and foreign airlines 35 per cent. The key requirement capping foreign ownership at 49 per cent remained intact.

Dressed in a dark suit, Joyce strode into an auditorium at Qantas' revamped headquarters near Sydney Airport with Evans in late August. The pair looked sombre as they stood motionless in front of photographers for several seconds. Less than an hour earlier, Qantas had lodged its annual accounts with the stock exchange. They revealed a $2.8 billion bottom-line loss, the worst in Qantas' 94-year history. A day after Air New Zealand had delivered a $NZ262 million annual profit, the bottom-line result for Qantas was far worse than anyone had expected. Standing in front of a podium, Joyce started his explanation for one of the largest losses in global aviation history. 'This morning Qantas announced an underlying profit,' he began. Quickly realising his slip, he corrected himself to tell the room full of journalists that the airline had in fact made an underlying pre-tax loss of $646 million for the year. While much of the bottom-line loss was due to writing down the value of its international fleet of A380, A330 and Boeing 747 aircraft to their market value, the sea of red ink highlighted the cost of his strategy in the domestic market and its foray into Asia. 'There's no doubt that today's numbers are confronting,' Joyce said. 'But they represent the year that is past, and we have now come through the worst.'[37] It was a major reversal of fortunes from 2008, when Qantas had struck a record profit of almost $1 billion. Joyce pinned the blame for the latest loss on fuel costs and competitors flooding international and domestic markets.

The massive write-down in the value of Qantas' international fleet was a way for Joyce to clear the decks. He offered investors hope by forecasting that Qantas would return to pre-tax profits in the first six months of the new financial year – typically when the airline earned the bulk of its earnings. 'We believe the worst is over for us now,' he declared. His crystal ball lay in Qantas' forward bookings for the next few months, which gave him enough confidence to forecast earnings for the first half. Investors focused on the short-term horizon saw a buying opportunity for a stock that had been languishing for months. However, concerns about the longer-term prognosis for the Flying Kangaroo remained. Joyce's plan for Qantas seemed to lack a longer-term vision beyond the $2 billion cost-cutting program. His so-called 'transformation plan' was about reducing Qantas' cost base to make it more competitive but it risked diminishing further its products and services.

Joyce's challenge was to convince investors, his workforce and the wider Australian public sceptical of his rhetoric. Over the years he had been long on promises but short on delivery. A year after declaring that Qantas' international flying arm was 'on track towards our target of a return to profit' by 2014–15, he moved the goalposts by declaring that 'we are not going to be giving an expectation of when it will be back to break even'. He had altered his targets for good reason. The latest annual result had revealed that Qantas' international losses had blown out to almost half a billion dollars, from $246 million a year earlier. Joyce was also no longer resolute about holding a 65 per cent share of the domestic market. In fact, Qantas would extend the freeze on capacity for another three months. He refuted suggestions it was a strategic mistake of the board and management to pursue a strategy focused on holding market share. The line-in-the-sand strategy had stripped hundreds of millions of dollars from what historically had been a highly profitable part of the business. 'You have to look at the strategic position in the domestic market and say, is Qantas still number one for business and has it maintained 80 per cent revenue of the corporate market? The strategy has been right,' Joyce said. 'People in the past have actually questioned whether Jetstar was the right strategy when we first started it.'

The four-pillar strategy he had rolled out in 2011 also seemed to ring hollow three years later. Jetstar's rapid expansion in Asia was spluttering, with losses from its offshoots in Singapore, Vietnam and Japan hitting $110 million. Jetstar Hong Kong was still grounded almost eighteen months after it had been supposed to be flying. The plans for an ultra-premium airline in Asia had been shelved in early 2012, less than a year after they were made public. The rhetoric in 2011 about building a 'strong, viable business' did not match the financial reality that now confronted Qantas. An aim for Qantas' international and domestic flying businesses to exceed their cost of capital by 2016 had quietly been dropped from the executive team's talking points. Joyce also told journalists that Qantas' alliance with Emirates was 'absolutely fantastic for us' but declined to show tangible financial evidence to back up the statement. Earlier in the year, the campaign to gain financial assistance from the federal government had also failed, and in the process Qantas had suffered the ignominy of a downgrade in its all-important investment-grade credit rating to junk status.

Qantas executives blamed everything and everyone else but themselves. The question was to what extent Qantas' losses were self-inflicted, and it again shone the spotlight on Joyce's tenure. 'There are always people out after my neck,' Joyce said. 'It hasn't changed for a long time.' He was battle-hardened, and his ability to withstand knocks could not be doubted. Under attack, his senior management team had tightened its defences around its leader. The board was also hitched to the strategy of the man they had selected six years earlier. Those integral to him remaining in the top job, such as Clifford and his fellow directors, as well as large shareholders such as Balanced Equity Management, would be admitting their own failings if they forced him out. Likewise, Joyce's loyal lieutenants would face an uncertain future if he went. They owed their positions to him. A new chief executive would be certain to push the broom through the top ranks at Qantas. They had been at the helm during some of the darkest days in Qantas' long history.

A day after Joyce revealed the record loss, Borghetti strolled into a room in the Four Seasons Hotel, just a stone's throw from Virgin's corporate head office overlooking the waterfront in Sydney's Circular Quay. Out the window, commuter trains glided to and from the nearby station. Standing at the podium flanked by teleprompters, Borghetti outlined Virgin's biggest loss since the airline had begun flying 14 years earlier. The $356 million loss was three times greater than the year before, and revealed that the battle for domestic passengers had been as punishing for Virgin as for Qantas. But Borghetti again had a surprise for investors, unveiling the sale of a slice of Virgin's loyalty program, Velocity, to a private-equity firm. This helped to overshadow the loss and upstage his rival.

Borghetti did not shy away from subtle digs at Joyce. 'It is the war that had to happen, I suppose, when you have a dominant player who wants to ensure he maintains his position,' he said of the battle in the domestic market. He also sought to contrast his strategy for Virgin with that pursued by Qantas. 'In aviation you can do one of two things. You can either go down the path that most airlines seem to go in times of trouble, and that is slash and burn. And inevitably no matter how much you try, you will impact the service, and you will impact the product,' he declared. 'Or you can go through a process that says we will absolutely be prudent on costs . . . but not at the expense of the consumer experience because the consumer will choose you or someone else.'[38]

After one of the most costly battles in the history of Australian aviation, Borghetti and Joyce showed no sign of relenting in what had become a deeply personal battle. It had become a question of who would last the distance – an Italian or an Irish migrant. The sea of red ink at both airlines highlighted the impact of the contest between the two men. By late 2014, the scorecard was firmly in Borghetti's favour. The record loss for Qantas capped off one of the most tumultuous periods in its 94-year history. Without a doubt, it reflected intense competition on international routes that Qantas had once dominated, and a pitched battle in the domestic market against a major challenger steered by Joyce's main adversary. Depending on one's frame of reference, a multitude of other reasons can be given for Qantas' predicament, ranging from management missteps to a desire by successive governments to open up the country's aviation market to a workforce unwilling to bend to their bosses' will. 'The genesis of Qantas' problems internationally really stemmed from the government's decision to open the skies. It's the right decision, absolutely, for the people of Australia but not necessarily if you are a shareholder of Qantas,' said Grant Fenn, a former Qantas strategy chief and deputy chief financial officer. 'You only have to be out by a fraction in timing, pricing or whatever and you can lose bucketloads of business.'[39] As Qantas nears its centenary, the future of its international arm, which once flew to a long list of overseas destinations such as Rome, Frankfurt, Beijing and Sapporo, is bleak. Competitors such as Emirates, Etihad, Singapore Airlines and Cathay Pacific have stolen a march on Qantas that will be difficult to catch. The inability by successive management teams to find a suitable airline partner to help overcome Qantas' tag as an end-of-the-line carrier is partly responsible.

But it is also a story of a corporate tragedy as big personalities have battled for control of the airline's future. If nothing else, Qantas serves as a reminder of the need to handle succession with care. Qantas had become a company of tribes whose divisions deepened over time. So-called legacy airlines around the world have poor track records setting up low-cost offshoots. Many tried the experiment only to fail – twice, in the case of many large American airlines. Qantas was able to avoid the worst of its peers' problems with budget airlines: Jetstar expanded aggressively, turning profits and helping Qantas rebuff Virgin's advance. 'Qantas' right to exist really revolved around its brand strength and the fact that it could command, whether it be internationally or domestically, a significantly higher fare. That premium offset any cost differential. There was always a question of how long that would be sustainable,' Fenn said. 'There had been really no other full-service airline that had been able to run with a low cost carrier and keep that premium. Qantas was doing that because it was very carefully managed. But there was always a question about what would be the future of Qantas – would it be Qantas or would it be Jetstar? And it was always in two camps.'[40]

Rod Eddington, the former chief executive of British Airways and briefly a Qantas director, believed in the rationale for setting up a new low-cost airline in the domestic market as a response to Virgin. However, he long harboured concerns about it leading to a loss of focus on reshaping Qantas. 'The problem with embracing the no-frills carrier is that you don't devote as much resource, in the enthusiasm to set up the new, to fix the old. It's much more fun setting up a new business than to fix the old one. Fixing the old one involves tackling outdated work practices; tackling tough union opposition,' he said. 'I spent my first five-and-a-half years at BA doing that. When I got there we had 65 000 staff and when I left we had less than 50 000. We had to make some radical changes.'[41] Jetstar grew way beyond its original intentions. At one stage, its executives had ambitions for Jetstar to fly as far afield as Greece and Italy. Eddington believed Qantas would survive due to the strength of its domestic network but conceded that the days of it maintaining an extensive international network appeared over. 'It will survive, but the question is in what form will it survive?' he said. 'At the heart of Qantas will be the domestic airline, not the international airline. That might disappoint many Australians but the brutal facts of life are that Qantas is no longer the dominant national carrier it once was. When I first got into the industry it was all about Pan American Airways, TWA and Northwest Airlines. The industry has changed enormously and in our part of the world it is the dominant hubs in the Middle East and Asia that have helped transform it.' Qantas' retreat has mirrored that of European airlines on long-haul routes to Australia over the previous two decades. In May 2014, British Airways became the only European airline to still fly to Australia after Virgin Atlantic withdrew from the route.

Halfway through the second decade of the twenty-first century Qantas still dominates Australia's domestic market. The market has been a natural duopoly. The hope for Qantas is that a lasting truce will be declared in its battle with Virgin as both nurse their wounds and are once again able to turn substantial profits. However, Borghetti is forever mindful of the need to keep adapting to a fast-changing game, and he remains intent on eating away at his rival's dominance of the domestic market. It raises the prospect of the market returning to a more even split, like that shared between Qantas and Ansett in the 1990s.

The heady mix of personalities at the top played a key role in determining Qantas' flight path. The tenures of Joyce and Clifford have been marked by a highly confrontational approach. They have never shied away from pushing the thermonuclear button, which was highlighted by the grounding of the Qantas fleet in 2011. In the process, they have made enemies or, at the very least, strained their relationship with governments, the Qantas workforce, travellers and anyone who has questioned their strategy. Despite their approach, they had little to show for it. Major restructuring seldom happens successfully with a big stick. Joyce may have retained support from large institutional investors for his strategy, but his standing among many Australians was almost beyond repair. On the other side, the Qantas duo has faced equally determined individuals who were like jilted lovers as they sought to right the ledger. None could completely let go of an airline that had played such a major role in their lives.

Joyce served at Ansett towards the end of its days. He learnt first hand how easy it was for once-venerable airlines to go bust. In Qantas' case, politicians of either strip would be highly unlikely to allow Australia to lose its de facto flag carrier. It holds a special place in the country's identity. The airline founded by Hudson Fysh, Paul McGinness and Fergus McMaster is set to remain a feature of Australian skies, but as a shadow of its former self. By their nature, airlines are amazing examples of human endeavour but make for lousy businesses. The capacity of an airline to survive in a volatile sector relies on the agility and capability of its management team. Qantas is no different. The Qantas story has had many twists and turns. It has been one hell of a ride.

ENDNOTES

Prologue

1 Hudson Fysh, *Qantas Rising: The Autobiography of the Flying Fysh*, Angus & Robertson, 1965

2 Author interview with Rod Eddington, a former chief executive of British Airways and Ansett, May 15, 2014

Chapter 1

1 Author interview with Peter Gregg, a former Qantas chief financial officer, June 30, 2014

2 Author interview with Grant Fenn, a former Qantas deputy chief financial officer and strategy chief, August 27, 2014

3 Author interview with Trevor Jensen, a former Ansett chief pilot, July 28, 2014

4 Brad Norrington, 'Jobless win 11th-hour pay dispute', *Sydney Morning Herald*, September 15, 2001

5 Frank Walker, 'For Albert, delayed trip to Sydney proves fatal', *Sun Herald*, September 16, 2001

6 Author interview with Richard Cantor, a former Qantas dispatch duty manager, October 27, 2014

7 Author interview with Warren Truss, the deputy prime minister, October 16, 2014

8 Author interview with Rod Eddington, a former chief executive of British Airways and Ansett, August 19, 2014

9 Author interview with Peter Gregg, August 18, 2014

10 Lachlan Johnston, 'Branson nearly makes trading blue with hoax', *Australian Financial Review*, September 5, 2001

11 Emiliya Mychasuk and Sarah Crichton, 'Kiwi PM trudges home by propeller after protesters block her jets', *Sydney Morning Herald*, September 15, 2001

12 Author interview with Peter McLaughlin, a former Qantas executive, August 12, 2014

13 Katrina Nicholas, 'Cleared for take-off', *Australian Financial Review*, March 30, 2007

14 Author interview with Ian Woods, a former president of the Australian and International Pilots Association, October 12, 2014

15 Report from Cameron & Company to New Zealand's Treasury, July 2001

16 Letter from Geoff Dixon, Qantas chief executive, to the New Zealand Finance Minister, June 25, 2001

17 Jason Koutsoukis, 'How Howard killed off Ansett's bid for survival', *Australian Financial Review*, September 29, 2001

18 Geoff Easdown and Peter Wilms, *Ansett: The Collapse*, Lothian, 2002
19 Darren Goodsir and Brad Norrington, 'Ansett dead as wealthy saviours get cold feet', *Sydney Morning Herald*, February 28, 2002

Chapter 2

1 Author interview with Grant Fenn, a former Qantas deputy chief financial officer and strategy chief, August 27, 2014
2 Author interview with Peter Gregg, a former Qantas chief financial officer, June 30, 2014
3 Ibid.
4 Author interview with Grant Fenn, August 27, 2014
5 Darren Goodsir and Brian Robins, 'Watch your tail, Virgin warns Qantas', *Sydney Morning Herald*, March 13, 2002
6 Author interview with Peter Gregg, June 30, 2014
7 Author interview with Geoff Dixon, a former Qantas chief executive, March 2012
8 Author interview with Rod Eddington, a former chief executive of British Airways and Ansett, May 15, 2014
9 Malcolm Knox, 'Air pressure', *Sydney Morning Herald*, June 24, 2010
10 Steve Creedy, 'Jetstar's Joyce ready for the Virgin dogfight', *Australian*, May 24, 2004
11 Jane Boyle, 'Ansett gets new flight crew', *Australian Financial Review*, August 11, 2000
12 Author interview with Trevor Jensen, a former Ansett chief pilot, August 18, 2014
13 Author interview with Peter Gregg, August 19, 2014
14 Author interview with Chris Manning, a former Qantas chief pilot, August 15, 2014
15 Geoff Easdown, 'Qantas meets Virgin head on', *Herald Sun*, December 2, 2003
16 Selma Milovanovic and Kenneth Nguyen, 'Runway lights, cameras, action: Jetstar takes off', *The Age*, May 26, 2004
17 Author interview with a former Jetstar executive, May 9, 2014
18 Author interview with Grant Fenn, August 27, 2014
19 Author interview with another former Jetstar executive, May 9, 2013
20 Author interview with Chris Manning, August 15, 2014

Chapter 3

1 Author interview with Warren Truss, the deputy prime minister, October 16, 2014
2 Lisa Allen and Kean Wong, 'PM puts Qantas merger on table', *Australian Financial Review*, June 23, 2005
3 Angela Macdonald-Smith, 'Singapore open to a Qantas merger', *Bloomberg*, July 10, 2005
4 Author interview with Peter Stainlay, a former Qantas deputy chief executive, July 14, 2014
5 Scott Rochfort, 'Dixon says there'll be opportunities for other airline mergers', *Sydney Morning Herald*, October 31, 2005
6 Author interview with a former Qantas executive, May 2014
7 Author interview with Peter Gregg, a former Qantas chief financial officer, June 30, 2014

Chapter 4

1 Scott Rochfort, '$5.60 offer for Qantas final: APA', *Sydney Morning Herald*, February 3, 2007
2 Kate Askew, 'Mental as anything', *Sydney Morning Herald*, May 12, 2007
3 Scott Rochfort and Phillip Coorey, 'Qantas boss plays down fears of cuts', *Sydney Morning Herald*, December 15, 2006
4 Kate Askew and Scott Rochfort, 'If you knew Suzie', *Sydney Morning Herald*, May 26, 2007
5 Richard J Connors, *Warren Buffett on Business: Principles from the Sage of Omaha*, Wiley, 2009
6 Author interview with a former Allco director, May 2014
7 Airline Partners Australia bidder's statement released to the ASX, February 2, 2007
8 Stuart Washington, Mark Davis and Scott Rochfort, 'Millions for Qantas chiefs', *Sydney Morning Herald*, February 21, 2007
9 John Durie, 'Frustrated and appalled: Qantas chair lashes critics', *Australian Financial Review*, March 21, 2007
10 Stuart Washington, 'Deal maker or breaker gives board a serve', *Sydney Morning Herald*, March 17, 2007
11 Scott Rochfort, 'Consortium's $4.5b Qantas cash grab sparks call for review of bid', *Sydney Morning Herald*, April 14, 2007
12 Author interview with a former Qantas executive, May 2014
13 Kate Askew, 'How MacBank tanked on the numbers', *Sydney Morning Herald*, May 7, 2007
14 Takeovers Panel decision, May 6, 2007
15 Scott Rochfort, 'Qantas farce: heads will roll', *Sydney Morning Herald*, May 7, 2007
16 Ibid.
17 Author interview with Ian Woods, a former president of the Australian and International Pilots Association, October 12, 2014
18 Matt O'Sullivan, 'Ex-Qantas freight chief pays heavy price for cartel', *Sydney Morning Herald*, May 4, 2009
19 'The Liberalisation of Aviation': speech by British Airways chief executive Willie Walsh on May 7, 2008

Chapter 5

1 Damon Kitney, Ingrid Mansell and Vesna Poljak, 'How secret London talks sealed deal', *Australian Financial Review*, December 4, 2008
2 Richard Webb, 'Flying higher', *Sunday Age*, July 30, 2006
3 Damon Kitney, Katrina Nicholas and Vesna Poljak, 'Joyce promotion to top job breaks up Qantas club', *Australian Financial Review*, August 18, 2008
4 Ibid.
5 Michael Bachelard and Mark Russell, 'Relief as QF30 passengers fly in to Melbourne', *Sunday Age*, July 27, 2008
6 Ibid.
7 Rachael Angley, 'Lucky escape', *Sunday Mail*, July 27, 2008

8 Final report on oxygen cylinder failure and depressurisation 475 km north-west of Manila, Philippines, on July 25, 2008, ATSB, November 22, 2010
9 Author interview with Chris Manning, a former Qantas chief pilot, August 15, 2014
10 Liam Houlihan and Shannon Deery, 'Exploding oxygen tank one theory', *Sunday Herald Sun*, July 27, 2008
11 Michael Evans, 'Scars of sky wars', *Sydney Morning Herald*, July 29, 2008
12 Qantas annual reports, 2008 and 2009
13 Damon Kitney, Katrina Nicholas and Vesna Poljak, 'Joyce promotion to top job breaks up Qantas club', *Australian Financial Review*, August 18, 2008
14 Author interview with Peter Gregg, a former Qantas chief financial officer, June 30, 2014
15 Scott Rochfort and Matt O'Sullivan, 'Gregg quits after top job goes to Joyce', *Sydney Morning Herald*, August 20, 2008
16 Matt O'Sullivan and Scott Rochfort, 'Turbulance ahead', *Sydney Morning Herald*, December 6, 2008
17 Arjun Ramachandran, 'Ex-fighter pilot saved QF72', *Sydney Morning Herald*, October 15, 2008
18 Final report on in-flight upset 154 km west of Learmouth, WA, on October 7, 2008, Australian Transport Safety Bureau, December 2011
19 Cherie Howie, 'Flight terror lawsuit rages on', *Herald on Sunday*, March 16, 2014
20 Paul Bibby with AAP, 'Qantas autopilot blamed for jet plunge', *Sydney Morning Herald*, October 9, 2008
21 Geoff Dixon address to Qantas annual general meeting, November 28, 2008
22 Leigh Clifford address to Qantas annual general meeting, November 28, 2008
23 Matt O'Sullivan, 'Shareholders vent anger at Qantas AGM', *Sydney Morning Herald*, November 26, 2008
24 Matt O'Sullivan and Scott Rochfort, 'Turbulance ahead', *Sydney Morning Herald*, December 6, 2008
25 Matt O'Sullivan, 'Qantas baulks at BA pensioners', *Sydney Morning Herald*, December 9, 2008
26 Matt O'Sullivan, 'Joyce ready for great leap at Qantas', *Sydney Morning Herald*, October 10, 2009
27 Author interview with Warren Truss, the deputy prime minister, October 16, 2014
28 Author interview with Chris Manning, a former Qantas chief pilot, August 15, 2014

Chapter 6

1 Declassified media talking points, Department of Foreign Affairs and Trade, June 30, 2010, released following Freedom of Information application by *Sydney Morning Herald*
2 Matt O'Sullivan, 'Qantas reassurance on Vietnam', *Sydney Morning Herald*, July 2, 2010
3 Author interview with Bruce Buchanan, Jetstar chief executive, January 14, 2010
4 Tom Allard and Matt O'Sullivan, 'Jetstar engulfed in surreal Vietnam ordeal', *Sydney Morning Herald*, January 16, 2010
5 Scott Rochfort, 'Qantas increases stake in Asian aviation', *Sydney Morning Herald*, April 27, 2007

6 Jetstar press release, April 14, 2008
7 Geoff Easdown, 'Ideology clash as Jetstar Pacific chief quits', *Herald Sun*, April 19, 2008
8 Tom Allard and Matt O'Sullivan, 'Whistleblowers will bring us down', *Sydney Morning Herald*, January 15, 2010
9 Formal conclusion of Civil Aviation Administration of Vietnam regarding safety inspection at Jetstar Pacific Airlines, January 5, 2010
10 Matt O'Sullivan and Jonathan Pearlman, 'Two Qantas executives held in Vietnam', *Sydney Morning Herald*, January 9, 2010
11 Author interview with a former Jetstar executive, May 5, 2014
12 Matt O'Sullivan, 'Grounded: the rescue of Qantas execs in Vietnam', *Sydney Morning Herald*, July 30, 2010
13 Declassified media talking points, Department of Foreign Affairs and Trade, June 30, 2010, released following Freedom of Information application by *Sydney Morning Herald*
14 Author interview with friend of Jetstar Pacific executives, July 2010
15 Author interview with David Epstein, Qantas head of corporate and government affairs, July 1, 2010
16 Declassified media talking points, Department of Foreign Affairs and Trade, June 30, 2010, released following Freedom of Information application by *Sydney Morning Herald*
17 Ibid.

Chapter 7

1 Tim Robinson, 'Qantas QF32 flight from the cockpit', *Royal Aeronautical Society Industry News* (blog), December 8, 2010
2 Author interview with QF32 flight attendant Emma Teres, August 13, 2014
3 Preliminary report on in-flight uncontained engine failure overhead Batam Island, Indonesia, on November 4, 2010, Australian Transport Safety Bureau (ATSB), December 3, 2010
4 Author interview with QF32 passenger Judith Friederich, August 12, 2014
5 Final report on in-flight uncontained engine failure overhead Batam Island, Indonesia, on November 4, 2010, ATSB, June 27, 2013
6 Sarah Ferguson interview with Michael von Reth, QF32 cabin service manager, *Four Corners*, ABC Television, March 28, 2011
7 Author interview with QF32 passenger Sheena Fenton, August 13, 2014
8 Matt O'Sullivan and Ellie Harvey, 'Is the plane going to go down?', *Sydney Morning Herald*, November 5, 2010
9 Emails from Strategic Forecasting senior officer, November 4, 2010, released by WikiLeaks
10 Matt O'Sullivan, 'Qantas jet engine fails: witnesses tell of hearing explosion', *Sydney Morning Herald*, November 4, 2010
11 Author interview with a former senior Qantas manager, April 17, 2014
12 Sarah Ferguson, interview with Mark Johnson, QF32 second officer, *Four Corners*, ABC Television, March 28, 2011
13 Author interview with Judith Friederich, August 12, 2014
14 Author interview with QF32 passenger Hon Mok, August 21, 2014

15 Sarah Ferguson, interview with Matt Hicks, QF32 first officer *Four Corners*, ABC Television, March 28, 2011
16 Ibid.
17 Tim Robinson, 'Qantas QF32 flight from the cockpit', *Royal Aeronautical Society Industry News* (blog), December 8, 2010
18 Author interview with QF32 passenger Donald Friederich on August 12, 2014
19 Author interview with QF32 passenger Hon Mok, August 21, 2014
20 Matt O'Sullivan, 'Pockets of turbulence for Rolls-Royce', *Sydney Morning Herald*, November 20, 2011
21 Alan Joyce at media conference, November 4, 2010
22 Emails from Strategic Forecasting senior officers, November 4, 2010, released by WikiLeaks
23 Author interview with the ATSB chief commissioner, Martin Dolan, March 11, 2014
24 Author interview with QF32 flight attendant Emma Teres, August 13, 2014
25 Matt O'Sullivan, 'More safety checks ordered on grounded A380s', *Sydney Morning Herald,* November 11, 2010
26 Matt O'Sullivan, 'Rolls-Royce reveals A380 engine redesign, takes blame for failure', *Sydney Morning Herald*, November 13, 2010
27 Matt O'Sullivan, 'Qantas hijacks Rolls-Royce claim', *Sydney Morning Herald*, December 10, 2010
28 Andrew Heasley and Matt O'Sullivan, 'Oil pipe fault led to Qantas fire, say investigators', *Sydney Morning Herald*, December 4, 2010
29 Final report on in-flight uncontained engine failure overhead Batam Island, Indonesia, on November 4, 2010, ATSB, June 27, 2013
30 Matt O'Sullivan, 'Qantas aircraft punt comes unstuck', *Sydney Morning Herald*, January 25, 2011
31 Author interview with a former senior Qantas manager, April 17, 2014
32 Author interview with Emma Teres, August 13, 2014

Chapter 8

1 Alan Joyce speech to Melbourne Press Club, February 3, 2011
2 Author interview with Jayne Hrdlicka, Jetstar chief executive, September 3, 2012
3 Matt O'Sullivan, 'RedQ firms as name for Qantas' new premium airline in Asia', *Sydney Morning Herald*, September 13, 2011
4 John Durie, 'Qantas eyes Asia', *Australian*, May 11, 2011
5 Matt O'Sullivan, 'Airline passengers face strike action', *Sydney Morning Herald*, May 10, 2011
6 Author interview with Ian Woods, a former president of the Australian and International Pilots Association, October 12, 2014
7 Alan Joyce speech to the Wings Club, Dublin, March 10, 2009
8 Pamela Williams, 'Come fly with Leigh', *Australian Financial Review*, June 28, 2009
9 Helen Trinca, 'The art of war', *Sydney Morning Herald*, December 8, 1997
10 Matt O'Sullivan, 'Unions backing us into corner with ridiculous claims, says Joyce', *Sydney Morning Herald*, May 17, 2011
11 Author interview with Richard Branson, Virgin Group founder, March 2, 2010

12 Matt O'Sullivan, 'Virgin's new link adds to Qantas woes', *Sydney Morning Herald*, June 8, 2011
13 Alan Joyce speech, 'Building a stronger Qantas', August 16, 2011
14 Ibid.
15 Matt O'Sullivan, 'Bumpy ride on the shrinking kangaroo', *Sydney Morning Herald*, August 20, 2011
16 Ibid.
17 Ibid.
18 Author interview with Conor McCarthy, a co-founder of AirAsia, January 5, 2012
19 Andrew Cleary, 'Qantas flies into row with regional rival', *Australian Financial Review*, October 24, 2011
20 Author interview with a former Qantas executive, May 28, 2014

Chapter 9

1 Matt O'Sullivan, 'Qantas engineers call off strikes', *Sydney Morning Herald*, May 13, 2011
2 Based on author interviews with present and former Qantas executives, May–October 2014
3 Author interview with an executive, May 7, 2014
4 Ibid.
5 Andrew Heasley and Matt O'Sullivan, 'Strike threat over Qantas plans to cut 1000 jobs', *Sydney Morning Herald*, August 17, 2011
6 Matt O'Sullivan, 'Qantas Asia push to cost $500m', *Sydney Morning Herald*, August 17, 2011
7 Author interview with a former Qantas executive, May 2014
8 Matt O'Sullivan and Mark Hawthorne, 'Qantas sends secret strike breakers to train in LA', *Sydney Morning Herald*, April 5, 2011
9 Author interview with a former Qantas senior manager, March 24, 2014
10 Matt O'Sullivan, 'Unions lash out as Qantas boosts CEO Joyce's pay packet to $5m', *Sydney Morning Herald*, September 8, 2011
11 Simon Benson, 'Guards for Qantas boss over threat', *Daily Telegraph*, October 5, 2011
12 Matt O'Sullivan, 'Qantas death threat probe . . . dies', *Sydney Morning Herald*, November 23, 2011
13 Matt O'Sullivan, 'Qantas stoush casts pall over Christmas', *Sydney Morning Herald*, October 14, 2011
14 Author interview with a former Qantas executive, May 20, 2014
15 Ewin Hannan, 'Flight chaos to last until Christmas, unions warn', *The Australian*, October 11, 2011
16 Post by Steve Purvinas, ALAEA federal secretary, on PPRuNe, August 24, 2011
17 Debra Jopson, 'Timing of the essence for Qantas', *Sydney Morning Herald*, November 5, 2011
18 Matt O'Sullivan and Andrew Heasley, 'Behind the scenes: how Joyce saddled up for battle', *Sydney Morning Herald*, October 31, 2011
19 Author interview with Tony Sheldon, national secretary of the Transport Workers Union, June 2, 2014

20 Hansard, House of Representatives, October 31, 2014
21 Author interview with former federal transport minister Anthony Albanese, April 30, 2014
22 Matt O'Sullivan, 'Qantas looked at farming out jobs', *Sydney Morning Herald*, October 24, 2011
23 Author interview with Richard Woodward, a vice-president of Australian and International Pilots Association, November 2011
24 Author interview with a former Qantas senior manager, April 17, 2014
25 Author interview with a former Qantas senior manager, October 4, 2014
26 Ibid.
27 Matt O'Sullivan and Jessica Wright, 'Airport security for Qantas meeting', *Sydney Morning Herald*, October 27, 2011
28 Staff reporters, 'Qantas troubles come to a head at AGM', *Sydney Morning Herald*, October 28, 2011
29 Author interview with a former Qantas executive, May 2014
30 Qantas media conference following annual shareholder meeting, October 28, 2011

Chapter 10

1 Alan Joyce at Qantas media conference on October 28, 2011
2 Simon Benson, Stephen Drill and Vanda Carson, 'The Dying Kangaroo: Jobs warning as unions threaten to ground Qantas', *Herald Sun*, October 29, 2011
3 Questions on notice to Senate Rural Affairs and Transport Legislative Committee, November 4, 2011
4 Author interview with anonymous source, July 4, 2014
5 Hansard, House of Representatives, October 31, 2011
6 Author interview with Anthony Albanese, former federal transport minister, April 30, 2014
7 Ibid.
8 Alan Joyce on ABC Radio National, October 31, 2011
9 Hansard, House of Representatives, November 1, 2011
10 Debra Jopson, 'Fasten your seat belts', *Sydney Morning Herald*, November 5, 2011; and Hansard, House of Representatives, October 31, 2011

Chapter 11

1 Author interviews with former Qantas executives, May-October 2014
2 Alan Joyce speech at Qantas head office, Sydney, October 29, 2011
3 Steve Creedy and Matthew Franklin, 'Eight minutes to ground a fleet, ignite battle', *The Australian*, October 31, 2011
4 Recording of conversation between air-traffic controller and a pilot on Qantas Flight 453, LiveATC.net, October 29, 2011
5 Gareth Hutchens, 'Traveller misses her best friend's wedding', *Sun Herald*, October 30, 2011
6 Tim Barlass and Gareth Hutchens, 'Nightmare unfolds at airport', *Sun Herald*, October 30, 2011
7 Andrew Heasley and Matt O'Sullivan, 'That Saturday morning meeting', *The Age*, October 31, 2011

8 Message from Samantha Taranto, Qantas executive manager of cabin crew, October 29, 2011
9 Author interview with a former Qantas staff member, October 13, 2014
10 Media conference for Anthony Albanese, federal infrastructure and transport minister, October 29, 2011
11 Decision of full bench of Fair Work, Melbourne, October 31, 2011
12 Author interview with a former Qantas executive, May 2014
13 Phillip Coorey and Matt O'Sullivan, 'Qantas takes off, political flak flies', *Sydney Morning Herald*, November 1, 2011
14 Author interview with Anthony Albanese, April 30, 2011
15 Hansard, House of Representatives, October 31, 2011
16 Leigh Sales interview with Shadow Treasurer Joe Hockey, *7.30 Report* on ABC Television, November 1, 2011
17 Gemma Daley, 'Hockey forced to clarify Qantas comments', *Australian Financial Review*, November 3, 2011
18 Matt O'Sullivan and Lenore Taylor, 'More pay for Qantas chiefs and more union unrest', *Sydney Morning Herald*, October 29, 2011
19 Qantas' response to questions on notice from Senate Rural Affairs and Transport Legislative Committee on November 4, 2011
20 Clare Harvey, 'The numbers man', *Sunday Telegraph*, November 6, 2011
21 Author interview with Anthony Albanese, April 30, 2011
22 Author interview with a former Qantas executive, May 28, 2014

Chapter 12

1 Author interview with a Qantas executive, May 12, 2014
2 Matt O'Sullivan, 'A name dropped in Barcelona', *Sydney Morning Herald*, March 3, 2010
3 Author interview with John Borghetti, Virgin Australia chief executive, May 9, 2014
4 Matt O'Sullivan, 'Virgin looks for cash in a crisis', *Sydney Morning Herald*, July 28, 2009
5 Author interview with John Borghetti, May 9, 2014
6 Matt O'Sullivan, 'Another regulator thwarts Virgin Blue', *Sydney Morning Herald*, September 11, 2010
7 Matt O'Sullivan, 'Discount dogfight', *Sydney Morning Herald*, September 18, 2010
8 Matt O'Sullivan, 'High flyer makes his connections', *Sydney Morning Herald*, December 4, 2010
9 Matt O'Sullivan, 'Virgin shares take off on Delta alliance ruling', *Sydney Morning Herald*, May 11, 2011
10 Author interview with John Borghetti, May 9, 2014
11 Matt O'Sullivan, 'Come fly with us . . . and visit our VIP lounges . . . and have a seat upgrade . . . and bend an air', *Sydney Morning Herald*, March 1, 2014
12 Author interview with a former Qantas executive, May 1, 2014
13 Matt O'Sullivan, 'Adviser urges vote against pay at Virgin AGM', *Sydney Morning Herald*, November 8, 2013
14 Author interview with a former Qantas executive, May 28, 2014
15 Author interview with John Borghetti, May 9, 2014

Chapter 13

1 Steve Lewis and Mark Davis, 'Airline access reform opens up the skies', *Australian Financial Review*, June 1, 1999
2 Mark Davis, 'Strong words on flights', *Australian Financial Review*, July 14, 1999
3 Author interview with Barry Brown, Emirates vice-president Australasia, June 21, 2013
4 Author interview with Barry Brown, May 9, 2014
5 Andrew Cleary, 'Smooth take-off for alliance of like minds', *Australian Financial Review*, September 8, 2012
6 Matt O'Sullivan, 'Emirates chief rules out Qantas stake', *Sydney Morning Herald*, June 12, 2012
7 Qantas briefing paper to federal politicians, June 2012
8 Alan Joyce speech, September 6, 2012
9 Matt O'Sullivan, 'Emirates alliance a flying leap of faith', *Sydney Morning Herald*, September 7, 2012
10 Matt O'Sullivan, 'Virgin throws down challenge to Qantas', *Sydney Morning Herald*, November 3, 2012
11 Andrew Cleary, 'Qantas tried to split Virgin alliance', *Australian Financial Review*, September 14, 2012
12 John Sharpe, 'Time flies', *Sydney Morning Herald*, November 28, 2007
13 Matt O'Sullivan, 'Singapore sling as pilots look to dine in Dubai', *Sydney Morning Herald*, March 30, 2013
14 International Airline Activity 2013, Bureau of Infrastructure, Transport and Regional Development
15 Author interview with Flight Centre managing director Graham Turner, February 2014

Chapter 14

1 Jonathan Chancellor, 'Title Deeds', *Sydney Morning Herald*, November 30, 2008
2 Paul McIntyre, 'Singo flying high with Qantas', *Australian Financial Review*, April 4, 1995
3 Andrew White and Joyce Moullakis, 'Dixon & Coe start in Flying High 2', *Australian Financial Review*, June 3, 2010
4 Matt O'Sullivan, 'Rumours of Flying Kangaroo takeover bid is just hot air, Joyce says,' *Sydney Morning Herald*, August 25, 2011
5 Damon Kitney, 'We eyed Qantas stake: ex-CEO', *The Australian*, November 26, 2011
6 Author interview with Peter Gregg, a former Qantas chief financial officer, August 19, 2014
7 Matt O'Sullivan, 'Qantas prepares for hostile takeover bids', *Sydney Morning Herald*, June 12, 2012
8 Andrew Cleary, 'The Qantas club is back', *Australian Financial Review*, November 24, 2012
9 Author interview with Richard Woodward, vice-president of the Australian and International Pilots Association, November 2012
10 Damon Kitney and Steve Creedy, 'Chinese airline in plan to buy stake in Qantas', *The Australian*, December 7, 2013

11 Matt O'Sullivan and Peter Cai, 'Airline targeted: China Southern had its eye on Qantas stake', *Sydney Morning Herald*, June 17, 2013
12 Adele Ferguson and Matt O'Sullivan, 'Mayday', *Sydney Morning Herald*, March 1, 2014
13 Damon Kitney, 'Former airline boss back in play', *The Australian*, December 17, 2012
14 Andrew Cleary and James Chessell, 'Rivals may challenge Joyce', *Australian Financial Review*, November 19, 2012
15 Matt O'Sullivan, 'Parting of the ways for the sorcerer and his apprentice', *Sydney Morning Herald*, November 24, 2012
16 Matt O'Sullivan, 'We will always defend our interests: Joyce', *Sydney Morning Herald*, November 28, 2012
17 Ibid.
18 Author interview with Peter Gregg, June 30, 2014
19 Author interview with a Qantas executive, November 22, 2012
20 Katrina Nicholas, 'Cleared for take-off', *Australian Financial Review*, March 30, 2007

Chapter 15

1 Matt O'Sullivan, 'Qantas to create Jetstar Hong Kong in Chinese joint venture', *Sydney Morning Herald*, March 27, 2012
2 Author interview with a former Qantas executive, May 28, 2014
3 Author interview with Alan Joyce, October 7, 2013
4 Special report of the Division of Gaming Enforcement to the Casino Control Commission, New Jersey, on its investigation of MGM Mirage's joint venture with Pansy Ho in Macau, May 18, 2009
5 Ibid.
6 Matt O'Sullivan, 'Destination Hong Kong – at any price', *Sydney Morning Herald*, October 5, 2013
7 Author interview with Peter Gregg, a former Qantas chief financial officer, June 30, 2014
8 Scott Rochfort, 'Qantas plots course with Jetstar Asia', *Sydney Morning Herald*, September 30, 2004
9 Matt O'Sullivan, 'Qantas belies tales of woe by doubling net profit', *Sydney Morning Herald*, August 25, 2011
10 Matt O'Sullivan, 'Cathay lets fly at Jetstar's Hong Kong plan', *Sydney Morning Herald*, September 6, 2013
11 Matt O'Sullivan, 'Destination Hong Kong – at any price', *Sydney Morning Herald*, October 5, 2013
12 Email from Jetstar Hong Kong's chief financial officer, Howard Cheung, to fellow executives, November 15, 2013
13 Matt O'Sullivan, 'Brakes on Jetstar's expansion in Asia', *Sydney Morning Herald*, February 28, 2014
14 Alan Joyce at Rural and Regional Affairs and Transport committee hearing, Sydney, March 14, 2014
15 Author interview with Andrew Pyne, a former Cathay Pacific executive and Viva Macau CEO, March 24, 2014

Chapter 16

1 Author interview with a former Qantas executive, May 12, 2014
2 Author interview with Anthony Albanese, a former federal transport minister, April 30, 2014
3 Richard Branson at media conference in Perth, May 7, 2013
4 Author interview with a former airline executive, February 2014
5 Matt O'Sullivan, 'Airlines battle for the pointy end', *Sydney Morning Herald*, May 5, 2012
6 Jane Boyle, 'Qantas braces for war fallout', *Australian Financial Review*, February 21, 2003
7 Author interview with Peter Stainlay, a former Qantas deputy chief executive, February 3, 2014
8 Letter from Anthony Albanese to the Qantas chief executive, Alan Joyce, August 2, 2013
9 Matt O'Sullivan, 'Airlines boost Virgin coffers', *Sydney Morning Herald*, November 15, 2013
10 Matt O'Sullivan, 'Sky's the limit in airline battle', *Sydney Morning Herald*, November 23, 2013
11 Author interview with Warren Truss, the deputy prime minister, October 16, 2014
12 Schedule of correspondence on Qantas between Treasurer's office and Treasury obtained under freedom-of-information laws by the *Sydney Morning Herald*
13 Matt O'Sullivan, 'Qantas gives thumbs up for Hockey debate on ownership', *Sydney Morning Herald*, November 28, 2013
14 Matt O'Sullivan, 'Virgin wants same support as Qantas', *Sydney Morning Herald*, November 29, 2013
15 Author interview with Warren Truss, deputy prime minister, October 16, 2014
16 Matt O'Sullivan, 'Rough warning for Qantas, whatever the flight path', *Sydney Morning Herald*, December 7, 2013
17 Matt O'Sullivan, 'Qantas rating cut to junk as woes mount', *Sydney Morning Herald*, December 7, 2013
18 Matt O'Sullivan and Mark Kenny, 'Qantas in crisis', *Sydney Morning Herald*, December 6, 2013
19 Author interview with Warren Truss, deputy prime minister, October 16, 2014
20 Cameron Stewart, 'The plane truth about Qantas' project Harbour', *The Australian*, March 1, 2014
21 Alan Joyce speech to 'friends of tourism' in Canberra, February 12, 2014
22 Matt O'Sullivan, 'Virgin attacks over Qantas monopoly fear', *Sydney Morning Herald*, February 14, 2014
23 Matt O'Sullivan, 'Joyce digs in as turbulence takes hold', *Sydney Morning Herald*, February 28, 2014
24 Hansard, House of Representatives, February 27, 2014
25 Author interview with Warren Truss, the deputy prime minister, October 16, 2014
26 Author interview with Alan Joyce, February 27, 2014
27 Leigh Clifford, 'Government policy must change to create a level playing field for Qantas', *Sydney Morning Herald*, March 1, 2014

28 Hansard, House of Representatives, March 4, 2014
29 Alan Joyce at Australia–Israel Chamber of Commerce lunch, Sydney, March 5, 2014
30 Harold Mitchell, 'No such thing as a level playing field – it's time to toughen up, Mr Clifford', *Sydney Morning Herald*, March 8, 2014
31 Author interview with a Qantas director, March 7, 2014
32 Author interview with a former Qantas executive, March 21, 2014
33 Internal Qantas email outlining organisation changes, March 19, 2014
34 Author interview with a former Qantas executive, May 28, 2014
35 Author interview with Ian Woods, a former president of the Australian and International Pilots Association, October 12, 2014
36 Gareth Evans, 'Armchair critics take flights of fancy on future of the air', *Sydney Morning Herald*, January 24, 2014
37 Alan Joyce at Qantas annual results in Sydney, August 28, 2014
38 John Borghetti at Virgin Australia's annual results, August 29, 2014
39 Author interview with Grant Fenn, a former Qantas deputy chief financial officer and strategy chief, August 27, 2014
40 Ibid.
41 Author interview with Rod Eddington, a former chief executive of British Airways and Ansett, May 15, 2014

ACKNOWLEDGEMENTS

Ever since Alan Joyce made the shock decision to ground the Qantas fleet, I had regularly thought about writing a book about one of the most tumultuous periods in the airline's long history. Two years after the grounding, I was in New Zealand with friends on New Year's Eve. As we counted down the hours to midnight, we joked about our resolutions for 2014. I told them mine was to write a book about Qantas. It was one of the few I have ever kept.

However, it would have become another resolution that I failed to keep without the love and support of my partner, Maki. At my lowest ebb, he reassured me and told me to stop doubting myself. He gave me invaluable advice and encouragement at key moments in this project, and is the reason my dream to write this book has finally become a reality.

The life of an author can be a daunting and isolating experience, especially when writing about a large company with substantial resources at its disposal. My thanks go to my good friend Greg Stutchbury, who twice read entire drafts and made valuable suggestions to improve the book. Vanda Carson and Julian Lee, both friends and former colleagues at the *Sydney Morning Herald*, helped and encouraged me at crucial stages. Brian Robins at the *Herald* gave generously of his time to read chapters, and imparted his wisdom to help overcome concerns about delicate subjects.

Other friends and present and former colleagues who supported me immeasurably include Eric Johnston, Michael West, Paddy Manning, Colin Kruger, Adele Ferguson, Scott Rochfort (who came to my rescue when it looked like the final manuscript would not reach the publisher on time), Kate McClymont, Linton Besser, Denise McNabb, Liz Knight, Mike Smith and Neil Chenoweth. Each played their part in different ways in helping me tell the story of Qantas.

My employer, Fairfax Media, was willing to give me time away from the office to pen this book. The company has experienced its own travails in recent years. Indeed, it has had three books published in just over a year about its decline. Yet the publisher remains the home of some of the best journalism in Australia. I want to thank my former business editor Eric Johnston and senior managing editors Darren Goodsir, Sean Aylmer, Paul Bailey, James Chessell and Mat Dunckley for allowing me to pursue my dream. I also want to pay tribute to several of my business editors over the years. Ian Verrender, Michael West and Eric Johnston gave endless counsel and encouragement, and remain champions of truth in covering the often ruthless world of business.

My parents, Kevin and Liz, have been my rock from the outset. Dad always had his nose in a newspaper, and with Mum encouraged my interest in current affairs as a young child. I wish to thank my large extended family, particularly those in Hong Kong who helped me with this book. Thanks also to James O'Sullivan, a fellow author and friend, who wrote to me at the start of this project to give me the courage to forge ahead.

Fiona Inglis, my literary agent at Curtis Brown, guided me expertly through the world of book publishing. At Penguin, the publishing director Ben Ball gave me significant latitude and encouragement from the day he agreed to take a large punt on an idea. He is one of the best in the business. The editor of this book at Penguin, Rachel Scully, deserves an award for her patience in putting up with my regular requests for changes and additions as the final deadline neared. My thanks also extend to designers Laura Thomas and Samantha Jayaweera, proofreaders Katie Purvis and Johannes Jakob, and indexer Fay Donlevy.

As a journalist, I have been granted a special privilege to cover a company that touches so many lives. I want to pay special tribute to countless former and present Qantas staff who have helped me to write about their airline over the years, and gave generously of their time to speak to me for this book – often at risk to their positions. The truth can often be elusive. This book would never have been more than an idea without their willingness to share accounts of their time at Qantas, and help separate fact from fiction. My thanks also to others in the wider aviation industry who have helped me enormously along the way. I wish I could acknowledge every one of you by name.

This book taught me that seemingly insurmountable projects are achievable. You just have to reach for the skies – and get on with it. To everyone, thank you.

INDEX